BASIC CASES IN CONSTITUTIONAL LAW

BASIC CASES IN CONSTITUTIONAL LAW

Second Edition

Duane Lockard
Walter F. Murphy
Princeton University

A Division of Congressional Quarterly Inc.
1414 22nd Street N.W., Washington, D.C. 20037

Printed in the United States of America

Library of Congress Cataloging-in-Publication Data

Lockard, Duane, 1921-
    Basic cases in constitutional law.

    1. United States—Constitutional law—Cases.
I. Murphy, Walter F., 1929-   II. Title.
KF4549.L55   1987   342.73'00264   87-5172
ISBN 0-87187-428-8   347.30200264

To June Traube,
Mother Superior to the Department of Politics

CONTENTS

Contents

PREFACE

We intend *Basic Cases in Constitutional Law* to serve as an adjunct to undergraduate education, most specifically in courses dealing with American politics. Without some understanding of the courts and the judicial process, one cannot hope to comprehend the stakes of politics or how particular public policies are made or mangled, or both. We hope this book, like the first edition, will help fill a void by providing a brief and inexpensive collection of leading Supreme Court decisions that have influenced the development of constitutional law and public policy.

We open this edition with a brief essay that sets out some of the reasons why political scientists are—or should be—concerned with the work of judges. We begin each of the succeeding eight chapters with an even briefer essay, in which we try to put the particular cases reprinted into a coherent perspective. But, like that great Italian scholar and statesman Italo Bombolini, we believe that the pasta of a book is in the readings it contains; editors' introductions provide only the sauce. Furthermore, we do not intend for our essays or even our organization of the cases to restrict choice. Indeed, we hope that professors will use the materials in any order that best suits the design of their own courses.

We are indebted to many people: to Jeffrey K. Tulis of Princeton University for nagging us to do a second edition, to Charles A. Miller of the Lake Forest College for editorial suggestions, to Suzette Marie Hemberger of Princeton University for typing parts of the manuscript, to Mrs. Helen Wright for proofreading, and to Stacie Scofield of Princeton University and Kelly McDermott for photocopying. Most of all, we are indebted to our wives for tolerating our many foibles, among which doing this book is only one.

Duane Lockard
Brewster, Massachusetts

Walter F. Murphy
Princeton, New Jersey

INTRODUCTION: POLITICS, THE CONSTITUTION, AND THE SUPREME COURT

Why bother to study judicial opinions if one's concerns are politics and public policy? What do black-robed judges deciding cases between individuals have to do with governance? Intelligent responses to these questions require thought not only about politics in general but also about constitutions and judges.

Politics is a much corrupted word, often misused to refer to petty matters. At root, however, politics addresses a society's most fundamental problems: how citizens identify, define, and justify their goals as a nation and how they choose means to achieve those goals—the ways in which a society allocates rights and responsibilities, costs and benefits. Politics is also very much concerned with the substantive content of such decisions. In sum, it deals with values: their meanings, their implications, their justifications, their preservation, and their changes over time.

A constitution is crucial to such a concept of politics, for in that instrument—whether conceived as a specific document, a bevy of practices, a tradition, a set of political theories, or a combination of some or all of these—societies typically try to enunciate their goals, specify governmental procedures, divide authority among officials, and mark off certain areas as beyond government's legitimate reach. In this sense, then, a constitution is an effort to limit power, even the power of "the People." In an even deeper sense, a constitution is an effort to control the future by structuring government. Those efforts are at least audacious, and one might well say foolish. But, in fact, constitutions have frequently provided frameworks that have heavily influenced, if not controlled, the procedures by which government has acted as well as the substance of public policy.

Who Shall Interpret?

The degree of a constitution's effectiveness as an instrument of governance depends on many factors, including the wisdom of its framers in assessing their society's values and in devising procedural and substantive provisions to enhance those values. In addition, a constitution's success depends on latter-day framers, its interpreters who translate the sacred document, sacred traditions, or both to cope with current problems.

And thus the question arises of who these interpreters of text and tradition will be. The standard answer of civics books is "the Supreme Court." But nothing in early American history and nothing in the constitutional document of 1787 or its amendments inevitably makes judges of any court the primary interpreters of the Constitution. Indeed, one might argue that judges are not in fact the primary constitutional interpreters. All public officials interpret the Constitution, usually before a case gets to a court. A police officer who sees a piece of evidence that might help convict a criminal is—however unconsciously—interpreting the Constitution when deciding whether or not to seize that evidence. Every time a legislator, state or federal, votes for a bill, he or she makes a judgment that the proposed law conforms to constitutional standards. Every time any public officer, from the president to the officer on the beat, decides he or she has authority to enforce (or not enforce) a particular piece of public policy, that official in effect if not intention interprets the Constitution.

Moreover, on occasion state or federal officials have balked at obeying particular judicial decisions and more often have refused to be bound in the future by the reasoning judges offered to justify their rulings. In 1832, for example, President Andrew Jackson vetoed legislation continuing federal support for the Bank of the United States because, in his opinion, establishing such a bank was beyond Congress's constitutional powers. In response to the argument that the Supreme Court had settled the issue of constitutionality in McCulloch v. Maryland (1819; see Case 3.1), Jackson wrote:

> Each public officer who takes an oath to support the Constitution swears that he will support it as he understands it, and not as it is understood by others. . . . The opinion of the judges has no more authority over Congress than the opinion of Congress has over judges, and on that point the President is independent of both.[1]

Other presidents, including Thomas Jefferson, Abraham Lincoln, Franklin D. Roosevelt, and Ronald Reagan, have agreed with Jackson, as have hundreds of senators and representatives over two centuries. Thus we warn readers of this book not to think the Supreme Court always has the last word. Whether it should is a matter about which reasonable people can—and do—reasonably differ.

With that much said, however, the usual—though not the inevitable or invariable—effect of the Supreme Court's constitutional interpretation has been willing or grudging acquiescence by the president, Congress, and state officials. Their opposition is less likely to be expressed in defiance than in selecting new justices with new ideas as older judges die or retire, in writing new legislation to circumvent the Court's constitutional objections, in confronting the Court with new cases in the hope of persuading judges to change their minds, or in proposing constitutional amendments. Sometimes these efforts achieve their aims, though the last has only rarely succeeded.

One need only recall a tiny portion of the last generation's history to see how far-reaching the effect of judicial rulings can be:

the end of the legitimacy if not the fact of governmentally mandated segregation by race (see Brown v. Board of Education [1954], Case 7.2);

a similar but not quite so sweeping invalidation of governmentally imposed distinctions based on gender (see Mississippi University for Women v. Hogan [1982], Case 7.5);[2]

requirements that government provide poor people who are arrested with lawyers to defend them and that police, when they arrest, inform the accused of their rights to silence and to counsel (see Miranda v. Arizona [1966], Case 8.1);

recognition of a right to privacy that protects the freedom of married and unmarried people to choose to use birth control and of women, at least in early stages of pregnancy, to have abortions (see Roe v. Wade [1973], Case 6.1); and

insistence that the democratic theory underpinning the Constitution requires that governors, state legislators, and members of the U.S. House of Representatives be chosen by electoral systems that as nearly as possible give equal weight to each citizen's vote (see Reynolds v. Sims [1964], Case 5.4).

One could multiply these examples; but, even if these were the only ones, the judiciary's impact on American society would have been little short of revolutionary. Today it is difficult to realize the extent to which the United States before World War II was a caste society, with harsh, governmentally imposed distinctions based on race, gender, and wealth; how little police needed to worry about the substantive or procedural commands of the Bill of Rights; or how perverted was the claim of most state legislatures and the U.S. House of Representatives to speak for "the People."

Reaction to Pressure

Judges, of course, did not bring about these changes single-handedly. They were reacting to pressures generated within society. But in each instance judges reacted favorably to those pressures *before* Congress did and in all but racial issues before the president. And, in the fight against racism, judicial decisions pressured Congress and the president to bring to bear the full authority and the physical force of the federal government. It was of crucial importance to this social and political revolution that judges grounded all of these rulings in the Constitution—in the document and tradition that profess to define the kind of people Americans are and wish to become.

By setting the ensuing political debates in terms of such fundamental principles, the judges made it difficult for opponents to gather support. For instance, in the context of a constitution that demands "equal protection of the laws" and a culture whose ideals include human equality, open appeals to racism or to assertions that men have a greater right to respect than women or that a person living in a rural area should have his or her vote count more than that of a person in a suburb are likely to embarrass or even anger rather than convert the uncommitted.

Yet reactions to these decisions illustrate the limited role that judges have in the American polity. Invoking the Constitution can be effective, but it provides no panacea. There has been resistance to most important Supreme Court decisions. Years of violent defiance, even bloodshed, followed the decisions on segregation; other rulings provoked much foot-dragging, attempts to maintain the old policy through new legislation, and efforts to amend the Constitution. And the fight is by no means over as far as abortion or the rights of the criminally accused are concerned. The Court's decisions do not end all controversy, but they do focus debate. Presidents will choose new judges with (perhaps) new ideas; new tides and currents will sweep through society, and these do not, as Justice Benjamin N. Cardozo once observed, "turn aside in their course and pass the judges by." [3] Sometimes these fresh tides will flow against, sometimes flow with, judicial interpretations of the Constitution.

Thus the picture that emerges is not simple. On the one hand, judicial decisions are important not only because they set the framework within which public policy is made, but also because they affect allocations of rights and duties, costs and benefits within society, even as they define society's goals and the legitimate means to achieve those goals. On the other hand, judicial rulings are sometimes wrong-headed about both the Constitution and public policy; and right or wrong they do not always succeed, in either the short or the long run. American society keeps contact with its traditional values as embodied in its constitutional document, yet at the same time modifies those values and even evolves new ones. Constitutional interpretation plays a significant role in processes both of continuity and of change.

Judicial decisions are also important because they mark out battlegrounds for continuing struggles over goals, over means, and over rights. Courts are agencies of government; and judges are rulers. They share power with a host of other officials; but, even as they share, they participate in governing the nation. Their claim to participate is based on reason, not force; on constitutional interpretation, not on winning elections or commanding police or armies. Their claim to obedience to their decisions is likewise based on reason, on using words to limit power. And much—not all but much—of the effect of their interpretations is based on their capacity to persuade citizens—elected representatives as well as "We, the People"—by reason. Thus, it is essential for anyone who would achieve even an elementary understanding of American politics to understand the Court's work in interpreting the Constitution, in setting boundaries on power, even the power of "the People," in defining and redefining the nation's goals, and in silhouetting issues on which there is sharp disagreement.

A Note on Reading Judicial Opinions

Most educated Americans can understand much of political discourse. Elected politicians may try to confuse voters on some issues, but those efforts are often transparent, for to win or retain office a candidate typically has to speak in language voters comprehend. We can read or watch much that passes for political debate and largely if not fully decode it, for most presidential messages as well as speeches by legislators, governors, and mayors are designed to be intelligible on television and radio and quoted in newspapers and popular magazines.

In contrast, judicial opinions are couched in what many people fear is a foreign language. That fear is exaggerated. Judges, it is true, seldom lighten their opinions with humor and invariably clutter them with references to previous decisions; but most cases involve the dramatic stuff of human conflict—whether married and unmarried individuals have a right to choose their own sexual partners, whether a state can execute convicted murderers, whether newspapers can publish classified governmental documents. And, whatever their failings, judges try to meet these problems by reasoning in a rigorously logical fashion within opinions and to apply the same rules to the same sorts of cases over time. To understand such arguments requires close attention.

The first and most important rule in reading judicial opinions is to understand what they are: justifications for decisions, not explanations of how courts arrived at decisions. The second rule is to read opinions carefully, for the choice of an adjective or adverb can shift the course of the law *and* public policy.

The third rule is to read critically, for judges are not infallible. One need go no further than judges themselves to learn that courts are often wrong in their decisions, in their reasoning, and even in their perceptions of the facts. The cases frequently provide lively—and occasionally bitter—debates about the meaning of the Constitution as well as about implications of its terms for public policy. For, on significant political issues, judges are as apt to disagree among themselves as are other public officials and private citizens. And, unlike courts in some countries, American judges publish several different kinds of opinions, most importantly:

opinions of the court—which justify the decision the entire court or a majority of its members reached in a case;

concurring opinions—in which one or several judges agree with the majority about the decision but justify it by different reasoning; and dissenting opinions—in which a minority of judges disagree with their colleagues about both the decision and the reasoning.

At times, the Supreme Court is so sharply divided that it is not possible for a majority of the justices to agree on common reasoning; thus there is sometimes no opinion of the Court, only a series of opinions. Usually in such instances, the opinion that commands the largest number of votes (the plurality opinion) announces the decision. That ruling is binding on the litigants in the case, but the various opinions remain those of individual justices, not of the Supreme Court, and so carry no weight as precedents.

Being able to decipher the numbers that judges use to cite previous judicial decisions helps to filter out static from opinions. Brown v. Board of Education, the school segregation case, is cited as 347 U.S. 483 (1954). The "347" refers to volume 347; the "U.S." to the *United States Reports*, the official publication of decisions of the Supreme Court; and "483" to the page in volume 347 on which the case begins. The "(1954)" explains that the decision was made public in 1954.

The additional numbers and letters that often appear are citations to unofficial reports put out by commercial publishers. The two most widely cited are S. Ct., short for *Supreme Court Reporter*, a product of the West Publishing Company, and L. Ed., *Lawyers Edition*, sold by the Lawyers Cooperative Publishing Company. Thus *Brown* is also cited as 74 S. Ct. 686, meaning it is located in volume 74 of the *Supreme Court Reporter*, beginning at page 686; and as 98 L. Ed. 873—that is, volume 98 of the *Lawyers Edition*, starting at page 873. The *Lawyers Edition* went into a second series in 1956, and cases since are cited as L. Ed. 2d.

Before 1816 the Court's opinions were published unofficially, and the volumes bear the compilers' names: A. J. Dallas (cited as Dall.) and William Cranch (cited as Cr.). In 1816 Congress created the Office of Reporter for the Court, and until 1875 decisions were published under the reporter's name:

Dates	Reporter	Citation
1816-1827	Wheaton	Wh.
1828-1843	Peters	Pet.
1843-1860	Howard	How.
1861-1862	Black	Bl.
1863-1874	Wallace	Wall.

1. James D. Richardson, ed., *A Compilation of the Messages and Papers of the Presidents* (Washington, D.C.: Bureau of National Literature and Art, 1908),

II, 581-582.

2. There are some who argue that the Supreme Court, by striking down such gender-based legislation as denials of equal protection of the laws required by the Fourteenth and Fifth amendments, actually weakened the case for ratification of an equal rights amendment to the Constitution.

3. Benjamin N. Cardozo, *The Nature of the Judicial Process* (New Haven: Yale University Press, 1921), 168.

1. COURTS AND THE CONSTITUTION

Americans have had a long love affair with written constitutions. A series of agreements—such as the Mayflower Compact of 1620, the various colonial charters granted by the king, and the constitutions most states adopted during the revolutionary period—nourished faith that words inscribed on paper can tame arbitrary political force. When the time came to establish a new nation, the founding generation chose to adopt first the Articles of Confederation and later the Constitution; they gave little serious thought to using the British notion of an unwritten basic law.

With the new Constitution came a period of economic prosperity and political expansion. The document's initial successes quickly cast a halo around it. One of the first senators from Pennsylvania complained that to hear some people talk one would have thought that "neither wood grew nor water ran in America before the happy adoption of the Constitution." The Constitution became and has remained sacrosanct, a form of higher law. For most Americans something that is "unconstitutional" is also morally evil. The Constitution, President Grover Cleveland said at the celebration of its first centennial, is the "ark of the people's covenant."

But Americans have also developed a love affair with democracy, believing both that, in the abstract, government derives its just powers from the consent of the governed and, specifically, that public officials should be chosen by, and held responsible to, the people. As in most multiple love affairs, there is great potential for conflict.[1] The very notion of constitutionalism—that individuals have certain rights that government must respect—exists in tension with the idea that the people should rule, for what a large majority of the people want at any particular time may trample on the rights of those in the minority.

Thus judges have played an ambivalent role in the American political system. On frequent occasions, they have spoken for constitutionalism against democracy's claims and have invalidated acts of Congress or the president through an authority called judicial review. But even more often judges have deferred to elected officials, as the third case in this chapter, *Korematsu v. United States* (1944), illustrates.

This latter kind of judicial activity attracts little attention because it tends to soothe rather than generate conflict.

By what authority do judges assert authority to invalidate presidential and congressional policy? The constitutional document provides no answer to the question of who is its ultimate interpreter, only a series of tantalizing hints that point toward "the People," the Congress, the president, and the courts. (Judicial control over state action is more obviously grounded in the plain words of Article VI.) In the first case we read, Marbury v. Madison (1803), Chief Justice John Marshall tried to reduce the argument for judicial review to a syllogism. How well he succeeded has been a matter of dispute. Thomas Jefferson, for instance, maintained that the chief justice had utterly failed to make a persuasive argument.

Nevertheless, Marshall's justification has been widely accepted, and Americans have cheerfully—and sometimes mindlessly—blended constitutionalism and democracy. The role of judges as important constitutional interpreters has become an integral part of the political system. What is not a part of the system—so presidents Jefferson, Andrew Jackson, Abraham Lincoln, Franklin Roosevelt, and Ronald Reagan have claimed—is that judges are the final *constitutional interpreters.*

---

1. *As Chapter 3 points out, Americans have simultaneously had other political love affairs—with localism, for instance, the idea that people in various parts of the country (or even within a single state) have somewhat different needs and outlooks and that diversity is something to be cherished, not merely tolerated. The notion of localism is instilled in the American constitutional system in the form of federalism.*

~ Case 1.1 ~

Chief Justice **MARSHALL:** "It is, emphatically, the province and duty of the judicial department, to say what the law is."

Marbury ˙v. Madison
5 U.S. (1 Cr.) 137, 2 L. Ed. 60 (1803)

In the election of 1800 the Jeffersonian Republicans crushed the Federalist party. But the Federalists, taking advantage of the fact that their terms of office would not expire until the following March (the expiration was changed to January by the Twentieth Amendment, adopted in 1933), passed the Judiciary Act of 1801. This statute created a large number of new judgeships, a move intended to give conservative judges the opportunity to curb the excesses expected of Thomas Jefferson. (One must realize that Federalists looked on Jefferson as a radical, much as modern Americans would view a Marxist.) As expected, President John Adams nominated, and the lame-duck Federalist majority in the Senate confirmed, deserving Federalists to these newly created posts.

Many of these appointments came, however, at the very last hours of Adams's term of office. John Marshall, who saw no ethical problems in simultaneously serving as chief justice of the United States and as secretary of state, was responsible for seeing that the new jurists received their commissions. But, during the last minute rush, Marshall's clerk—in a fine display of nepotism, his brother—misplaced several of the commissions; and when he took office the next day, Jefferson ordered the new secretary of state, James Madison, not to deliver them.

After some delay William Marbury, one of the disappointed judges, brought a lawsuit asking the Court to issue a mandamus *to James Madison, that is, to order him, in effect, to do his duty and deliver the commission. Marbury began his case not in one of the usual trial courts but in the U.S. Supreme Court. He claimed that sec. 13 of the Judiciary Act of 1789 authorized the Supreme Court to issue a* mandamus *under its original jurisdiction—its authority to hear cases as a trial court rather than, as was (and is) far more common, as an appellate tribunal reviewing decisions of lower courts.*

Because the terms of sec. 13 are quite general, the Supreme Court could have easily disposed of the case by pointing out that the statute allowed the Court to issue a mandamus *whenever its jurisdiction was properly invoked, and, under the terms of Article III of the Constitution, Marbury could not properly invoke that jurisdiction But John*

Marshall and the other Federalist justices decided to use the occasion for a bold assertion of judicial power, in essence to stake out their claim to power in the face of the Jeffersonians' control of Congress and the presidency.

Marshall's opinion for the Court began by asking two questions: Had Marbury a right to the commission? And did the law provide him a remedy? The chief justice's answer to both questions was a decided yes. In fact, he paused to deliver a long lecture about Jefferson's illegal and unethical action in refusing to allow the commission to be delivered. Then and only then did Marshall turn to what is normally the first question a judge asks: Had Marbury sought the proper remedy, that is, did the Supreme Court have original jurisdiction over the case? By accepting Marbury's interpretation of sec. 13 that the statute added to the original jurisdiction given to the Court by Article III of the Constitution, Marshall cleverly turned the case into a vehicle to analyze whether a judge should obey an act of Congress or the Constitution when the two were in conflict. In sum, he was asking whether federal judges had a legal power that we call judicial review—the authority of a court to declare invalid acts of a coordinate branch of government.

Mr. Chief Justice **MARSHALL** delivered the opinion of the Court. . . .

The question whether an act, repugnant to the constitution, can become the law of the land, is a question deeply interesting, but, happily, not of an intricacy proportioned to its interest. It seems only necessary to recognize certain principles . . . to decide it. That the people have an original right to establish for their future government, such principles as, in their opinion, shall most conduce to their own happiness, is the basis on which the whole American fabric has been erected. The exercise of this original right is a very great exertion; nor can it, nor ought it, to be frequently repeated. The principles, therefore, so established, are deemed fundamental; and as the authority from which they proceed is supreme, and can seldom act, they are designed to be permanent.

This original and supreme will organizes the government, and assigns to different departments their respective powers. It may either stop here, or establish certain limits not to be transcended by those departments. The government of the United States is of the latter description. The powers of the legislature are defined and limited; and that those limits may not be mistaken, or forgotten, the constitution is written. To what purpose are powers limited, and to what purpose is that limitation committed to writing, if these limits may, at any time, be passed by those intended to be restrained? . . . It is a proposition too plain to be contested, that the constitution controls any legislative act repugnant to it; or that the legislature may alter the constitution by an ordinary act.

Between these alternatives, there is no middle ground. The constitution is either a superior paramount law, unchangeable by ordinary means, or it is on a level with ordinary legislative acts, and, like other acts, is alterable when the legislature shall please to alter it. If the former part of the alternative be true, then a legislative act, contrary to the constitution, is not law; if the latter part be true, then written constitutions are absurd attempts . . . to limit a power, in its own nature, illimitable.

Certainly, all those who have framed written constitutions contemplate them as forming the fundamental and paramount law of the nation, and consequently, the theory of every such government must be, that an act of the legislature repugnant to the constitution is void. This theory is essentially attached to a written constitution, and is, consequently, to be considered, by this court, as one of the fundamental principles of our society. . . .

If an act of the legislature, repugnant to the constitution, is void, does it, notwithstanding its invalidity, bind the courts, and oblige them to give it effect? Or, in other words, though it not be law, does it constitute a rule as operative as if it was a law? This would be to overthrow, in fact, what was established in theory; and would seem, at first view, an absurdity too gross to be insisted on. It shall, however, receive a more attentive consideration.

It is, emphatically, the province and duty of the judicial department, to say what the law is. Those who apply the rule to particular cases, must of necessity expound and interpret that rule. If two laws conflict with each other, the courts must decide on the operation of each. So, if a law be in opposition to the constitution; if both the law and the constitution apply to a particular case, so that the court must either decide that case, conformably to the law, disregarding the constitution; or conformably to the constitution, disregarding the law; the court must determine which of these conflicting rules governs the case; this is of the very essence of judicial duty. If then, the courts are to regard the constitution, and the constitution is superior to any ordinary act of the legislature, the constitution, and not such ordinary act, must govern the case to which they both apply.

Those, then, who controvert the principle, that the constitution is to be considered, in court, as a paramount law, are reduced to the necessity of maintaining that courts must close their eyes on the constitution, and see only the law. This doctrine would subvert the very foundation of all written constitutions. . . . It would declare, that if the legislature shall do that which is expressly forbidden, such act, notwithstanding the express prohibition, is in reality effectual. It would be giving to the legislature a practical and real omnipotence, with the same breath which professes to restrict their powers within narrow limits. . . .

The judicial power of the United States is extended to all cases arising under the constitution. Could it be the intention of those who gave this power, to say, that in using it, the constitution should not be looked into? That a case arising under the constitution should be decided, without examining the instrument under which it arises? This is too extravagant to be maintained. In some cases, then, the constitution must be looked into by the judges. And if they can open it at all, what part of it are they forbidden to read or to obey?

There are many other parts of the constitution which serve to illustrate this subject. It is declared that "no tax or duty shall be laid on articles exported from any state." Suppose, a duty on the export of cotton, of tobacco, or of flour; and a suit intended to recover it. Ought judgment to be rendered in such a case? Ought the judges to close their eyes on the constitution, and only see the law?

The constitution declares "that no bill of attainder or *ex post facto* law shall be passed." If, however, such a bill should be passed, and a person should be prosecuted under it; must the court condemn to death those victims whom the constitution endeavors to preserve? . . .

From these, and many other selections which might be made, it is apparent that the framers of the constitution contemplated that instrument as a rule for the government of courts, as well as of the legislature. Why otherwise does it direct the judges to take an oath to support it? . . . How immoral to impose it on them, if they were to be used as the instruments, and the knowing instruments, for violating what they swear to support! . . . Why does a judge swear to discharge his duties agreeably to the constitution of the United States, if that constitution forms no rule for his government? If it is closed upon him, and cannot be inspected by him? If such be the real state of things, this is worse than solemn mockery. To prescribe, or to take the oath, becomes equally a crime.

It is also not entirely unworthy of observation, that in declaring what shall be the supreme law of the land, the constitution itself is first mentioned; and not the laws of the United States, generally, but those only which shall be made in pursuance of the constitution, have that rank.

Thus, the particular phraseology of the constitution of the United States confirms and strengthens the principle, supposed to be essential to all written constitutions, that a law repugnant to the constitution is void; and that *courts*, as well as other departments, are bound by that instrument.

The rule must be discharged.

Editors' Note: To delay a decision, the Jeffersonians, worried by Marbury's lawsuit, had pushed through Congress a statute changing the dates of the Supreme Court's sittings. Furthermore, they broadly and publicly hinted that, were the Court to order Madison to deliver the commission, Jefferson would not allow him to do so. But Marshall's cunning in holding the Court to be without jurisdiction, while at the same time asserting the power of judicial review, left Jefferson with no order to disobey. He could only fume in frustration and proceed with plans to impeach one or more Federalist members of the Court.

~ Case 1.2 ~

Justice **DAVIS:** "No doctrine, involving more pernicious consequences, was ever invented by the wit of man than that any of [the
Constitution's] provisions can be suspended during any of the great
exigencies of government."

Ex Parte* Milligan
71 U.S. (4 Wall.) 2, 18 L. Ed. 281 (1866)

*During the Civil War, President Lincoln authorized courts mar-
tial—tribunals staffed by military officers—to try persons for certain
offenses pertaining to the waging of war. In October 1864, federal
troops arrested Lambdin P. Milligan, an alleged member of an armed
pro-Southern guerrilla unit, on charges of conspiring against the United
States and giving aid and comfort to its enemies. He was tried later that
year by a court martial, as authorized by the president, convicted, and
sentenced to hang. His lawyers unsuccessfully sought a writ of* habeas
corpus—*an order from a judge directing a person who has custody of a
prisoner to bring that prisoner into court and show by what legal
authority the prisoner is being restrained—from a local federal court,
then appealed to the U.S. Supreme Court.*

Mr. Justice **DAVIS** delivered the opinion of the Court. . . .
The importance of the main question presented by this record cannot be
overstated, for it involves the very framework of the government and the
fundamental principles of American liberty.
During the late wicked Rebellion the temper of the times did not allow
that calmness in deliberation and discussion so necessary to a correct
conclusion of a purely judicial question. Then, considerations of safety were
mingled with the exercise of power, and feelings and interests prevailed
which are happily terminated. Now that the public safety is assured, this
question, as well as all others, can be discussed and decided without
passion. . . .

° *"Ex parte," Latin for "on behalf of," has several meanings as a legal term.
In the context of this case, it refers to litigation brought by a friend or lawyer on
behalf of a person who, because he is imprisoned, cannot himself file suit. For a
related but somewhat different usage, see United States v. United States
District Court (1972; Case 1.4)—Eds.*

The controlling question in the case is this: Upon the facts stated in Milligan's petition, and the exhibits filed, had the Military Commission mentioned in it jurisdiction, legally, to try and sentence him? Milligan, not a resident of one of the rebellious states, or a prisoner of war, but a citizen of Indiana for twenty years past, and never in the military or naval service, is, while at his home, arrested by the military power of the United States, imprisoned and, on certain criminal charges preferred against him, tried, convicted, and sentenced to be hanged by a military commission, organized under the direction of the military commander of the military district of Indiana. Had this tribunal the legal power and authority to try and punish this man?

No graver question was ever considered by this court, nor one which more nearly concerns the rights of the whole people; for it is the birthright of every American citizen when charged with crime, to be tried and punished according to law.... The decision of this question does not depend on argument or judicial precedents, numerous and highly illustrative as they are. These precedents inform us of the extent of the struggle to preserve liberty and to relieve those in civil life from military trials. The founders of our government were familiar with the history of that struggle; and secured in a written Constitution every right which the people had wrested from power during a contest of ages....

... The history of the world had taught them that what was done in the past might be attempted in the future. The Constitution of the United States is a law for rulers and people, equally in war and peace, and covers with the shield of its protection all classes of men, at all times, and under all circumstances. No doctrine, involving more pernicious consequences, was ever invented by the wit of man than that any of its provisions can be suspended during any of the great exigencies of government. Such a doctrine leads directly to anarchy or despotism, but the theory of necessity on which it is based is false; for the government, within the Constitution, has all the powers granted to it which are necessary to preserve its existence, as has been happily proved by the result of the great effort to throw off its just authority....

Every trial involves the exercise of judicial power; and from what source did the Military Commission that tried him derive their authority? Certainly no part of the judicial power of the country was conferred on them; because the Constitution expressly vests it "in one Supreme Court and such inferior courts as the Congress may from time to time ordain and establish," and it is not pretended that the commission was a court ordained and established by Congress. They cannot justify on the mandate of the President; because he is controlled by law, and has his appropriate sphere of duty, which is to execute, not to make, the laws; and there is "no unwritten criminal code to which resort can be had as a source of jurisdiction."

But it is said that the jurisdiction is complete under the "laws and usages of war." It can serve no useful purpose to inquire what those laws and usages are, whence they originated, where found, and on whom they operate; they can never be applied to citizens in states which have upheld the authority of the government, and where the courts are open and their process unobstructed. This court has judicial knowledge that in Indiana the Federal authority was always unopposed, and its courts always open to hear criminal accusations and redress grievances; and no usage of war could sanction a military trial there for any offense whatever of a citizen in civil life, in nowise connected with the military service. Congress could grant no such power; and to the honor of our national legislature be it said, it has never been provoked by the state of the country even to attempt its exercise. One of the plainest constitutional provisions was, therefore, infringed when Milligan was tried by a court not ordained and established by Congress, and not composed of judges appointed during good behavior. . . .

Another guarantee of freedom was broken when Milligan was denied a trial by jury. The great minds of the country have differed on the correct interpretation to be given to various provisions of the Federal Constitution; and judicial decision has been often invoked to settle their true meaning; but until recently no one ever doubted that the right of trial by jury was fortified in the organic law against the power of attack. It is now assailed; but if ideas can be expressed in words, and language has any meaning, this right—one of the most valuable in a free country—is preserved to everyone accused of crime who is not attached to the Army or Navy or Militia in actual service. The Sixth Amendment affirms that "in all criminal prosecutions the accused shall enjoy the right to a speedy and public trial by an impartial jury," language broad enough to embrace all persons and cases; but the Fifth, recognizing the necessity of an indictment, or presentment, before anyone can be held to answer for high crimes, "*excepts* cases arising in the land or naval forces, or in the militia, when in actual service, in time of war or public danger," and the framers of the Constitution, doubtless, meant to limit the right to trial by jury, in the Sixth Amendment, to those persons who were subject to indictment or presentment in the Fifth.

. . . This privilege is a vital principle, underlying the whole administration of criminal justice; it is not held by sufferance, and cannot be frittered away on any plea of state or political necessity. When peace prevails, and the authority of the government is undisputed, there is no difficulty in preserving the safeguards of liberty; for the ordinary modes of trial are never neglected, and no one wishes it otherwise; but if society is disturbed by civil commotion—if the passions of men are aroused and the restraints of law weakened, if not disregarded—these safeguards need, and should receive, the watchful care of those intrusted with the guardianship of the Constitution and laws. In no other way can we transmit to posterity unimpaired the blessings of liberty, consecrated by the sacrifices of the Revolution.

It is claimed that martial law covers with its broad mantle the proceedings of this Military Commission. The proposition is this: That in a time of war the commander of an armed force (if in his opinion the exigencies of the country demand it, and of which he is to judge), has the power, within the lines of his military district, to suspend all civil rights and their remedies, and subject citizens as well as soldiers to the rule of his will; and in the exercise of his lawful authority cannot be restrained, except by his superior officer or the President of the United States.

If this position is sound to the extent claimed, then when war exists, foreign or domestic, and the country is subdivided into military departments for mere convenience, the commander of one of them can, if he chooses, within the limits, on the plea of necessity, with the approval of the Executive, substitute military force for and to the exclusion of the laws, and punish all persons, as he thinks right and proper, without fixed or certain rules.

The statement of this proposition shows its importance; for, if true, republican government is a failure, and there is an end of liberty regulated by law. . . . Civil liberty and this kind of martial law cannot endure together; the antagonism is irreconcilable and, in the conflict, one or the other must perish.

This nation, as experience has proved, cannot always remain at peace, and has no right to expect that it will always have wise and humane rulers, sincerely attached to the principles of the Constitution. Wicked men, ambitious of power, with hatred of liberty and contempt of law, may fill the place once occupied by Washington and Lincoln; and if this right is conceded, and the calamities of war again befall us, the dangers to human liberty are frightful to contemplate. If our fathers had failed to provide for just such a contingency, they would have been false to the trust reposed in them. . . .

It follows, from what has been said on this subject, that there are occasions when martial rule can be properly applied. If, in foreign invasion or civil war, the courts are actually closed, and it is impossible to administer criminal justice according to law then, on the theater of actual military operations, where war really prevails, there is a necessity to furnish a substitute for the civil authority, thus overthrown, to preserve the safety of the army and society; and as no power is left but the military, it is allowed to govern by martial rule until the laws can have their free course. As necessity creates the rule, so it limits its duration; for, if this government is continued after the courts are reinstated, it is a gross usurpation of power. Martial rule can never exist where the courts are open, and in the proper and unobstructed exercise of their jurisdiction. It is also confined to the locality of actual war. . . .

[Mr. Chief Justice **CHASE** delivered a concurring opinion in which Justices **WAYNE**, **SWAYNE**, and **MILLER** joined. The justices concurred in the result of *Milligan* but reasoned that the majority opinion went too far in saying that Congress under no circumstances could have authorized trials by such a military tribunal. They thought that "the power of Congress in the government of the land and naval forces and of the militia, is not at all affected by the fifth or any other amendment" and were unwilling to say that circumstances could never exist that would justify such an action by Congress.]

Editors' Note: Justice Davis's opinion makes the issues seem crystal clear, but one should note: (1) the case was decided in 1866, a year after the war had ended; and (2) during the war the justices had cleverly dodged deciding several cases that presented much the same issue as Milligan. A similar case grew out of World War II. During the war the governor of Hawaii had declared martial law. Over the protest of the local federal district judge, which resulted in the military's threatening to arrest the judge and the judge's holding the commanding general in contempt of court, military tribunals conducted many trials of civilians. The judge and the general agreed on a truce until the Supreme Court had decided a test case. Once more the justices spoke out boldly in favor of trials for civilians in regular courts, but once more they waited until the war was over to speak boldly. Indeed, in this particular case, Duncan v. Kahanamoku, 327 U.S. 304 (1946), they relied totally upon statutory interpretation rather than basic constitutional principles.

~ Case 1.3 ~

Justice **BLACK:** "Here, as in *Hirabayashi*, we cannot reject as unfounded the judgment of the military authorities and of Congress that there were disloyal [Japanese-Americans]....' "

Justice **MURPHY:** "This exclusion ... goes over 'the very brink of constitutional power' and falls into the ugly abyss of racism."

Korematsu v. United States
323 U.S. 214, 65 S. Ct. 193, 89 L. Ed. 194 (1944)

When the Japanese bombed Pearl Harbor and made December 7, 1941, in Franklin D. Roosevelt's words, "a date that will live in infamy," Americans reacted with shock, anger, and an emotionally charged resolve to retaliate. Further spurred by economic interest groups on the Pacific Coast who feared the frugal, industrious Japanese immigrants and American citizens of Japanese ancestry, Congress made it a crime to "enter, remain in, leave, or commit any act in a military area" designated by the president or the secretary of war. Abetted by near hysteria among those (like the future chief justice Earl Warren) who should have known better and by his own outspoken racial bigotry, the commanding general of the West Coast ordered a curfew (8 p.m. to 6 a.m.) for all persons of Japanese ancestry. Then, asserting that "a Jap is a Jap" and describing World War II as "a war of the white race against the yellow race," the general used the authority delegated to him by the secretary of war to command all persons of Japanese ancestry to report to relocation centers for transportation to concentration camps. At the same time as he was incarcerating American citizens of Japanese ancestry, the general allowed German and Italian aliens to remain in their residences and follow more or less normal lives.

As would be expected, the general's policy provoked several lawsuits. Hirabayashi v. United States, decided by the Supreme Court in 1943, involved a conviction on counts of violating both the curfew and the order to report to a relocation center. The justices took advantage of the fact that the sentences ran concurrently to restrict their ruling to the validity of the curfew. (A decision on the constitutionality of the program of relocation would not have freed the Japanese-American if the curfew order had been valid.) On very narrow grounds, the Court sustained the curfew, likening it to a fire line, which police use to keep crowds out of danger and out of the way in an emergency. Then, in 1944, the justices agreed to review Fred Korematsu's case. He had been convicted solely for refusing to report to a relocation center.

Mr. Justice **BLACK** delivered the opinion of the Court. . . .

It should be noted . . . that all legal restrictions which curtail the civil rights of a single racial group are immediately suspect. That is not to say that all such restrictions are unconstitutional. It is to say that courts must subject them to more rigid scrutiny. Pressing public necessity may sometimes justify the existence of such restrictions; racial antagonism never can. . . .

In light of the principles we announced in the Hirabayashi Case, we are unable to conclude that it was beyond the war power of Congress and the Executive to exclude those of Japanese ancestry from the West Coast area. . . . True, exclusion from . . . one's home . . . is a far greater deprivation than constant confinement to the home from 8 p.m. to 6 p.m. . . . But exclusion from a threatened area, no less than curfew, has a definite and close relationship to the prevention of espionage and sabotage. The military authorities, charged with the primary responsibility of defending our shores, concluded that curfew provided inadequate protection and ordered exclusion. They did so, in accordance with congressional authority to the military to say who should, and who should not, remain in the threatened areas. . . .

Here, as in *Hirabayashi*, "we cannot reject as unfounded the judgment of the military authorities and of Congress that there were disloyal members of that population. . . ."

. . . It was because we could not reject the finding of the military authorities that it was impossible to bring about an immediate segregation of the disloyal from the loyal that we sustained the validity of the curfew order as applying to the whole group. In the instant case, temporary exclusion of the entire group was rested by the military on the same ground. . . .

. . . [W]e are not unmindful of the hardships imposed by it upon a large group of American citizens. . . . But hardships are part of war, and war is an aggregation of hardships. Compulsory exclusion of large groups of citizens from their homes, except under circumstances of direst emergency and peril, is inconsistent with our basic governmental institutions. But when under conditions of modern warfare our shores are threatened by hostile forces, the power to protect must be commensurate with the threatened danger. . . .

We are thus being asked to pass at this time upon the whole subsequent detention program in both assembly and relocation centers, although the only issues framed at the trial related to petitioner's remaining in the prohibited area in violation of the exclusion order. Had petitioner here left the prohibited area and gone to an assembly center we cannot say either as a matter of fact or law, that his presence in that center would have resulted in his detention in a relocation center.° Some who did report to the assembly center were not sent to relocation centers, but were released upon condition that they remain outside the prohibited zone until the military orders were modified or lifted. . . .

Since the petitioner has not been convicted of failing to report or to remain in an assembly or relocation center, we cannot in this case determine the validity of these separate provisions of the order. . . .

Some of the members of the Court are of the view that evacuation and detention in an Assembly Center were inseparable. . . . The power to exclude includes the power to do it by force if necessary. And any forcible measure must necessarily entail some degree of detention or restraint whatever method of removal is selected. But whichever view is taken, it results in holding that the order under which petitioner was convicted was valid.

It is said that we are dealing here with the case of imprisonment of a citi-

---

° *In its brief, the Justice Department conceded that had Korematsu gone to an assembly center he would have been placed in a detention camp.—Eds.*

zen in a concentration camp solely because of his ancestry. . . . Our task would be simple were this a case involving the imprisonment of a loyal citizen in a concentration camp because of racial prejudice. Regardless of the true nature of the assembly and relocation centers—and we deem it unjustifiable to call them concentration camps with all the ugly connotations that term implies—we are dealing specifically with nothing but an exclusion order. To cast this case into outlines of racial prejudice, without reference to the real military dangers which were presented, merely confuses the issue. Korematsu was not excluded from the Military Area because of hostility to him or his race. He *was* excluded because we are at war with the Japanese Empire, because the properly constituted military authorities feared an invasion of our West Coast and felt constrained to take proper security measures, because they decided that the military urgency of the situation demanded that all citizens of Japanese ancestry be segregated from the West Coast temporarily, and finally, because Congress, reposing its confidence in this time of war in our military leaders—as inevitably it must—determined that they should have the power to do just this. There was evidence of disloyalty on the part of some, the military authorities considered that the need for action was great, and time was short. We cannot—by availing ourselves of the calm perspective of hindsight—now say that at that time these actions were unjustified.

Affirmed.

Mr. Justice **FRANKFURTER,** concurring. . . .

The provisions of the Constitution which confer on the Congress and the President powers to . . . wage war are as much part of the Constitution as provisions looking to a nation at peace. . . . Therefore the validity of action under the war power must be judged wholly in the context of war. That action is not to be stigmatized as lawless because like action in times of peace would be lawless. To talk about a military order that expresses an allowable judgment of war needs by those entrusted with the duty of conducting war as "an unconstitutional order" is to suffuse a part of the Constitution with an atmosphere of unconstitutionality. The respective spheres of action of military authorities and of judges are of course very different. But within their sphere, military authorities are no more outside the bounds of obedience to the Constitution than are judges within theirs. . . .

To find that the Constitution does not forbid the military measures now complained of does not carry with it approval of that which the Congress and the Executive did. That is their business, not ours.

Mr. Justice **ROBERTS**, dissenting:

I dissent, because I think the indisputable facts exhibit a clear violation of Constitutional rights. . . . [E]xclusion was but a part of an over-all plan for forceable detention. . . . The two conflicting orders, one of which commanded him to stay and the other which commanded him to go, were nothing but a cleverly devised trap to accomplish the real purpose of the military authority, which was to lock him up in a concentration camp. . . . Why should we set up a figmentary and artificial situation instead of addressing ourselves to the actualities of the case? . . .

Mr. Justice **MURPHY,** dissenting:

This exclusion . . . goes over "the very brink of constitutional power" and falls into the ugly abyss of racism.

In dealing with matters relating to the prosecution and progress of a war, we must accord great respect . . . to the judgments of the military authorities. . . .

At the same time, however, it is essential that there be limits to military discretion. . . .

The judicial test of whether the Government, on a plea of military necessity, can validly deprive an individual of any of his constitutional rights is whether the deprivation is reasonably related to a public danger that is so "immediate, imminent, and impending" as not to admit of delay and not to permit the intervention of ordinary constitutional processes to alleviate the danger. . . .

Civilian Exclusion Order No. 34 . . . clearly does not meet that test. Being an obvious racial discrimination, the order deprives all those within its scope of the equal protection of the laws as guaranteed by the Fifth Amendment. It further deprives these individuals of their constitutional rights to live and work where they will, to establish a home where they choose and to move about freely. In excommunicating them without benefit of hearings, this order also deprives them of all their constitutional rights to procedural due process. Yet no reasonable relation to an "immediate, imminent, and impending" public danger is evident to support this racial restriction. . . .

It must be conceded that the military and naval situation in the spring of 1942 was such as to generate a very real fear of invasion of the Pacific Coast, accompanied by fears of sabotage and espionage in that area. The military command was therefore justified in adopting all reasonable means necessary to combat these dangers. In adjudging the military action taken in light of the then apparent dangers, we must not erect too high or too meticulous standards; it is necessary only that the action have some reasonable relation to the removal of the dangers. . . . But the exclusion . . . of all persons with Japanese blood in their veins has no such reasonable relation . . . because the ʼexclusion order necessarily must rely for its reasonableness upon the assumption that *all* persons of Japanese ancestry may have a dangerous tendency to commit sabotage and espionage and to aid our Japanese enemy in other ways. . . .

That this forced exclusion was the result in good measure of this erroneous assumption of racial guilt rather than bona fide military necessity is evidenced by the Commanding General's Final Report on the evacuation from the Pacific Coast area. In it he refers to all individuals of Japanese descent as "subversive," as belonging to "an enemy race" whose "racial strains are undiluted," and as constituting "over 112,000 potential enemies ... at large today" along the Pacific Coast. In support of this blanket condemnation of all persons of Japanese descent, however, no reliable evidence is cited. . . .

Justification ... is sought, instead, mainly upon questionable racial and sociological grounds not ordinarily within the realm of expert military judgment, supplemented by certain semi-military conclusions drawn from an unwarranted use of circumstantial evidence. . . .

The main reasons ... appear ... to be largely an accumulation of much of the misinformation, half-truths and insinuations that for years have been directed against Japanese Americans by people with racial and economic prejudices—the same people who have been among the foremost advocates of the evacuation. A military judgment based upon such racial and sociological considerations is not entitled to the great weight ordinarily given the judgments based upon strictly military considerations. Especially is this so when every charge relative to race, religion, culture, geographical location,. and legal and economic status has been substantially discredited by independent studies made by experts in these matters. . . .

I dissent, therefore, from this legalization of racism. Racial discrimination in any form and in any degree has no justifiable part whatever in our democratic way of life. It is unattractive in any setting but it is utterly revolting among a free people who have embraced the principles set forth in the Constitution of the United States. . . .

Mr. Justice **JACKSON,** dissenting:

Now if any fundamental assumption underlies our system, it is that guilt is personal and not inheritable. . . . But here is an attempt to make an otherwise innocent act a crime merely because this prisoner is the son of parents as to whom he had no choice, and belongs to a race from which there is no way to resign. . . .

. . . [T]he "law" which this prisoner is convicted of disregarding is not found in an act of Congress, but in a military order. Neither the Act of Congress nor the Executive Order of the President, nor both together, would afford a basis for this conviction. . . . And it is said that if the military commander had reasonable military grounds for promulgating the orders, they are constitutional and become law, and the Court is required to enforce them. . . .

It would be impracticable and dangerous idealism to expect or insist that each specific military command in an area of probable operations will conform to conventional tests of constitutionality. . . . The armed services must protect a society, not merely its Constitution. The very essence of the military job is to marshal physical force, to remove every obstacle to its effectiveness, to give it every strategic advantage. Defense measures will not, and often should not, be held within the limits that bind civil authority in peace. . . .

But if we cannot confine military expedients by the Constitution, neither would I distort the Constitution to approve all that the military may deem expedient. . . . I cannot say . . . that the orders of General DeWitt were not reasonably expedient military precautions, nor could I say that they were. But even if they were permissible military procedures, I deny that it follows that they are constitutional. If, as the Court holds, it does follow, then we may as well say that any military order will be constitutional and have done with it. . . .

Much is said of the danger to liberty from the Army program. . . . But a judicial construction of the due process clause that will sustain this order is a far more subtle blow to liberty. . . . A military order, however unconstitutional, is not apt to last longer than the military emergency. Even during that period a succeeding commander may revoke it all. But once a judicial opinion rationalizes such an order to show that it conforms to the Constitution, or rather rationalizes the Constitution to show that the Constitution sanctions such an order, the Court for all time has validated the principle of racial discrimination in criminal procedure and of transplanting American citizens. The principle then lies about like a loaded weapon ready for the hand of any authority that can bring forward a plausible claim of an urgent need. . . . All who observe the work of courts are familiar with what Judge Cardozo described as "the tendency of a principle to expand itself to the limit of its logic." A military commander may overstep the bounds of constitutionality, and it is an incident. But if we review and approve, that passing incident becomes the doctrine of the Constitution. There it has a generative power of its own, and all that it creates will be in its own image. Nothing better illustrates this danger than does the Court's opinion in this case. . . .

I should hold that a civil court cannot be made to enforce an order which violates constitutional limitations even if it is a reasonable exercise of military authority. The courts can exercise only the judicial power, can apply only law, and must abide by the Constitution, or they cease to be civil courts and become instruments of military policy.

. . . I would not lead people to rely on this Court for a review that seems to me wholly delusive. . . . If the people ever let command of the war power fall into irresponsible and unscrupulous hands, the courts wield no power equal to its restraint. The chief restraint upon those who command the physical forces of the country . . . must be their responsibility to the political judgments of their contemporaries and to the moral judgments of history.

My duties as a justice . . . do not require me to make a military judgment as to whether General DeWitt's evacuation and detention program was a reasonable military necessity. I do not suggest that the courts should have attempted to interfere with the Army in carrying out its task. But I do not think they may be asked to execute a military expedient that has no place in law under the Constitution. I would reverse the judgment and discharge the prisoner.

Editors' Note: On the same day the Court decided Korematsu, it also ruled on Ex parte Endo, 323 U.S. 283 (1944). Based on statutory rather than constitutional interpretation, Endo held that the government could not continue to detain any person whom it had investigated and found to be loyal. In effect, this decision marked the legal end of the internment program, because, with few exceptions, persons of Japanese ancestry were loyal to the United States. Some of the justices thought that Endo, because of its implications for the internment program, was the more important decision. However, Endo, as an interpretation of a no longer operative statute, is seldom recalled. Korematsu, as Justice Jackson warned, gives constitutional sanction to a policy based on racial discrimination.

∼ Case 1.4 ∼

Justice **POWELL:** "The Fourth Amendment does not contemplate the executive officers of Government as neutral and disinterested magistrates."

United States v. United States District Court
407 U.S. 297, 92 S. Ct. 2115, 32 L. Ed. 2d 752 (1972)

During the Vietnam War, the United States charged three antiwar activists with conspiring to destroy government property and one of the three with dynamiting a CIA office in Ann Arbor, Michigan. During pretrial proceedings, the defendants asked the judge to order the government to produce information gathered against them by means of electronic surveillance so that they could determine whether the government's case was "tainted" by illegally obtained evidence. The government conceded that it had used wiretaps without obtaining a warrant as provided by sec. III of the Omnibus Crime Control and Safe Streets Act, but asserted that such surveillance without a warrant was lawful in domestic security cases under the president's inherent power to protect national security. The district judge held that wiretaps without warrants violated the Fourth Amendment. The Court of Appeals for the Sixth Circuit agreed, and the government sought and obtained review from the U.S. Supreme Court.

Mr. Justice **POWELL** delivered the opinion of the Court.

The issue before us is an important one for the people of our country and their Government. It involves the delicate question of the President's power, acting through the Attorney General, to authorize electronic surveillance in internal security matters without prior judicial approval. Successive Presidents for more than one-quarter of a century have authorized such surveillance in varying degrees, without guidance from the Congress or a definitive decision of this Court. This case brings the issue here for the first time. Its resolution is a matter of national concern, requiring sensitivity both to the Government's right to protect itself from unlawful subversion and attack and to the citizen's right to be secure in his privacy against unreasonable Government intrusion. . . .

I

Title III of the Omnibus Crime Control and Safe Streets Act . . . authorizes the use of electronic surveillance for classes of crimes carefully specified. . . . Such surveillance is subject to prior court order. . . . The Act represents a comprehensive attempt by Congress to promote more effective control of crime while protecting the privacy of individual thought and expression. Much of Title III was drawn to meet constitutional requirements for electronic surveillance enunciated by this Court in Berger v. New York (1967), and Katz v. United States (1967).

Together with the elaborate surveillance requirements in Title III, there is the following proviso, 18 USC° § 2511 (3):

> "Nothing contained in this chapter or in section 605 of the Communications Act of 1934 shall limit the constitutional power of the President to take such measures as he deems necessary to protect the Nation against actual or potential attack or other hostile acts of a foreign power, to obtain foreign intelligence information deemed essential to the security of the United States, or to protect national security information against foreign intelligence activities. *Nor shall anything contained in this chapter be deemed to limit the constitutional power of the President to take such measures as he deems necessary to*

° *"USC" refers to the United States Code.—Eds.*

> *protect the United States against the overthrow of the Government by force or other unlawful means, or against any other clear and present danger to the structure or existence of the Government.* The contents of any wire or oral communication intercepted by authority of the President in the exercise of the foregoing powers may be received in evidence in any trial hearing or other proceeding only where such interception was reasonable, and shall not be otherwise used or disclosed except as is necessary to implement that power." (Emphasis is supplied.)

The Government relies on § 2511 (3). It argues that "in excepting national security surveillances from the Act's warrant requirement Congress recognized the President's authority to conduct such surveillances without prior judicial approval." . . . The section thus is viewed as a recognition or affirmance of a constitutional authority in the President to conduct warrantless domestic security surveillance such as that involved in this case.

We think the language of § 2511 (3), as well as the legislative history of the statute, refutes this interpretation. The relevant language is that: "Nothing contained in this chapter . . . shall limit the constitutional power of the President to take such measures as he deems necessary to protect . . ." against the dangers specified. At most, this is an implicit recognition that the President does have certain powers in the specified areas. Few would doubt this, as the section refers—among other things—to protection "against actual or potential attack or other hostile acts of a foreign power." But so far as the use of the President's electronic surveillance power is concerned, the language is essentially neutral.

Section 2511 (3) certainly confers no power. . . . It merely provides that the Act shall not be interpreted to limit or disturb such power as the President may have under the Constitution. In short, Congress simply left presidential powers where it found them. . . .

The express grant of authority to conduct surveillances is found in § 2516, which authorizes the Attorney General to make application to a federal judge when surveillance may provide evidence of certain offenses. These offenses are described with meticulous care and specificity.

Where the Act authorizes surveillance, the procedure to be followed is specified in § 2518. Subsection (1) thereof requires application to a judge of competent jurisdiction for a prior order of approval, and states in detail the information required in such application. Subsection (3) prescribes the necessary elements of probable cause which the judge must find before issuing an order authorizing an interception. Subsection (4) sets forth the required contents of such an order. Subsection (5) sets strict time limits on an order. Provision is made in subsection (7) for "an emergency situation" found to exist by the Attorney General (or by the principal prosecuting attorney of a State) "with respect to conspiratorial activities threatening the national security interest." In such a situation, emergency surveillance may be conducted "if an application for an order approving the interception is made

... within forty-eight hours." If such an order is not obtained, or the application therefore is denied, the interception is deemed to be a violation of the Act.

In view of these and other interrelated provisions delineating permissible interceptions of particular criminal activity upon carefully specified conditions, it would have been incongruous for Congress to have legislated with respect to the important and complex area of national security in a single brief and nebulous paragraph. This would not comport with the sensitivity of the problem involved or with the extraordinary care Congress exercised in drafting other sections of the Act. We therefore think the conclusion inescapable that Congress only intended to make clear that the Act simply did not legislate with respect to national security surveillances.

The legislative history of § 2511 (3) supports this interpretation. . . .

II

It is important at the outset to emphasize the limited nature of the question before the Court. This case raises no constitutional challenge to electronic surveillance as specifically authorized by Title III of the Omnibus Crime Control and Safe Streets Act of 1968. Nor is there any question or doubt as to the necessity of obtaining a warrant in the surveillance of crimes unrelated to the national security interest. . . . Further, the instant case requires no judgment on the scope of the President's surveillance power with respect to the activities of foreign powers, within or without this country. The Attorney General's affidavit in this case states that the surveillances were "deemed necessary to protect the nation from attempts of *domestic organizations* to attack and subvert the existing structure of Government" (emphasis supplied).

There is no evidence of any involvement, directly or indirectly, of a foreign power. Our present inquiry, though important, is therefore a narrow one. . . .

"Whether safeguards other than prior authorization by a magistrate would satisfy the Fourth Amendment is a situation involving the national security. . . ."

We begin the inquiry by noting that the President . . . has the fundamental duty, under Art. II, § 1 of the Constitution, to "preserve, protect, and defend the Constitution of the United States." Implicit in that duty is the power to protect our Government against those who would subvert or overthrow it by unlawful means. In the discharge of this duty, the President—through the Attorney General—may find it necessary to employ electronic surveillance to obtain intelligence information on the plans of those who plot unlawful acts against the Government. . . . The price of lawful public dissent must not be dread of subjection to an unchecked surveillance power. Nor must the fear of unauthorized official eavesdropping deter vigorous citizen dissent and discussion of Government action in private conversation. For private dissent, no less than open public discourse, is essential to our free society.

III

As the Fourth Amendment is not absolute in its terms, our task is to examine and balance the basic values at stake in this case: the duty of Government to protect the domestic security, and the potential danger posed by unreasonable surveillance to individual privacy and free expression. If the legitimate need of Government to safeguard domestic security requires the use of electronic surveillance, the question is whether the needs of citizens for privacy and free expression may not be better protected by requiring a warrant before such surveillance is undertaken. We must also ask whether a warrant requirement would unduly frustrate the efforts of Government to protect itself from acts of subversion and overthrow directed against it.

Though the Fourth Amendment speaks broadly of "unreasonable searches and seizures," the definition of "reasonableness" turns, at least in part, on the more specific commands of the warrant clause. . . . The warrant clause of the Fourth Amendment . . . has been "a valued part of our constitutional law for decades, and it has determined the result in scores and scores of cases in courts all over this country. It is not an inconvenience to be somehow 'weighed' against the claims of police efficiency. It is, or should be, an important working part of our machinery of government, operating as a matter of course to check the 'well-intentioned but mistakenly overzealous executive officers' who are a part of any system of law enforcement." Coolidge v. New Hampshire (1971).

Over two centuries ago, Lord Mansfield held that common-law principles prohibited warrants that ordered the arrest of unnamed individuals whom the *officer* might conclude were guilty of seditious libel. "It is not fit," said Mansfield, "that the receiving or judging of the information should be left to the discretion of the officer. The magistrate ought to judge; and should give certain directions to the officer." . . .

Lord Mansfield's formulation touches the very heart of the Fourth Amendment directive: that, where practical, a governmental search and seizure should represent both the efforts of the officer to gather evidence of wrongful acts and the judgment of the magistrate that the collected evidence is sufficient to justify invasion of a citizen's private premises or conversation. Inherent in the concept of a warrant is its issuance by a "neutral and detached magistrate." . . . The further requirement of "probable cause" instructs the magistrate that baseless searches shall not proceed.

These Fourth Amendment freedoms cannot properly be guaranteed if domestic security surveillances may be conducted solely within the discretion of the executive branch. The Fourth Amendment does not contemplate the executive officers of Government as neutral and disinterested magistrates. . . . The historical judgment, which the Fourth Amendment accepts, is that unreviewed executive discretion may yield too readily to pressures to obtain incriminating evidence and overlook potential invasions of privacy and protected speech.

It may well be that, in the instant case, the Government's surveillance . . . was a reasonable one which readily would have gained prior judicial approval. . . . The Fourth Amendment [, however,] contemplates a prior judicial judgment, not the risk that executive discretion may be reasonably exercised. This judicial role accords with our basic constitutional doctrine that individual freedoms will be best preserved through a separation of powers and division of functions among the different branches and levels of Government. . . . The independent check upon executive discretion is not satisfied, as the Government argues, by "extremely limited" post-surveillance judicial review. Indeed, post-surveillance review would never reach the surveillances which failed to result in prosecutions. . . .

It is true that there have been some exceptions to the warrant requirement. . . . But those exceptions are few in number and carefully delineated. . . . In general, they serve the legitimate needs of law enforcement officers to protect their own well-being and preserve evidence from destruction. . . .

The Government argues that the special circumstances applicable to domestic security surveillances necessitate a further exception to the warrant requirement. It is urged that the requirement of prior judicial review would obstruct the President in the discharge of his constitutional duty to protect domestic security. We are told further that these surveillances are directed primarily to the collecting and maintaining of intelligence with respect to subversive forces, and are not an attempt to gather evidence for specific criminal prosecutions. . . .

The Government further insists that courts "as a practical matter would have neither the knowledge nor the techniques necessary to determine whether there was probable cause to believe that surveillance was necessary to protect national security." . . .

As a final reason for exemption . . . the Government believes that disclosure to a magistrate of all or even a significant portion of the information involved in domestic security surveillances "would create serious potential dangers to the national security and to the lives of informants and agents . . . requiring prior judicial authorization would create a greater danger of leaks. . . ."

. . . [W]e do not think a case has been made for the requested departure from Fourth Amendment standards. The circumstances described do not justify complete exemption of domestic security surveillance from prior judicial scrutiny. Official surveillance, whether its purpose be criminal investigation or ongoing intelligence gathering, risks infringement of constitutionally protected privacy of speech. Security surveillances are especially sensitive because of the inherent vagueness of the domestic security concept, the necessarily broad and continuing nature of intelligence gathering, and the temptation to utilize such surveillances to oversee political dissent. We recognize, as we have before, the constitutional basis of the President's domestic security role, but we think it must be exercised in a manner compatible with the Fourth Amendment. In this case we hold that this requires an appropriate prior warrant procedure.

We cannot accept the Government's argument that internal security matters are too subtle and complex for judicial evaluation. Courts regularly deal with the most difficult issues of our society. There is no reason to believe that federal judges will be insensitive to or uncomprehending of the issues involved in domestic security cases. . . .

Nor do we believe prior judicial approval will fracture the secrecy essential to official intelligence gathering. The investigation of criminal activity has long involved imparting sensitive information to judicial officers who have respected the confidentialities involved. . . . Moreover, a warrant application involves no public or adversary proceedings: it is an ex parte° request before a magistrate or judge. . . .

Thus, we conclude that the Government's concerns do not justify departure in this case from the customary Fourth Amendment requirement of judicial approval prior to initiation of a search or surveillance. Although some added burden will be imposed upon the Attorney General, this inconvenience is justified in a free society to protect constitutional values. . . .

IV

We emphasize . . . the scope of our decision. . . . [T]his case involves only the domestic aspects of national security. We have not addressed, and express no opinion as to, the issues which may be involved with respect to activities of foreign powers or their agents. . . .

Moreover, we do not hold that the same type of standards and procedures prescribed by Title III are necessarily applicable to this case. We recognize that domestic security surveillance may involve different policy and practical considerations from the surveillance of "ordinary crime." . . .

Given these potential distinctions between . . . criminal surveillances and those involving the domestic security, Congress may wish to consider protective standards for the latter which differ from those already prescribed for specified crimes in Title III. Different standards may be compatible with the Fourth Amendment if they are reasonable both in relation to the

---

° *Here "ex parte" means only one side offers evidence and argument. See also footnote to Case 1.2.—Eds.*

legitimate need of Government for intelligence information and the protected rights of our citizens. . . .

The judgment of the Court of Appeals is hereby

Affirmed.

The Chief Justice [**BURGER**] concurs in the result.

Mr. Justice **REHNQUIST** took no part in the consideration or decision of this case.

Mr. Justice **DOUGLAS**, concurring. . . .

This is an important phase in the campaign of the police and intelligence agencies to obtain exemptions from the Warrant Clause of the Fourth Amendment. For, due to the clandestine nature of electronic eavesdropping, the need is acute for placing on the Government the heavy burden to show that "exigencies of the situation [make its] course imperative." Other abuses, such as the search incident to arrest, have been partly deterred by the threat of damage actions against offending officers, the risk of adverse publicity, or the possibility of reform through the political process. These latter safeguards, however, are ineffective against lawless wiretapping and "bugging" of which their victims are totally unaware. Moreover, even the risk of exclusion of tainted evidence would here appear to be of negligible deterrent value inasmuch as the United States frankly concedes that the primary purpose of these searches is to fortify its intelligence collage rather than to accumulate evidence to support indictments and convictions. If the Warrant Clause were held inapplicable here, then the federal intelligence machine would literally enjoy unchecked discretion.

Here, federal agents wish to rummage for months on end through every conversation, no matter how intimate or personal, carried over selected telephone lines, simply to seize those few utterances which may add to their sense of the pulse of a domestic underground.

We are told that one national security wiretap lasted for 14 months and monitored over 900 conversations. Senator Edward Kennedy found recently that "warrantless devices accounted for an average of 78 to 209 days of listening per device, as compared with a 13-day per device average for those devices installed under court order." . . .

Such gross invasions of privacy epitomize the very evil to which the Warrant Clause was directed. . . .

That "domestic security" is said to be involved here does not draw this case outside the mainstream of Fourth Amendment law. Rather, the recurring desire of reigning officials to employ dragnet techniques to intimidate their critics lies at the core of that prohibition. For it was such excesses as the use of general warrants and the writs of assistance that led to the ratification of the Fourth Amendment. In Entick v. Carrington . . . decided [in England] in 1765, one finds a striking parallel. . . . The Secretary of State had issued general executive warrants to his messengers authorizing them to roam about and to seize libelous material and libellants of the sovereign. Entick, a critic of the Crown, was the victim of one such general search during which his seditious publications were impounded. He brought a successful damage action for trespass against the messengers. The verdict was sustained on appeal. Lord Camden wrote that if such sweeping tactics were validated, then "the secret cabinets and bureaus of every subject in this kingdom will be thrown open to the search and inspection of a messenger, whenever the secretary of state shall think fit to charge, or even to suspect, a person to be the author, printer, or publisher of a seditious libel." . . .

Mr. Justice **WHITE,** concurring in the judgment. . . .

2. SEPARATE INSTITUTIONS SHARING POWERS

A mericans tend to speak of their political system as one of "separation of powers," allocating legislative authority to Congress, executive authority to the president and judicial authority to courts. In fact, however, the constitutional document and political practice have combined to create a system that Richard E. Neustadt described as one of "separated institutions sharing powers." [1]

Article I of the Constitution begins, "All legislative power herein granted shall be vested in a Congress of the United States"; but that article, as well as Article II, go on to make the president an integral part of the legislative process. He functions not only as chief executive, but also as chief legislator, who can veto bills, call Congress into special session, and adjourn the two houses when they disagree on a date. Although the president cannot formally introduce legislation, executive agencies draft many bills; furthermore, few important proposals can become law without at least the president's tacit cooperation.

More than the veto is involved here. Each house of Congress elects its own leadership; but no one can speak for both houses, and few legislators feel a heavy obligation to follow their congressional leadership. Given his automatic access to the mass media, the president can present a legislative program to the country as a whole and, as Lyndon B. Johnson claimed, put legislators' "feet to the fire." Moreover, not only can he reason with individual legislators; he can use his powers of patronage to reward or punish them and their constituents.

Congress, in turn, exercises a great deal of executive power. The Senate must consent to all important appointments. Moreover, all executive officials except the president and vice president hold offices created or authorized by statutes, and Congress may abolish those offices either directly or by refusing to appropriate money for their operations. That body may also take the less drastic course and stymie any agency's policies by reducing its budget.

Further, both Congress and the president exercise some judicial power. Congress creates all federal courts except the Supreme Court and specifies the number and salaries of all federal judges [2] as well as the amount of assistance they will have. In addition, congressional investi-

gating committees can severely punish people by parading their sins before television cameras. Presidents, by choosing judges, and the Senate, by confirming or not confirming them, often try to influence judicial decisions. And a president can pardon anyone convicted of a federal crime. In a negative way, the president can influence the impact of a decision by refusing to enforce it.

For their part, courts have some legislative and executive powers. Often the broad terms of the Constitution, more often the congressionalese of statutes, and most often the bureaucratese of executive orders cry out for creative interpretation. One cannot mechanically interpret such constitutional clauses as: Article I, sec. 8, which authorizes Congress to enact laws "necessary and proper" to carry out any power delegated to any branch of the national government; the Fifth and Fourteenth amendments, which forbid the federal and state governments to take "life, liberty, or property without due process of law"; the Fourteenth Amendment, which demands that states accord all persons "the equal protection of the laws"; or the Ninth Amendment, which says, "The enumeration in the Constitution of certain rights shall not be construed to deny or disparage others retained by the people."

There is, one likes to believe, one core of legislative powers, a second of executive powers, and a third of judicial powers. But, given the Constitution's requirement for sharing powers, those cores are elusive. And the founding generation was well aware that sharing and elusiveness would create distrust, jealousy, and conflict among public officials, thus limiting government by keeping power divided in fact as well as on paper. As Madison explained in Federalist No. 51:

> [T]he great security against a gradual concentration of the several powers in the same department consists in giving those who administer each department the necessary constitutional means and personal motives to resist encroachments of the others. . . . Ambition must be made to counteract ambition. The interest of the man must be connected with the constitutional rights of the place.

The system has worked pretty much as the framers foresaw. To get anything important accomplished, the various branches must cooperate to some extent; but friction among them has been the norm, and conflict frequent. To settle interbranch disputes Madison, like Jefferson, preferred negotiation rather than adjudication. As he told the First Congress:

> There is not one Government on the face of the earth . . . in which provision is made for a particular authority to determine the limits of the constitutional division of power between the branches of Government. In all systems there are points which must be adjusted by the departments themselves, to which no one of them is competent. If it

cannot be determined in this way, there is no recourse left but the will of the community.[3]

Here, however, practice has proven Madison only partly correct. Many interbranch disputes are indeed settled by negotiation—sometimes by open and clear discussion, sometimes by tacit bargaining. Still, many important disputes are settled by adjudication, by lawsuits filed by private citizens against public officials or by one set of public officials against another set. And, despite dangers inherent in getting between combatants—"Blessed are the peacemakers, for they will be reviled by both sides"—the Supreme Court has usually accepted the role of constitutional referee. Whether such a role is compatible with the basic purpose of shared and overlapping powers as a limitation on all government remains an open question.

---

1. *Richard E. Neustadt,* Presidential Power *(New York: Wiley, 1960), 33.*
2. *Article III, sec. 1 says that Congress shall not lower a judge's salary during his or her tenure; but in providing or not providing for increases in salaries Congress can affect the attractiveness of judicial service.*
3. Annals of Congress, *I, 521 (June 17, 1789).*

~ Case 2.1 ~

Justice **BLACK:** "[T]he Constitution is neither silent nor equivocal about who shall make laws which the President is to execute."

Chief Justice **VINSON:** "[I]f the President has any power under the Constitution to meet a critical situation in the absence of express statutory authorization, there is no basis whatever for criticizing the exercise of such power in this case."

Youngstown Sheet & Tube Co. v. Sawyer
343 U.S. 579, 72 S. Ct. 863, 96 L. Ed. 1153 (1952)

When the Korean War first broke out in June 1950 President Harry S. Truman and his advisers gambled that the conflict would be brief and that the United States could rely heavily on military supplies left over from World War II. But the Korean conflict dragged on, and initial slowness in ordering production of ammunition placed severe restrictions on American forces in combat. Then, in the spring of 1952, a bitter dispute over wages between the United Steel Workers and the steel industry threatened a strike that would have crippled war production. Despite Herculean efforts by the White House to negotiate a settlement, the parties remained in fundamental dispute. Literally hours before a strike was scheduled, the president issued Executive Order 10340, directing the secretary of commerce, Charles Sawyer, to "seize" the mills and operate them. In this context, seizure meant only that the secretary sent telegrams to all the firms affected, appointing the president of each as the government's manager. All operating details, including profits and losses, were to remain under each company's control. But Secretary Sawyer also announced that he intended to negotiate an agreement with the union, action that might well have affected future earnings. The steel companies went into federal courts, and, claiming they would suffer irreparable injury, asked various judges to forbid Sawyer to carry out Executive Order 10340. After several unsuccessful efforts, the companies finally found a district judge willing to issue the injunction. The Department of Justice persuaded a court of appeals to stay—that is, suspend—the force of the writ, and obtained review from the U.S. Supreme Court.

Mr. Justice **BLACK** delivered the opinion of the Court. . . .

The President's power, if any, to issue the order must stem either from an act of Congress or from the Constitution itself. There is no statute that expressly authorizes the President to take possession of property as he did here. Nor is there any act of Congress to which our attention has been directed from which such a power can fairly be implied. Indeed, we do not understand the Government to rely on statutory authorization for this seizure. There are two statutes which do authorize the President to take both personal and real property under certain conditions.° However, the Government admits that these conditions were not met and that the President's order was not rooted in either of the statutes. The Government refers to the seizure provisions of one of the statutes (§ 201(b) of the Defense Production Act) as "much too cumbersome, involved, and time-consuming for the crisis which was at hand."

Moreover, the use of the seizure technique to solve labor disputes . . . was not only unauthorized by any congressional enactment; prior to this controversy, Congress had refused to adopt that method of settling labor disputes. When the Taft-Hartley Act was under consideration in 1947, Congress rejected an amendment which would have authorized such governmental seizures in cases of emergency. Apparently it was thought that the technique of seizure, like that of compulsory arbitration, would interfere with the process of collective bargaining. Consequently, the plan Congress adopted in that Act did not provide for seizure under any circumstances. Instead, the plan sought to bring about settlements by use of the customary devices of mediation, conciliation, investigation by boards of inquiry, and public reports. In some instances temporary injunctions were authorized to provide cooling-off periods. All this failing, the unions were left free to strike if the majority of the employees, by secret ballot, expressed a desire to do so.

It is clear that if the President had authority to issue the order he did, it must be found in some provisions of the Constitution. And it is not claimed that express constitutional language grants this power to the President. The contention is that presidential power should be implied from the aggregate of his powers under the Constitution. Particular reliance is placed on provisions in Art. II which say that "the executive Power shall be vested in a President. . . ."; that "he shall take Care that the Laws be faithfully executed"; and that he "shall be Commander in Chief of the Army and Navy of the United States."

The order cannot properly be sustained as an exercise of the President's military power as Commander in Chief of the Armed Forces. The govern-

---

° *The Selective Service Act of 1948 and the Defense Production Act of 1950.—Eds.*

ment attempts to do so by citing a number of cases upholding broad powers in military commanders engaged in day-to-day fighting in a theater of war. Such cases need not concern us here. Even though "theater of war" be an expanding concept, we cannot with faithfulness to our constitutional system hold that the Commander in Chief of the Armed Forces has the ultimate power as such to take possession of private property in order to keep labor disputes from stopping production. This is a job for the Nation's lawmakers, not for its military authorities.

Nor can the seizure order be sustained because of the several constitutional provisions that grant executive power to the President. In the framework of our Constitution, the President's power to see that the laws are faithfully executed refutes the idea that he is to be a lawmaker. The Constitution limits his functions in the law-making process to the recommending of laws he thinks wise and the vetoing of laws he thinks bad. And the Constitution is neither silent nor equivocal about who shall make laws which the President is to execute. The first section of the first article says that "All legislative Powers herein granted shall be vested in a Congress of the United States. . . ."

The President's order does not direct that a congressional policy be executed in a manner prescribed by Congress—it directs that a presidential policy be executed in a manner prescribed by the President. The preamble of the order itself, like that of many statutes, sets out reasons why the President believes certain policies should be adopted, proclaims these policies as rules of conduct to be followed, and again, like a statute, authorizes a government official to promulgate additional rules and regulations consistent with the policy proclaimed and needed to carry that policy into execution. The power of Congress to adopt such public policies as those proclaimed by the order is beyond question. It can authorize the taking of private property for public use. It can make laws regulating relationships between employers and employees, prescribing rules designed to settle labor disputes, and fixing wages and working conditions in certain fields of our economy. The Constitution did not subject this law-making power of Congress to presidential or military supervision or control.

It is said that other Presidents without congressional authority have taken possession of private business enterprises in order to settle labor disputes. But even if this be true, Congress has not thereby lost its exclusive constitutional authority to make laws necessary and proper to carry out the powers vested by the Constitution "in the Government of the United States, or any Department or Officer thereof."

The Founders of this Nation entrusted the law-making power to the Congress alone in both good and bad times. It would do no good to recall the historical events, the fears of power and the hopes for freedom that lay behind their choice. Such a review. would but confirm our holding that this seizure order cannot stand.

The judgment of the District Court is

Affirmed.

Mr. Justice **FRANKFURTER,** concurring. . . .

The question before the Court comes in this setting. Congress has frequently—at least 16 times since 1916—specifically provided for executive seizure of production, transportation, communications, or storage facilities. In every case it has qualified this grant of power with limitations and safeguards. . . . The power to seize has uniformly been given only for a limited period or for a defined emergency, or has been repealed after a short period. Its exercise has been restricted to particular circumstances such as "time of war or when war is imminent," the needs of "public safety" or of "national security or defense," or "urgent and impending need."

Congress in 1947 was again called upon to consider whether governmental seizure should be used to avoid serious industrial shutdowns. Congress decided against conferring such power. . . .

It cannot be contended that the President would have had power to issue this order had Congress explicitly negated such authority in formal legislation. Congress has expressed its will to withhold this power from the President as though it has said so in so many words. . . .

By the Labor Management Relations Act of 1947, Congress said to the President, "You may not seize. Please report to us and ask for seizure power if you think it is needed in a specific situation." . . .

No authority that has since been given to the President can by any fair process of statutory construction be deemed to withdraw the restriction or change the will of Congress as expressed by a body of enactments, culminating in the Labor Management Relations Act of 1947. . . .

A scheme of government like ours no doubt at times feels the lack of power to act with complete all-embracing, swiftly moving authority. No doubt a government with distributed authority, subject to be challenged in the courts of law, at least long enough to consider and adjudicate the challenge, labors under restrictions from which other governments are free. It has not been our tradition to envy such governments. In any event our government was designed to have such restrictions. The price was deemed not too high in view of the safeguards which these restrictions afford. . . .

Mr. Justice **DOUGLAS,** concurring.

There can be no doubt that the emergency which caused the President to seize these steel plants was one that bore heavily on the country. But the emergency did not create power; it merely marked an occasion when power should be exercised. And the fact that it was necessary that measures be taken to keep steel in production does not mean that the President rather than the

Congress, had the constitutional authority to act. The Congress, as well as the President, is trustee of the national welfare. The President can act more quickly than the Congress.... All executive power—from the reign of ancient kings to the rule of modern dictators—has the outward appearance of efficiency.

Legislative power, by contrast, is slower to exercise. There must be delay while the ponderous machinery of committees, hearings, and debates is put into motion. That takes time; and while the Congress slowly moves into action, the emergency may take its toll in wages, consumer goods, war production, the standard of living of the people, and perhaps even lives....

The method by which industrial peace is achieved is of vital importance not only to the parties but to society as well.... In some nations that [legislative] power is entrusted to the executive branch as a matter of course or in case of emergencies. We chose another course. We chose to place the legislative power of the Federal Government in the Congress. The language of the Constitution is not ambiguous or qualified. It places not *some* legislative power in the Congress; Art. I, § 1 says "All legislative Powers herein granted shall be vested in a Congress of the United States...."

The legislative nature of the action taken by the President seems to me to be clear. When the United States takes over an industrial plant to settle a labor controversy, it is condemning property. The seizure of the plant is a taking in the constitutional sense....

The President has no power to raise revenues. That power is in the Congress by Art. I, § 8 of the Constitution. The President might seize and the Congress by subsequent action might ratify the seizure. But until and unless Congress acted, no condemnation would be lawful. The branch of government that has the power to pay compensation for a seizure is the only one able to authorize a seizure or make lawful one that the President had effected. That seems to me to be the necessary result of the condemnation provision in the Fifth Amendment. It squares with the theory of checks and balances expounded by Mr. Justice Black in the opinion of the Court in which I join....

We pay a price for our system of checks and balances, for the distribution of power among the three branches of government. It is a price that today may seem exorbitant to many. Today a kindly President uses the seizure power to effect a wage increase and to keep the steel furnaces in production. Yet tomorrow another President might use the same power to prevent a wage increase, to curb trade unionists, to regiment labor as oppressively as industry thinks it has been regimented by this seizure.

Mr. Justice **JACKSON,** concurring in the judgment and opinion of the Court....

A judge, like an executive adviser, may be surprised at the poverty of really useful and unambiguous authority applicable to concrete problems of executive power as they actually present themselves. Just what our forefathers did envision, or would have envisioned had they foreseen modern conditions, must be divined from materials almost as enigmatic as the dreams Joseph was called upon to interpret for Pharaoh. A century and a half of partisan debate and scholarly speculation yields no net result but only supplies more or less apt quotations from respected sources on each side of any question. They largely cancel each other. And court decisions are indecisive because of the judicial practice of dealing with the largest questions in the most narrow way.

The actual art of governing under our Constitution does not and cannot conform to judicial definitions of the power of any of its branches based on isolated clauses or even single Articles torn from context. While the Constitution diffuses power the better to secure liberty, it also contemplates that practice will integrate the dispersed powers into a workable government. It enjoins upon its branches separateness but interdependence, autonomy but reciprocity. Presidential powers are not fixed but fluctuate, depending upon their disjunction or conjunction with those of Congress. We may well begin by a somewhat oversimplified grouping of practical situations in which a President may doubt, or others may challenge, his powers, and by distinguishing roughly the legal consequences of this factor of relativity.

1. When the President acts pursuant to an express or implied authorization of Congress, his authority is at its maximum, for it includes all that he possesses in his own right plus all that Congress can delegate. . . . A seizure executed by the President pursuant to an Act of Congress would be supported by the strongest of presumptions. . . .

2. When the President acts in absence of either a congressional grant or denial of authority, he can only rely upon his own independent powers, but there is a zone of twilight in which he and Congress may have concurrent authority, or in which its distribution is uncertain. . . . In this area any actual test of power is likely to depend on the imperatives of events and contemporary imponderables rather than on abstract theories of law.

3. When the President takes measures incompatible with the expressed or implied will of Congress, his power is at its lowest ebb, for then he can rely only upon his own constitutional powers minus any constitutional powers of Congress over the matter. Courts can sustain exclusive Presidential control in such a case only by disabling the Congress from acting upon the subject. Presidential claim to a power at once so conclusive and preclusive must be scrutinized with caution, for what is at stake is the equilibrium established by our constitutional system.

Into which of these classifications does this executive seizure of the steel industry fit? It is eliminated from the first by admission, for it is conceded that no congressional authorization exists for this seizure. . . .

Can it then be defended under flexible texts available to the second category? It seems clearly eliminated from that class because Congress has not left seizure of private property an open field but has covered it by three statutory policies inconsistent with this seizure. . . .

This leaves the current seizure to be justified only by the severe tests under the third grouping, where it can be supported only by any remainder of executive power after subtraction of such powers as Congress may have over the subject. In short, we can sustain the President only by holding that seizure of such strike-bound industries is within his domain and beyond control by Congress. . . .

Mr. Justice **BURTON,** concurring in both the opinion and judgment of the Court. . . .

The controlling fact here is that Congress, within its constitutionally delegated power, has prescribed for the President specific procedures, exclusive of seizure, for his use in meeting the present type of emergency. Congress has reserved to itself the right to determine where and when to authorize the seizure of property in meeting such an emergency. Under these circumstances, the President's order of April 8 invaded the jurisdiction of Congress. It violated the essence of the principle of the separation of governmental powers. Accordingly, the injunction against its effectiveness should be sustained.

Mr. Justice **CLARK**, concurring in the judgment of the Court. . . .

One of this Court's first pronouncements upon the powers of the President under the Constitution was made by Chief Justice John Marshall some one hundred and fifty years ago. In Little v. Barreme, he used this characteristically clear language in discussing the power of the President to instruct the seizure of the "Flying-Fish," a vessel bound from a French port:

> "It is by no means clear that the president of the United States whose high duty it is to 'take care that the laws be faithfully executed,' and who is commander in chief of the armies and navies of the United States, might not, without any special authority for that purpose, in the then existing state of things, have empowered the officers commanding the armed vessels of the United States, to seize and send into port for ad-judication, American vessels which were forfeited by being engaged in this illicit commerce. But when it is observed that [an Act of Congress] gives a special authority to seize on the high seas, and limits that authority to the seizure of vessels bound or sailing *to* a French port, the legislature seem to have prescribed that the manner in which this law shall be carried into execution, was to exclude a seizure of any vessel *not* bound *to* a French port."

Accordingly, a unanimous Court held that the President's instructions had been issued without authority and that they could not "legalize an act which without those instructions would have been a plain trespass." I know of no subsequent holding of this Court to the contrary. . . .

I conclude that where Congress has laid down specific procedures to deal with the type of crisis, confronting the President, he must follow those procedures in meeting the crisis; but that in the absence of such action by Congress, the President's independent power to act depends upon the gravity of the situation confronting the nation. I cannot sustain the seizure in question because here, as in Little v. Barreme, Congress had prescribed methods to be followed by the President in meeting the emergency at hand. . . .

Mr. Chief Justice **VINSON**, with whom Mr. Justice **REED** and Mr. Justice **MINTON** join, dissenting. . . .

In passing upon the question of Presidential powers in this case, we must first consider the context in which those powers were exercised.

Those who suggest that this is a case involving extraordinary powers should be mindful that these are extraordinary times. A world not yet recovered from the devastation of World War II has been forced to face the threat of another and more terrifying global conflict. . . .

. . . As an illustration of the magnitude of the over-all program, Congress has appropriated $130 billion for our own defense and for military assistance to our allies since the June, 1950 attack in Korea.

Even before Korea, steel production at levels above theoretical 100% capacity was not capable of supplying civilian needs alone. Since Korea, the tremendous military demand for steel has far exceeded the increases in productive capacity. . . .

The President has the duty to execute the foregoing legislative programs [of military development and foreign aid, some by statute, and some by treaty]. Their successful execution depends upon continued production of steel and stabilized prices for steel. . . .

. . . The Union and the steel companies may well engage in a lengthy struggle. Plaintiff's counsel tells us that "sooner or later" the mills will operate again. That may satisfy the steel companies and, perhaps, the Union. But our soldiers and our allies will hardly be cheered with the assurance that the ammunition upon which their lives depend will be forthcoming—"sooner or later," or, in other words, "too little and too late."

Accordingly, if the President has any power under the Constitution to meet a critical situation in the absence of express statutory authorization, there is no basis whatever for criticizing the exercise of such power in this case.

The steel mills were seized for a public use. . . . Plaintiffs cannot complain that any provision in the Constitution prohibits the exercise of the power of eminent domain in this case. The Fifth Amendment provides: "nor shall private property be taken for public use, without just compensation." It is no bar to this seizure for, if the taking is not otherwise unlawful, plaintiffs are assured of receiving the required just compensation. . . .

Admitting that the Government could seize the mills, plaintiffs claim that the implied power of eminent domain can be exercised only under an Act of Congress. . . .

Under this view, the President is left powerless at the very moment when the need for action may be most pressing and when no one, other than he, is immediately capable of action. . . . [H]e is left powerless because a power not expressly given to Congress is nevertheless found to rest exclusively with Congress. . . .

. . . [I]n this case, we need only look to history and time-honored principles of constitutional law—principles that have been applied consistently by all branches of the Government throughout our history. It is those who assert the invalidity of the Executive Order who seek to amend the Constitution in this case.

A review of executive action demonstrates that our Presidents have on many occasions exhibited the leadership contemplated by the Framers when they made the President Commander in Chief, and imposed upon him the trust to "take Care that the Laws be faithfully executed." With or without explicit statutory authorization, Presidents have at such times dealt with national emergencies by acting promptly and resolutely to enforce legislative programs, at least to save those programs until Congress could act. Congress and the courts have responded to such executive initiative with consistent approval. . . .

[Vinson then cited a long list of instances in which presidents had taken the initiative when, in their judgments, national welfare demanded immediate action. Without explicit congressional authorization Washington had used military force against the Whiskey Rebellion of 1794; Jefferson bought Louisiana; Lincoln ordered a blockade of Southern ports when the Civil War began; Hayes and later Cleveland used troops to cope with railroad strikes; and Franklin Roosevelt, six months before Pearl Harbor, seized a plant manufacturing airplanes, a move—as the dissenters emphasized—ardently defended by Justice Jackson, who had then been FDR's attorney general.]

Focusing now on the situation confronting the President on the night of April 8, 1952, we cannot but conclude that the President was performing his duty under the Constitution "to take Care that the Laws be faithfully executed"—a duty described by President Benjamin Harrison as "the central idea of the office."

The President reported to Congress the morning after the seizure that he acted because a work stoppage in steel production would immediately imperil the safety of the Nation by preventing execution of the legislative programs for procurement of military equipment. . . .

. . . The President's action served the same purpose as a judicial stay entered to maintain the status quo in order to preserve the jurisdiction of a court. . . .

Plaintiffs place their primary emphasis on the Labor Management Relations Act of 1947 . . . but do not contend that that Act contains any provision prohibiting seizure. . . .

The diversity of views expressed in the six opinions of the majority, the lack of reference to authoritative precedent, the repeated reliance upon prior dissenting opinions, the complete disregard of the uncontroverted facts showing the gravity of the emergency and the temporary nature of the taking all serve to demonstrate how far afield one must go to affirm the order of the District Court.

The broad executive power granted by Art. II to an officer on duty 365 days a year cannot, it is said, be invoked to avert disaster. Instead, the President must confine himself to sending a message to Congress recommending action. Under this messenger-boy concept of the Office, the President cannot even act to preserve legislative programs from destruction so that Congress will have something left to act upon. . . .

As the District Judge stated, this is no time for "timorous" judicial action. But neither is this a time for timorous executive action. . . . The President immediately informed Congress of his action and clearly stated his intention to abide by the legislative will. No basis for claims of arbitrary action, unlimited powers or dictatorial usurpation of congressional power appears from the facts of this case. . . .

~ Case 2.2 ~

Chief Justice **BURGER:** "To ensure that justice is done, it is imperative to the function of courts that compulsory process be available for the production of evidence needed either by the prosecution or by the defense."

United States v. Nixon
418 U.S. 683, 94 S. Ct. 3090, 41 L. Ed. 2d 1039 (1974)

Since the time of George Washington, some presidents have claimed a right to keep from Congress certain kinds of information. Usually presidents have asserted the privilege—generally called "executive privilege" in recent decades—in foreign affairs. Although there, as in most other phases of policy making, the president and Congress share authority, the president's sources of information are typically far superior to those of Congress. Moreover, those sources—agents of the Central Intelligence Agency, for example, or a disgruntled foreign official—must remain secret lest the source be killed. Even revelation of the information itself, without the name or nature of the source, might blow the source's cover or destroy the value of the information. Further, like senators and representatives, presidents have staffs of personal and official advisers who would hesitate to speak candidly and offer advice were they subject to being hauled before a congressional committee to explain their recommendations, given possibly in the heat of crisis when emotions were high and the level of information low.

Obviously, an assertion of executive privilege can conflict with the authority of the Senate to understand and accept or reject a treaty or of Congress as a whole to adopt or not adopt legislation regarding foreign or domestic affairs. A claim of executive privilege might also conflict with judicial authority to conduct a fair trial, as well as with the right of a defendant to such a trial.

Specifically, it is the last kind of situation out of which these cases grew, although the opinion reaches out to touch other possibilities. As a result of the Watergate scandals, seven of Richard Nixon's top aides from the White House were indicted on charges of defrauding the United States government and obstructing justice. Nixon, of course, was personally implicated in these felonies and had secretly taped conversations with his aides that showed their, as well as his own, conspiracy. The special prosecutor asked the trial judge to issue to Nixon a subpoena duces tecum,° *demanding some of those tapes. The prosecutor asked only that the trial judge receive the tapes, examine them, and give to the prosecution and defense those portions relevant to the issues that would be tried. The trial judge would seal and return the remainder to the White House.*

Nixon produced some of the subpoenaed material, but, realizing other portions would clearly prove that he was both a liar and a felon, invoked executive privilege, claiming that confidential presidential documents were beyond judicial control. The trial judge, John Sirica, denied Nixon's claim, and he appealed to the U.S. court of appeals. The special prosecutor persuaded the U.S. Supreme Court to hear the case before the court of appeals had passed judgment.

Mr. Chief Justice **BURGER** delivered the opinion of the Court. . . .

° *Literally an order, under (sub) threat of punishment (poena), for the named person to bring certain documents (duces tecum: "bring with you") to court.—Eds.*

The Claim of Privilege

A

...[W]e turn to the claim that the subpoena should be quashed [dismissed] because it demands "confidential conversations between a President and his close advisors that it would be inconsistent with the public interest to produce."... The first contention is a broad claim that the separation of powers doctrine precludes judicial review of the President's claim of privilege. The second contention is that if he does not prevail on the claim of absolute privilege, the court should hold as a matter of constitutional law that the privilege prevails over the subpoena *duces tecum*.

In the performance of assigned constitutional duties each branch of the Government must initially interpret the Constitution, and the interpretation of its powers by any branch is due great respect from the others. The President's counsel ... reads the Constitution as providing an absolute privilege of confidentiality for all presidential communications. Many decisions of this Court, however, have unequivocally reaffirmed the holding of Marbury v. Madison (1803) that "it is emphatically the province and duty of the judicial department to say what the law is."

No holding of the Court has defined the scope of judicial power specifically relating to the enforcement of a subpoena for confidential presidential communications for use in a criminal prosecution, but other exercises of power by the Executive Branch and the Legislative Branch have been found invalid as in conflict with the Constitution. Powell v. McCormack (1969). *Youngstown* (1952). Since this Court has consistently exercised the power to construe and delineate claims arising under express powers, it must follow that the Court has authority to interpret claims with respect to powers alleged to derive from enumerated powers....

B

In support of his claim of absolute privilege, the President's counsel urges two grounds, one of which is common to all governments and one of which is peculiar to our system of separation of powers. The first ground is the valid need for protection of communications between high government officials and those who advise and assist them in the performance of their manifold duties; the importance of this confidentiality is too plain to require further discussion.... Whatever the nature of the privilege of confidentiality of presidential communications in the exercise of Art. II powers, the privilege can be said to derive from the supremacy of each branch within its own assigned area of constitutional duties. Certain powers and privileges flow from the nature of enumerated powers; the protection of the confidentiality of presidential communications has similar constitutional underpinnings.

The second ground asserted by the President's counsel in support of the claim of absolute privilege rests on the doctrine of separation of powers. Here it is argued that the independence of the Executive Branch within its own sphere ... insulates a President from a judicial subpoena in an ongoing criminal prosecution. . . .

However, neither the doctrine of separation of powers, nor the need for confidentiality of high level communications, without more, can sustain an absolute, unqualified presidential privilege of immunity from judicial process under all circumstances. The President's need for complete candor and objectivity from advisers calls for great deference from the courts. However, when the privilege depends solely on the broad, undifferentiated claim of public interest in the confidentiality of such conversations, a confrontation with other values arises. Absent a claim of need to protect military, diplomatic or sensitive national security secrets, we find it difficult to accept the argument that even the very important interest in confidentiality of presidential communications is significantly diminished by production of such material for *in camera*° inspection with all the protection that a district court will be obliged to provide.

The impediment that an absolute, unqualified privilege would place in the way of the primary constitutional duty of the Judicial Branch to do justice in criminal prosecutions would plainly conflict with the function of the courts under Art. III. In designing the structure of our Government and dividing and allocating the sovereign power among three coequal branches, the Framers of the Constitution sought to provide a comprehensive system, but the separate powers were not intended to operate with absolute independence.

> "While the Constitution diffuses power the better to secure liberty, it also contemplates that practice will integrate the dispersed powers into a workable government. It enjoins upon its branches separateness but interdependence, autonomy but reciprocity." Youngstown Sheet & Tube Co. v. Sawyer (1952) (Jackson, J., concurring). . . .

C

Since we conclude that the legitimate needs of the judicial process may outweigh presidential privilege, it is necessary to resolve those competing interests in a manner that preserves the essential functions of each branch. The right and indeed the duty to resolve that question does not free the

---

° In camera *means in the judge's chambers rather than in open court. In the sort of situation referred to here, the judge would receive the relevant documents from the government, read them, and decide which to give to the private parties.—Eds.*

judiciary from according high respect to the representations made on behalf of the President. United States v. Burr (1807).

The expectation of a President to the confidentiality of his conversations and correspondence, like the claim of confidentiality of judicial deliberations, for example, has all the values to which we accord deference for the privacy of all citizens and added to those values the necessity for protection of the public interest in candid, objective, and even blunt or harsh opinions in presidential communications. The privilege is fundamental to the operation of government and inextricably rooted in the separation of powers under the Constitution. In Nixon v. Sirica (1973), the Court of Appeals held that such presidential communications are "presumptively privileged,"... and this position is accepted by both parties in the present litigation. We agree with Mr. Chief Justice Marshall's observation, therefore; that "in no case of this kind would a court be required to proceed against the President as against an ordinary individual." United States v. Burr.

But this presumptive privilege must be considered in light of our historic commitment to the rule of law. This is nowhere more profoundly manifest than in our view that "the twofold aim [of criminal justice] is that guilt shall not escape or innocence suffer." Berger v. United States (1935). We have elected to employ an adversary system of criminal justice in which the parties contest all issues before a court of law. The need to develop all relevant facts in the adversary system is both fundamental and comprehensive.... The very integrity of the judicial system and public confidence in the system depend on full disclosure of all the facts, within the framework of the rules of evidence. To ensure that justice is done, it is imperative to the function of courts that compulsory process be available for the production of evidence needed either by the prosecution or by the defense.

In this case the President ... does not place his claim of privilege on the ground they are military or diplomatic secrets. As to these areas of Art. II duties the courts have traditionally shown the utmost deference to presidential responsibilities.... No case of the Court ... has extended this high degree of deference to a President's generalized interest in confidentiality. Nowhere in the Constitution ... is there any explicit reference to a privilege of confidentiality, yet to the extent this interest relates to the effective discharge of a President's powers, it is constitutionally based.

The right to the production of all evidence at a criminal trial similarly has constitutional dimensions. The Sixth Amendment explicitly confers upon every defendant in a criminal trial the right "to be confronted with the witnesses against him" and "to have compulsory process for obtaining witnesses in his favor." Moreover, the Fifth Amendment also guarantees that no person shall be deprived of liberty without due process of law. It is the manifest duty of the courts to vindicate those guarantees and to accomplish that it is essential that all relevant and admissible evidence be produced.

In this case we must weigh the importance of the general privilege of confidentiality of presidential communications . . . against the inroads of such a privilege on the fair administration of criminal justice. The interest in preserving confidentiality is weighty indeed and entitled to great respect. However, we cannot conclude that advisers will be moved to temper the candor of their remarks by the infrequent occasions of disclosure because of the possibility that such conversations will be called for in the context of a criminal prosecution.

On the other hand, the allowance of the privilege to withhold evidence that is demonstrably relevant in a criminal trial would cut deeply into the guarantee of due process of law and gravely impair the basic function of the courts. A President's acknowledged need for confidentiality in the communications of his office is general in nature, whereas the constitutional need for production of relevant evidence in a criminal proceeding is specific and central to the fair administration of justice. Without access to specific facts a criminal prosecution may be totally frustrated. . . .

We conclude that when the ground for asserting privilege as to subpoenaed material sought for use in a criminal trial is based only on the generalized interest in confidentiality, it cannot prevail over the fundamental demands of due process of law in the fair administration of criminal justice. The generalized assertion of privilege must yield to the demonstrated specific need for evidence in a pending criminal trial. . . .

E

Enforcement of the subpoena *duces tecum* was stayed pending this Court's resolution of the issues. . . . Those issues now having been disposed of, the matter of implementation will rest with the District Court. . . . Statements that meet the test of admissibility and relevance must be isolated; all other material must be excised. . . . We have no doubt that the District Judge will at all times accord to presidential records that high degree of deference suggested in United States v. Burr. . . .

Affirmed.

Mr. Justice **REHNQUIST** took no part in the consideration or decision of these cases.

~ Case 2.3 ~

Chief Justice **BURGER:** "The structure of the Constitution does not permit Congress to execute the laws; it follows that Congress cannot grant to an officer under its control what it does not possess."

Justice **WHITE** (dissenting): "The deficiencies in the Court's reasoning are apparent. . . . [T]he substantial role played by the President in the process of removal through joint resolution reduces . to utter insignificance the possibility that the threat of removal will induce subservience to the Congress."

Bowsher v. Synar
478 U.S. ___, 106 S. Ct. 3181, 92 L. Ed. 2d 583 (1986)

In 1985, faced with a fiscal crisis caused by escalating federal deficits, Congress passed and the president signed into law the Gramm-Rudman-Hollings Act (the Balanced Budget and Emergency Deficit Control Act). Because of severe differences between the White House and Capitol Hill about spending priorities for federal funds, Congress would not allow the president to choose levels of funding for various programs. Instead, it provided for across-the-board cuts in federal spending, if in any year the deficit were to exceed a specified maximum. Sec. 251 required the Office of Management and Budget (OMB), an executive agency, and the Congressional Budget Office (CBO), a legislative agency, to submit to the comptroller general their estimates of deficits and, if needed, their calculations of cuts in spending for each program. That official would review these estimates, make independent decisions, and then instruct the president to sequester certain funds.

The constitutionality of sec. 251's delegation of power was much debated in Congress; and Ronald Reagan, in signing the law, said he thought sec. 251 was invalid because it allowed the comptroller general to exercise supervisory authority over the president, an opinion his aides had voiced earlier. As a compromise, Congress had provided a quick means for legislators to challenge the act. In addition, sec. 274(f) contained fallback procedures for reducing the deficit were the Supreme Court to declare sec. 251 unconstitutional. In essence, these required OMB and CBO to submit their estimates to a joint congressional committee and Congress to pass a joint resolution—subject to a presidential veto—embodying its own decisions as to cuts in spending.

Almost as soon as Gramm-Rudman became law, twelve senators and representatives filed suit in a federal district court attacking the validity of sec. 251. In a separate action, a group of employees of the De-partment of the Treasury, who were going to lose benefits if cuts in spending were made, filed a separate suit. The district court declared sec. 251 unconstitutional and the comptroller general appealed directly to the Supreme Court.

Chief Justice **BURGER** delivered the opinion of the Court. . . .

III

We noted recently that "[t]he Constitution sought to divide the delegated powers of the new Federal Government into three defined categories, Legislative, Executive, and Judicial." INS v. Chadha (1983). The declared purpose of separating and dividing the powers of government, of course, was to "diffus[e] power the better to secure liberty." Youngstown Sheet & Tube Co. v. Sawyer (1952) (Jackson, J., concurring). Justice Jackson's words echo the famous warning of Montesquieu, quoted by James Madison in *The Federalist* No. 47, that " 'there can be no liberty where the legislative and ex-ecutive powers are united in the same person, or body of magistrates.' . . ."

Even a cursory examination of the Constitution reveals the influence of Montesquieu's thesis that checks and balances were the foundation of a structure of government that would protect liberty. The Framers provided a vigorous legislative branch and a separate and wholly independent executive branch, with each branch responsible ultimately to the people. The Framers also provided for a judicial branch equally independent with "[t]he judicial Power . . . extend[ing] to all Cases, in Law and Equity, arising under this Constitution, and the Laws of the United States." Art. III, § 2.

Other, more subtle, examples of separated powers are evident as well. Unlike parliamentary systems such as that of Great Britain, no person who is an officer of the United States may serve as a Member of the Congress. Art. I, § 6. Moreover, unlike parliamentary systems, the President, under Article II, is responsible not to the Congress but to the people, subject only to impeachment proceedings which are exercised by the two Houses as repre-sentatives of the people. Art. II, § 4. And even in the impeachment of a President the presiding officer of the ultimate tribunal is not a member of the legislative branch, but the Chief Justice of the United States. Art. I, § 3.

That this system of division and separation of powers produces conflicts, confusion, and discordance at times is inherent, but it was deliberately so structured to assure full, vigorous and open debate on the great issues affecting the people and to provide avenues for the operation of checks on the exercise of governmental power.

The Constitution does not contemplate an active role for Congress in the supervision of officers charged with the execution of the laws it enacts. The

President appoints "Officers of the United States" with the "Advice and Consent of the Senate . . ." Article II, § 2. Once the appointment has been made and confirmed, however, the Constitution explicitly provides for removal of Officers of the United States by Congress only upon impeachment by the House of Representatives and conviction by the Senate. An impeachment by the House and trial by the Senate can rest only on "Treason, Bribery or other high Crimes and Misdemeanors." Article II, § 4. A direct congressional role in the removal of officers charged with the execution of the laws beyond this limited one is inconsistent with separation of powers.

This was made clear in debate in the First Congress in 1789. When Congress considered an amendment to a bill establishing the Department of Foreign Affairs, the debate centered around whether the Congress "should recognize and declare the power of the President under the Constitution to remove the Secretary of Foreign Affairs without the advice and consent of the Senate." James Madison urged rejection of a congressional role in the removal of Executive Branch officers, other than by impeachment. . . . Madison's position ultimately prevailed, and a congressional role in the removal process was rejected. This "Decision of 1789" provides "contemporaneous and weighty evidence" of the Constitution's meaning since many of the Members of the first Congress "had taken part in framing that instrument." Marsh v. Chambers (1983).

This Court first directly addressed this issue in Myers v. United States (1925). At issue in *Myers* was a statute providing that certain postmasters could be removed only "by and with the advice and consent of the Senate." The President removed one such postmaster without Senate approval, and a lawsuit ensued. Chief Justice Taft, writing for the Court, declared the statute unconstitutional on the ground that for Congress to "draw to itself, or to either branch of it, the power to remove or the right to participate in the exercise of that power . . . would be . . . to infringe the constitutional principle of the separation of governmental powers."

A decade later, . . . Humphrey's Executor v. United States (1935) . . . [upheld] the power of Congress to limit the President's powers of removal of a Federal Trade Commissioner. The relevant statute permitted removal "by the President," but only "for inefficiency, neglect of duty, or malfeasance in office." Justice Sutherland, speaking for the Court, upheld the statute, holding that "illimitable power of removal is not possessed by the President [with respect to Federal Trade Commissioners]." The Court distinguished *Myers*, reaffirming its holding that congressional participation in the removal of executive officers is unconstitutional. . . . The Court reached a similar result in Wiener v. United States (1958), concluding that, under *Humphrey's Executor*, the President did not have unrestrained removal authority over a member of the War Crimes Commission.

In light of these precedents, we conclude that Congress cannot reserve for itself the power of removal of an officer charged with the execution of the laws except by impeachment. To permit the execution of the laws to be vested in an officer answerable only to Congress would, in practical terms, reserve in Congress control over the execution of the laws. . . . The structure of the Constitution does not permit Congress to execute the laws; it follows that Congress cannot grant to an officer under its control what it does not possess. . . .

IV

. . . The critical factor lies in the provisions of the statute defining the Comptroller General's office relating to removability. Although the Comptroller General is nominated by the President from a list of three individuals recommended by the Speaker of the House of Representatives and the President pro tempore of the Senate, and confirmed by the Senate, he is removable only at the initiative of Congress. He may be removed not only by impeachment but also by Joint Resolution of Congress "at any time" resting on any one of the following bases:

"(i) permanent disability;
"(ii) inefficiency;
"(iii) neglect of duty;
"(iv) malfeasance; or
"(v) a felony or conduct involving moral turpitude."

This provision was included, as one Congressman explained in urging passage of the Act, because Congress "felt that [the Comptroller General] should be brought under the sole control of Congress, so that Congress at the moment when it found he was inefficient and was not carrying on the duties of his office as he should and as the Congress expected, could remove him without the long, tedious process of a trial by impeachment."

The removal provision was an important part of the legislative scheme, as a number of Congressmen recognized. Representative Hawley commented: "[H]e is our officer, in a measure, getting information for us. . . . If he does not do his work properly, we, as practically his employers, ought to be able to discharge him from office." Representative Sisson observed that the removal provisions would give "[t]he Congress of the United States . . . absolute control of the man's destiny in office." The ultimate design was to "give the legislative branch of the Government control of the audit, not through the power of appointment, but through the power of removal." (Rep. Taylor.)

Justice White contends that "[t]he statute does not permit anyone to remove the Comptroller at will; removal is permitted only for specified cause, with the existence of cause to be determined by Congress following a hearing. Any removal under the statute would presumably be subject to post-termination judicial review to ensure that a hearing had in fact been held and the finding of cause for removal was not arbitrary." That observation . . . rests on at least two arguable premises: (a) that the enumeration of certain specified causes of removal excludes the possibility of removal for other causes and (b) that any removal would be subject to judicial review, a position that appellants were unwilling to endorse.

Glossing over these difficulties, the dissent's assessment of the statute fails to recognize the breadth of the grounds for removal. The statute permits removal for "inefficiency," "neglect of duty," or "malfeasance." These terms are very broad and, as interpreted by Congress, could sustain removal of a Comptroller General for any number of actual or perceived transgressions of the legislative will. The Constitutional Convention chose to permit impeachment of executive officers only for "Treason, Bribery, or other high Crimes and Misdemeanors." It rejected language that would have permitted impeachment for "maladministration," with Madison arguing that "[s]o vague a term will be equivalent to a tenure during pleasure of the Senate." ...

... Surely no one would seriously suggest that judicial independence would be strengthened by allowing removal of federal judges only by a joint resolution finding "inefficiency," "neglect of duty," or "malfeasance."

... The separated powers of our government can not be permitted to turn on judicial assessment of whether an officer exercising executive power is on good terms with Congress. The Framers recognized that, in the long term, structural protections against abuse of power were critical to preserving liberty. In constitutional terms, the removal powers over the Comptroller General's office dictate that he will be subservient to Congress.

This much said, we must also add that the dissent is simply in error to suggest that the political realities reveal that the Comptroller General is free from influence by Congress. The Comptroller General heads the General Accounting Office, "an instrumentality of the United States Government independent of the executive departments," which was created by Congress in 1921 as part of the Budget and Accounting Act of 1921. Congress created the office because it believed that it "needed an officer, responsible to it alone, to check upon the application of public funds in accordance with appropriations." H. Mansfield, *The Comptroller General.*

It is clear that Congress has consistently viewed the Comptroller General as an officer of the Legislative Branch. The Reorganization Acts of 1945 and 1949, for example, both stated that the Comptroller General and the GAO are "a part of the legislative branch of the Government." Similarly, in the Accounting and Auditing Act of 1950, Congress required the Comptroller General to conduct audits "as an agent of the Congress."

Over the years, the Comptrollers General have also viewed themselves as part of the Legislative Branch. In one of the early Annual Reports of Comptroller General, the official seal of his office was described as reflecting:

> "the independence of judgment to be exercised by the General Accounting Office, subject to the control of the legislative branch.... The combination represents an agency of the Congress independent of other

authority auditing and checking the expenditures of the Government as required by law and subjecting any questions arising in that connection to quasijudicial determination."

Later, Comptroller General Warren, who had been a member of Congress for 15 years before being appointed Comptroller General, testified that: "During most of my public life, . . . I have been a member of the legislative branch. Even now, although heading a great agency, it is an agency of the Congress, and *I am an agent of the Congress.*" And, in one conflict during Comptroller General McCarl's tenure, he asserted his independence of the Executive Branch, stating:

"Congress . . . is . . . the only authority to which there lies an appeal from the decision of this office. . . ."

Against this background, we see no escape from the conclusion that, because Congress had retained removal authority over the Comptroller General, he may not be entrusted with executive powers. The remaining question is whether the Comptroller General has been assigned such powers. . . .

V

The primary responsibility of the Comptroller General under the instant Act is the preparation of a "report." This report must contain detailed estimates of projected federal revenues and expenditures. The report must also specify the reductions, if any, necessary to reduce the deficit to the target for the appropriate fiscal year. The reductions must be set forth on a program-by-program basis.

In preparing the report, the Comptroller General is to have "due regard" for the estimates and reductions set forth in a joint report submitted to him by the Director of CBO and the Director of OMB, the President's fiscal and budgetary advisor. However, the Act plainly contemplates that the Comptroller General will exercise his independent judgment and evaluation with respect to those estimates. The Act also provides that the Comptroller General's report "shall explain fully any differences between the contents of such report and the report of the Directors."

. . . Under § 251, the Comptroller General must exercise judgment concerning facts that affect the application of the Act. He must also interpret the provisions of the Act to determine precisely what budgetary calculations are required. Decisions of that kind are typically made by officers charged with executing a statute.

The executive nature of the Comptroller General's functions under the Act is revealed in § 252(a)(3) which gives the Comptroller General the ultimate authority to determine the budget cuts to be made. Indeed, the Comptroller General commands the President himself to carry out, without the slightest variation (with exceptions not relevant to the constitutional issues presented), the directive of the Comptroller General as to the budget reductions. . . .

Congress of course initially determined the content of the Balanced Budget and Emergency Deficit Control Act; and undoubtedly the content of the Act determines the nature of the executive duty. However, as *Chadha* makes clear, once Congress makes its choice in enacting legislation, its participation ends. Congress can thereafter control the execution of its enactment only indirectly—by passing new legislation. By placing the responsibility for execution of the Balanced Budget and Emergency Deficit Control Act in the hands of an officer who is subject to removal only by itself, Congress in effect has retained control over the execution of the Act and has intruded into the executive function. The Constitution does not permit such intrusion.

VI

We now turn to the final issue of remedy. . . .

. . . The language of the Balanced Budget and Emergency Deficit Control Act itself settles the issue. In § 274(f), Congress has explicitly provided "fallback" provisions in the Act that take effect "[i]n the event . . . *any* of the reporting procedures described in section 251 are invalidated." § 274(f)(1) (emphasis added). The fallback provisions are " 'fully operative as a law.' " . . .

. . . [O]ur holding simply permits the fallback provisions to come into play.

VII

No one can doubt that Congress and the President are confronted with fiscal and economic problems of unprecedented magnitude, but "the fact that a given law or procedure is efficient, convenient, and useful in facilitating functions of government, standing alone, will not save it if it is contrary to the Constitution. Convenience and efficiency are not the primary objectives—or the hallmarks—of democratic government. . . ." *Chadha*. . . .

Our judgment is stayed for a period not to exceed 60 days to permit Congress to implement the fallback provisions.

Justice **STEVENS**, with whom Justice **MARSHALL** joins, concurring in the judgment.

. . . I agree with the Court that the "Gramm-Rudman-Hollings" Act contains a constitutional infirmity so severe that the flawed provision may not stand. I disagree with the Court, however, on the reasons why. . . . It is not the dormant, carefully circumscribed congressional removal power that represents the primary constitutional evil. Nor do I agree ... that the analysis depends on a labeling of the functions assigned to the Comptroller General as "executive powers." Rather, I am convinced that the Comptroller General must be characterized as an agent of Congress because of his longstanding statutory responsibilities; that the powers assigned to him under the Gramm-Rudman-Hollings Act require him to make policy that will bind the Nation; and that, when Congress, or a component or an agent of Congress, seeks to make policy that will bind the Nation, it must follow the procedures mandated by Article I of the Constitution—through passage by both Houses and presentment to the President. In short, Congress may not exercise its fundamental power to formulate national policy by delegating that power to one of its two Houses, to a legislative committee, or to an individual agent of the Congress such as the Speaker of the House of Representatives, the Sergeant at Arms of the Senate, or the Director of the Congressional Budget Office. INS v. Chadha (1983). That principle, I believe, is applicable to the Comptroller General. . . .

Justice **WHITE,** dissenting.

The Court, acting in the name of separation of powers, takes upon itself to strike down the Gramm-Rudman-Hollings Act, one of the most novel and far-reaching legislative responses to a national crisis since the New Deal. The basis of the Court's action is a solitary provision of another statute that was passed over sixty years ago and has lain dormant since that time. I cannot concur in the Court's action. Like the Court, I will not purport to speak to the wisdom of the policies incorporated in the legislation the Court invalidates; that is a matter for the Congress and the Executive, *both* of which expressed their assent to the statute barely half a year ago. I will, however, address the wisdom of the Court's willingness to interpose its distressingly formalistic view of separation of powers as a bar to the attainment of governmental objectives through the means chosen by the Congress and the President in the legislative process established by the Constitution. . . . [T]he Court's decision rests on a feature of the legislative scheme that is of minimal practical significance and that presents no substantial threat to the basic scheme ·of separation of powers. In attaching dispositive significance to what should be regarded as a triviality, the Court neglects what has in the past been recognized as a fundamental principle governing consideration of disputes over separation of powers:

> "The actual art of governing under our Constitution does not and cannot conform to judicial definitions of the power of any of its branches based on isolated clauses or even single Articles torn from context. While the Constitution diffuses power the better to secure liberty, it also contemplates that.practice will integrate the dispersed

powers into a workable government." Youngstown Sheet & Tube Co. v.
Sawyer (1952) (Jackson, J. concurring).

I

... Before examining the merits of the Court's argument, I wish to
emphasize what it is that the Court quite pointedly and correctly does *not*
hold: namely, that "executive" powers of the sort granted the Comptroller by
the Act may only be exercised by officers removable at will by the President.
The Court's apparent unwillingness to accept this argument, which has been
tendered in this Court by the Solicitor General, is fully consistent with the
Court's longstanding recognition that it is within the power of Congress under
the "Necessary and Proper" Clause, Art. I, § 8, to vest authority that falls
within the Court's definition of executive power in officers who are not
subject to removal at will by the President and are therefore not under the
President's direct control. See, e.g., Humphrey's Executor v. United States
(1935); Wiener v. United States (1958). . . . [W]ith the advent and triumph of
the administrative state and the accompanying multiplication of the tasks
undertaken by the Federal Government, the Court has been virtually
compelled to recognize that Congress may reasonably deem it "necessary and
proper" to vest some among the broad new array of governmental functions
in officers who are free from the partisanship that may be expected of agents
wholly dependent upon the President.

The Court's recognition of the legitimacy of legislation vesting "executive" authority in officers independent of the President does not imply
derogation of the President's own constitutional authority—indeed, duty—to
"take Care that the Laws be faithfully executed," Art. II, § 3, for any such
duty is necessarily limited to a great extent by the content of the laws enacted
by the Congress. . . . In determining whether a limitation on the President's
power to remove an officer performing executive functions constitutes a
violation of the constitutional scheme of separation of powers, a court must
"focu[s] on the extent to which [such a limitation] prevents the Executive
Branch from accomplishing its constitutionally assigned functions." Nixon v.
Administrator of General Services (1977). . . . This inquiry is, to be sure, not
one that will beget easy answers; it provides nothing approaching a bright-
line rule or set of rules. Such an inquiry, however, is necessitated by the
recognition that "formalistic and unbending rules" . . . may "unduly constrict
Congress' ability to take needed and innovative action pursuant to its Article I
powers." Commodity Futures Trading Commission v. Schor (1986).

It is evident . . . that the powers exercised by the Comptroller General
under the Gramm-Rudman Act are not such that vesting them in an officer
not subject to removal at will by the President would in itself improperly
interfere with Presidential powers. Determining the level of spending by the
Federal Government is not by nature a function central either to the exercise

of the President's enumerated powers or to his general duty to ensure execution of the laws; rather, appropriating funds is a peculiarly legislative function, and one expressly committed to Congress by Art. I, § 9, which provides that "[n]o Money shall be drawn from the Treasury, but in Consequence of Appropriations made by Law." . . . [T]he result of such a delegation, from the standpoint of the President, is no different from the result of more traditional forms of appropriation: under either system, the level of funds available to the Executive branch to carry out its duties is not within the President's discretionary control. To be sure, if the budget-cutting mechanism required the responsible officer to exercise a great deal of policymaking discretion, one might argue that having created such broad discretion Congress had some obligation based upon Art. II to vest it in the Chief Executive or his agents. In Gramm-Rudman, however, Congress has done no such thing; instead, it has created a precise and articulated set of criteria designed to minimize the degree of policy choice exercised by the officer executing the statute and to ensure that the relative spending priorities established by Congress in the appropriations it passes into law remain unaltered. Given that the exercise of policy choice by the officer executing the statute would be inimical to Congress' goal in enacting "automatic" budget-cutting measures, it is eminently reasonable and proper for Congress to vest the budget-cutting authority in an officer who is to the greatest degree possible nonpartisan and independent of the President and his political agenda. . . . Such a delegation deprives the President of no authority that is rightfully his.

II

. . . The Court's decision . . . is based on a syllogism: the Act vests the Comptroller with "executive power"; such power may not be exercised by Congress or its agents; the Comptroller is an agent of Congress because he is removable by Congress; therefore the Act is invalid. I have no quarrel with the proposition that the powers exercised by the Comptroller under the Act may be characterized as "executive" in that they involve the interpretation and carrying out of the Act's mandate. I can also accept the general proposition that although Congress has considerable authority in designating the officers who are to execute legislation, the constitutional scheme of separated powers does prevent Congress from reserving an executive role for itself or for its "agents." I cannot accept, however, that the exercise of authority by an officer removable for cause by a joint resolution of Congress is analogous to the impermissible execution of the law by Congress itself, nor would I hold that the congressional role in the removal process renders the Comptroller an "agent" of the Congress, incapable of receiving "executive" power. . . .

. . . Because the Comptroller is not an appointee of Congress but an officer of the United States appointed by the President with the advice and consent of the Senate, Buckley [v. Valeo (1976)] neither requires that he be characterized as an agent of the Congress nor in any other way calls into question his capacity to exercise "executive" authority. . . .

The deficiencies in the Court's reasoning are apparent. First, the Court baldly mischaracterizes the removal provision when it suggests that it allows Congress to remove the Comptroller for "executing the laws in any fashion found to be unsatisfactory"; in fact, Congress may remove the Comptroller only for one or more of five specified reasons. . . . Second . . . the Court overlooks or deliberately ignores the decisive difference between the congressional removal provision and the legislative veto struck down in *Chadha:* under the Budget and Accounting Act, Congress may remove the Comptroller only through a joint resolution, which by definition must be passed by both Houses and signed by the President. In other words, a removal of the Comptroller under the statute *satisfies the requirements of bicameralism and presentment laid down in* Chadha. . . .

. . . The question to be answered is whether the threat of removal of the Comptroller General for cause through joint resolution as authorized by the Budget and Accounting Act renders the Comptroller sufficiently subservient to Congress that investing him with "executive" power can be realistically equated with the unlawful retention of such power by Congress itself; more generally, the question is whether there is a genuine threat of "encroachment or aggrandizement of one branch at the expense of the other," *Buckley.* Common sense indicates that the existence of the removal provision poses no such threat to the principle of separation of powers.

The statute does not permit anyone to remove the Comptroller at will; removal is permitted only for specified cause, with the existence of cause to be determined by Congress following a hearing. Any removal under the statute would presumably be subject to post-termination judicial review to ensure that a hearing had in fact been held and that the finding of cause for removal was not arbitrary. These procedural and substantive limitations on the removal power militate strongly against the characterization of the Comptroller as a mere agent of Congress by virtue of the removal authority. Indeed, similarly qualified grants of removal power are generally deemed to protect the officers to whom they apply and to establish their independence from the domination of the possessor of the removal power. See Humphrey's Executor v. United States. . . . That the agent enforcing the standard is Congress may be of some significance to the Comptroller, but Congress' substantively limited removal power will undoubtedly be less of a spur to subservience than Congress' unquestionable and unqualified power to enact legislation reducing the Comptroller's salary, cutting the funds available to his department, reducing his personnel, limiting or expanding his duties, or even abolishing his position altogether.

More importantly, the substantial role played by the President in the process of removal through joint resolution reduces to utter insignificance the possibility that the threat of removal will induce subservience to the Congress. . . . [A] joint resolution must be presented to the President and is ineffective if it is vetoed by him, unless the veto is overridden by the constitutionally prescribed two-thirds majority of both Houses of Congress. The requirement of presidential approval obviates the possibility that the Comptroller will perceive himself as so completely at the mercy of Congress that he will function as its tool. If the Comptroller's conduct in office is not so unsatisfactory to the President as to convince the latter that removal is required under the statutory standard, Congress will have no independent power to coerce the Comptroller unless it can muster a two-thirds majority in both Houses—a feat of bipartisanship more difficult than that required to impeach and convict. . . .

The practical result of the removal provision is not to render the Comptroller unduly dependent upon or subservient to Congress, but to render him one of the most independent officers in the entire federal establishment. . . . As one scholar put it nearly fifty years ago, "Under the statute the Comptroller General, once confirmed, is safe so long as he avoids a public exhibition of personal immorality, dishonesty, or failing mentality." H. Mansfield, *The Comptroller General* (1939). The passage of time has done little to cast doubt on this view: of the six Comptrollers who have served since 1921, none has been threatened with, much less subjected to, removal. . . .

Realistic consideration of the nature of the Comptroller General's relation to Congress thus reveals that the threat to separation of powers conjured up by the majority is wholly chimerical. . . .

The majority's contrary conclusion rests on the rigid dogma that, outside of the impeachment process, any "direct congressional role in the removal of officers charged with the execution of the laws . . . is inconsistent with separation of powers." Reliance on such an unyielding principle to strike down a statute posing no real danger of aggrandizement of congressional power is extremely misguided and insensitive to our constitutional role. The wisdom of vesting "executive" powers in an officer removable by joint resolution may indeed be debatable—as may be the wisdom of the entire scheme of permitting an unelected official to revise the budget enacted by Congress—but such matters are for the most part to be worked out between the Congress and the President through the legislative process, which affords each branch ample opportunity to defend its interests. The Act vesting budget-cutting authority in the Comptroller General represents Congress' judgment that the delegation of such authority to counteract ever-mounting deficits is "necessary and proper" to the exercise of the powers granted the Federal Government by the Constitution; and the President's approval of the statute signifies his unwillingness to reject the choice made by Congress. Under such circumstances, the role of this Court should be limited to determining whether the Act so alters the balance of authority among the branches of government as to pose a genuine threat to the basic division between the lawmaking power and the power to execute the law. Because I see no such threat, I cannot join the Court in striking down the Act. . . .

Justice **BLACKMUN,** dissenting. . . .

3. FEDERALISM

The term federalism *refers to a political system in which there are two levels of government, central and regional, each with its own authority independent of the other's, but with each operating directly on the same citizenry. A federal structure differs from a* unitary system, *in which regional governments exist only at the will of the central government, and a* confederation, *in which the central government is the creature of regional governments and cannot operate directly on individual citizens.*

Each of these definitions is vague. To say that regional governments—in this country, the states—have authority independent of the national government tells nothing at all about where lines of authority between the two levels should be drawn, who should do the drawing, and what standards linedrawers should use. The American constitutional document provides little additional information. The two most directly relevant parts speak in broad terms. Article VI, par. 2 says:

> This Constitution, and the Laws of the United States which shall be made in Pursuance thereof; and all Treaties made, or which shall be made, under the Authority of the United States, shall be the supreme Law of the Land; and the Judges in every State shall be bound thereby, any Thing in the Constitution or Laws of any State to the Contrary notwithstanding.

But the Tenth Amendment reads:

> The powers not delegated to the United States by the Constitution, nor prohibited by it to the States, are reserved to the States respectively, or to the people.

Reinforcing the notion of national supremacy is the delegation of power by the so-called elastic clause of Article I, sec. 8:

> The Congress shall have power ... To make all Laws which shall be necessary and proper for carrying into Execution the foregoing [delegated] Powers, and all other Powers vested by this Constitution in the Government of the United States, or in any Department or Officer thereof.

67

Despite the sweep of this clause, the framing generation apparently believed that the Constitution's delegating powers imposed real limits on the national government's authority vis-à-vis the states as well as individual citizens. Other constitutional clauses shed more light on federalism, but only a bit more.[1] Article I, sec. 8 enumerates specific delegations of power to the national government; Article I, sec. 9 contains a few restrictions on national power; Article I, sec. 10 lists some specific restrictions on state authority; and Article IV catalogs several positive duties of state and national governments.[2] These clauses remove some issues from the realm of serious dispute, but they provide no precise definitions of boundaries between state and national authority.

One can see in this imprecision the same strategy the framers used in setting up overlapping grants of power among the three branches of the federal government. Blurred divisions of authority will inevitably engender friction, even conflict, and thus further limit government.

How to maintain federalism without removing friction poses a critical question for the political system. Thomas Jefferson and later John C. Calhoun would have allowed the states to interpose their authority to nullify federal action they thought unconstitutional. At root nullification denied national supremacy, and ultimately it led to secession. It took a bloody civil war to settle these issues.

A second response places protection of national authority in the hands of courts, a function the plain words of Article VI require judges to perform in enforcing national supremacy. In the early days of the Republic, state action far more often and seriously threatened federal authority than federal authority threatened the states. As the first two cases in this chapter, McCulloch v. Maryland (1819) and Gibbons v. Ogden (1824), show, Chief Justice John Marshall led his Court to protect national supremacy. On the other hand, Marshall saw the real protection for states in the structure of the Constitution. Each representative, like each senator, is elected from a single state. National legislators are dependent on their states for reelection; if the states do not approve of their representatives' use of federal power, the states can vote them out of office.

Marshall's successor, Roger Brooke Taney, and his colleagues took a more expansive view of state power. For a century after Taney's appointment in 1837 the Court offered a third response to maintaining federalism: Judges are the arbiters of federal-state relations, with the dual function of protecting states from the nation and the nation from the states. As Chapter 5 demonstrates, during the period 1890-1937, the justices used this role to etch an economic theory of laissez faire into the margins of the Constitution; they restricted both Congress's power to regulate "commerce among the several states" because of "invisible radiations" from the Tenth Amendment, and state authority to regulate business by calling on the due process clause of the Fourteenth Amendment.

Since 1937 the justices have taken a very wide view of national power under the commerce clause.[3] (See United States v. Darby Lumber Co. [1941], Case 3.3.) More generally they have returned to Marshall's theory, protecting national power against the states and largely leaving protection of state authority to the way the Constitution structures the national legislative process. (See Garcia v. San Antonio Metropolitan Transit Authority [1985], Case 3.4.)

Still, as we have noted, that judicial decisions settle specific cases does not mean they settle underlying issues of public policy or constitutional theory. Friction and even conflict between state and nation will remain as long as the Constitution functions to limit government.

---

1. *No part of the constitutional document has so altered the nature of federalism as secs. 1 and 5 of the Fourteenth Amendment:*

   Sec. 1. . . . No State shall make or enforce any law which shall abridge the privileges or immunities of citizens of the United States; nor shall any State deprive any person of life, liberty, or property, without due process of law; nor deny to any person within its jurisdiction the equal protection of the laws.
   Sec. 5. The Congress shall have power to enforce, by appropriate legislation, the provisions of this article.

2. *In addition, the Fifteenth, Nineteenth, Twenty-fourth, and Twenty-sixth amendments forbid Congress and the states to discriminate against potential voters on the basis of race, sex, payment of taxes, or age (if voters are 18 or older). The Twenty-fourth Amendment applies only to elections of federal officials, but the Supreme Court has ruled that the equal protection clause of the Fourteenth Amendment forbids states to discriminate, in general, among potential voters on the basis of wealth or taxes paid. Harper v. Virginia State Board of Elections, 383 U.S. 663 (1966).*

3. *And also of state authority to regulate business. See Chapter 5.*

∼ Case 3.1 ∼

Chief Justice **MARSHALL**: "[T]he government of the Union, though limited in its powers, is supreme within its sphere of action."

McCulloch v. Maryland
17 U.S. (4 Wh.) 316, 4 L. Ed. 579 (1819)

In 1811, during James Madison's first administration, the Jefferso-nians allowed the Bank of the United States, originally chartered in 1791 at the urging of the arch-Federalist, Alexander Hamilton, to die. But, in 1816, national fiscal difficulties following the War of 1812 persuaded the Jeffersonians to recharter the bank, which quickly became an aggressive financial institution successful in attracting much of the business of competing state banks. Local banks sought relief from their own legislatures, and many states, including Maryland, began to tax the national bank. Maryland required banks not chartered by its legislature to issue notes only on special stamped paper which the state would supply at an annual fee of $15,000 plus an additional charge for each note. James McCulloch, cashier of the Baltimore branch of the Bank of the United States, took time out from his systematic looting of the bank's resources to refuse to pay the tax. Maryland then obtained a judgment for the taxes from the Baltimore County court, and the state's Court of Appeals sustained the ruling. McCulloch sought a writ of error from the U.S. Supreme Court.

MARSHALL, Ch. J., delivered the opinion of the court:
In the case now to be determined, the defendant, a sovereign state, denies the obligation of a law enacted by the legislature of the Union, and the plaintiff, on his part, contests the validity of an act which has been passed by the legislature of that state. The constitution of our country, in its most interesting and vital parts, is to be considered; the conflicting powers of the government of the Union and of its members, as marked in that constitution, are to be discussed; and an opinion given, which may essentially influence the great operations of the government. No tribunal can approach such a question without a deep sense of its importance, and of the awful responsibility involved in its decision. But it must be decided peacefully, or remain a source of hostile legislation, perhaps of hostility of a still more serious nature; and if it is to be so decided, by this tribunal alone can the decision be made. On the Supreme Court of the United States has the constitution of our country devolved this important duty.

The first question made in the cause is, has Congress power to incorporate a bank?

It ... can scarcely be considered as an open question, entirely unprejudiced by the former proceedings of the nation respecting it. The principle now contested was introduced at a very early period of our history, has been recognized by many successive legislatures, and has been acted upon by the judicial department, in cases of peculiar delicacy, as a law of undoubted obligation.

It will not be denied that a bold and daring usurpation might be resisted, after an acquiescence still longer and more complete than this. But it is conceived that a doubtful question, one on which human reason may pause, and the human judgment be suspended, in the decision of which the great principles of liberty are not concerned, but the respective powers of those who are equally the representatives of the people, are to be adjusted; if not put at rest by the practice of the government, ought to receive a considerable impression from that practice. An exposition of the constitution, deliberately established by legislative acts, on the faith of which an immense property has been advanced, ought not to be lightly disregarded.

The power now contested was exercised by the first Congress elected under the present constitution.

The bill for incorporating the bank of the United States did not steal upon an unsuspecting legislature, and pass unobserved. Its principle was completely understood, and was opposed with equal zeal and ability. . . . The original act was permitted to expire; but a short experience of the embarrassments to which the refusal to revive it exposed the government, convinced those who were most prejudiced against the measure of its necessity and induced the passage of the present law. It would require no ordinary share of intrepidity to assert that a measure adopted under these circumstances was a bold and plain usurpation, to which the constitution gave no countenance.

These observations belong to the cause; but they are not made under the impression that, were the question entirely new, the law would be found irreconcilable with the constitution.

In discussing this question, the counsel for the state of Maryland have deemed it of some importance in the construction of the constitution, to consider that instrument not as emanating from the people, but as the act of sovereign and independent states. The powers of the general government, it has been said, are delegated by the states, who alone are truly sovereign; and must be exercised in subordination to the states, who alone possess supreme dominion.

It would be difficult to sustain this proposition. The convention which framed the constitution was indeed elected by the state legislatures. But the instrument, when it came from their hands, was a mere proposal, without obligation, or pretensions to it. It was reported to the then existing Congress of the United States, with a request that it might "be submitted to a convention of delegates, chosen in each state by the people thereof, under the recommendation of its legislature, for their assent and ratification." This mode of proceeding was adopted; and by the convention, by Congress, and by the state legislatures, the instrument was submitted to the people. They acted upon it in the only manner in which they can act safely, effectively, and wisely, on such a subject, by assembling in convention. It is true, they assembled in their several states—and where else should they have assembled? No political dreamer was ever wild enough to think of breaking down the lines which separate the states, and of compounding the American people into one common mass. Of consequence, when they act, they act in their states. But the measures they adopt do not, on that account, cease to be the measures of the people themselves, or become the measures of the state governments.

From these conventions the constitution derives its whole authority. The government proceeds directly from the people; is "ordained and established" in the name of the people.... The assent of the states, in their sovereign capacity, is implied in calling a convention, and thus submitting that instrument to the people. But the people were at perfect liberty to accept or reject it; and their act was final. It required not the affirmance, and could not be negatived, by the state governments. The constitution, when thus adopted, was of complete obligation, and bound the state sovereignties.

It has been said that the people had already surrendered all their powers to the state sovereignties, and had nothing more to give. But, surely, the question whether they may resume and modify the powers granted to government does not remain to be settled in this country.... To the formation of a league, such as was the confederation, the state sovereignties were certainly competent. But when, "in order to form a more perfect union," it was deemed necessary to change this alliance into an effective government, possessing great and sovereign powers, and acting directly on the people, the necessity of referring it to the people, and of deriving its powers directly from them, was felt and acknowledged by all.

The government of the Union, then (whatever may be the influence of this fact on the case), is, emphatically, and truly, a government of the people. In form and in substance it emanates from them. Its powers are granted by them, and are to be exercised directly on them, and for their benefit.

This government is acknowledged by all to be one of enumerated powers.... But the question respecting the extent of the powers actually granted, is perpetually arising, and will probably continue to arise, as long as our system shall exist.

In discussing these questions, the conflicting powers of the general and state governments must be brought into view, and the supremacy of their respective laws, when they are in opposition, must be settled.

If any one proposition could command the universal assent of mankind, we might expect it would be this—that the government of the Union, though limited in its powers, is supreme within its sphere of action. This would seem to result necessarily from its nature. It is the government of all; its powers are delegated by all; it represents all, and acts for all. Though any one state may be willing to control its operations, no state is willing to allow others to control them. The nation, on those subjects on which it can act, must necessarily bind its component parts. But this question is not left to mere reason; the people have, in express terms, decided it by saying, "this constitution, and the laws of the United States, which shall be made in pursuance thereof," "shall be the supreme law of the land," and by requiring that the members of the state legislatures, and the officers of the executive and judicial departments of the states shall take the oath of fidelity to it.

The government of the United States, then, though limited in its powers, is supreme; and its laws, when made in pursuance of the constitution, form the supreme law of the land, "anything in the constitution or laws of any state to the contrary notwithstanding."

Among the enumerated powers, we do not find that of establishing a bank or creating a corporation. But there is no phrase in the instrument which, like the articles of confederation, excludes incidental or implied powers; and which requires that everything granted shall be expressly and minutely described. Even the 10th amendment, which was framed for the purpose of quieting the excessive jealousies which had been excited, omits the word "expressly," and declares only that the powers "not delegated to the United States, nor prohibited to the states, are reserved to the states or to the people;" thus leaving the question, whether the particular power which may become the subject of contest has been delegated to the one government, or prohibited to the other, to depend on a fair construction of the whole instrument. The men who drew and adopted this amendment had experienced the embarrassments resulting from the insertion of this word in the articles of confederation, and probably omitted it to avoid those embarrassments. A constitution, to contain an accurate detail of all the subdivisions of which its great powers will admit, and of all the means by which they may be carried into execution, would partake of a prolixity of a legal code, and could scarcely be embraced by the human mind. It would probably never be understood by the public. Its nature, therefore, requires, that only its great outlines should be marked, its important objects designated, and the minor ingredients which compose those objects be deduced from the nature of the objects themselves. That this idea was entertained by the framers of the American constitution, is not only to be inferred from the nature of the instrument, but from the language. Why else were some of the limitations, found in the ninth section of the 1st article, introduced? It is also, in some degree, warranted by their having omitted to use any restrictive term which might prevent its receiving a fair and just interpretation. In considering this question, then, we must never forget that it is *a constitution* we are expounding.

Although, among the enumerated powers of government, we do not find the word "bank" or "incorporation," we find the great powers to lay and collect taxes; to borrow money; to regulate commerce; to declare and conduct a war; and to raise and support armies and navies. The sword and the purse, all the external relations, and no inconsiderable portion of the industry of the nation, are entrusted to its government. It can never be pretended that these vast powers draw after them others of inferior importance, merely because they are inferior.... But it may with great reason be contended, that a government, entrusted with such ample powers, on the due execution of which the happiness and prosperity of the nation so vitally depends, must also be entrusted with ample means for their execution. The power being given, it is the interest of the nation to facilitate its execution. It can never be their interest, and cannot be presumed to have been their intention, to clog and embarrass its execution by withholding the most appropriate means. Throughout this vast republic, from the St. Croix to the Gulf of Mexico, from the Atlantic to the Pacific, revenue is to be collected and expended, armies are to be marched and supported.... Is that construction of the constitution to be preferred which would render these operations difficult, hazardous, and expensive? Can we adopt that construction (unless the words imperiously require it) which would impute to the framers of that instrument, when granting these powers for the public good, the intention of impeding their exercise by withholding a choice of means? If, indeed, such be the mandate of the constitution, we have only to obey; but that instrument does not profess to enumerate the means by which the powers it confers may be executed; nor does it prohibit the creation of a corporation, if the existence of such a being be essential to the beneficial exercise of those powers. It is, then, the subject of fair inquiry, how far such means may be employed. It is not denied that the powers given to the government imply the ordinary means of execution.... But it is denied that the government has its choice of means; or, that it may employ the most convenient means, if, to employ them, it be necessary to erect a corporation.

On what foundation does this argument rest? On this alone: The power of creating a corporation, is one appertaining to sovereignty, and is not expressly conferred on Congress. This is true. But all legislative powers appertain to sovereignty....

The government which has a right to do an act, and has imposed on it the duty of performing that act, must, according to the dictates of reason, be allowed to select the means; and those who contend that it may not select any appropriate means, that one particular mode of effecting the object is excepted, take upon themselves the burden of establishing that exception....

... The power of creating a corporation, though appertaining to sovereignty, is not, like the power of making war, or levying taxes, or of regulating commerce, a great substantive and independent power, which cannot be implied as incidental to other powers, or used as a means of executing them.

It is never the end for which other powers are exercised, but a means by which other objects are accomplished. . . . No sufficient reason is, therefore, perceived, why it may not pass as incidental to those powers which are expressly given, if it be a direct mode of executing them.

But the constitution of the United States has not left the right of Congress to employ the necessary means for the execution of the powers conferred on the government to general reasoning. To its enumeration of powers is added that of making "all laws which shall be necessary and proper, for carrying into execution the foregoing powers, and all other powers vested by this constitution, in the government of the United States, or in any department thereof."

The counsel for the State of Maryland have urged . . . that this clause, though in terms a grant of power, is not so in effect; but is really restrictive of the general right, which might otherwise be implied, of selecting means for executing the enumerated powers.

In support of this proposition, they have found it necessary to contend, that this clause was inserted for the purpose of conferring on Congress the power of making laws. . . .

. . . [W]ould it have entered into the mind of a single member of the convention that an express power to make laws was necessary to enable the legislature to make them? That a legislature, endowed with legislative powers, can legislate, is a proposition too self-evident to have been questioned.

But the argument on which most reliance is placed, is drawn from the peculiar language of this clause. Congress is not empowered by it to make all laws, which may have relation to the powers conferred on the government, but such only as may be *"necessary and proper"* for carrying them into execution. The word *"necessary"* is considered as controlling the whole sentence, and as limiting the right to pass laws for the execution of the granted powers, to such as are indispensable, and without which the power would be nugatory. That it excludes the choice of means, and leaves to Congress, in each case, that only which is most direct and simple.

Is it true that this is the sense in which the word "necessary" is always used? Does it always import an absolute physical necessity, so strong that one thing, to which another may be termed necessary, cannot exist without that other? We think it does not. If reference be had to its use, in the common affairs of the world, or in approved authors, we find that it frequently imports no more than that one thing is convenient, or useful, or essential to another. To employ the means necessary to an end, is generally understood as employing any means calculated to produce the end, and not as being confined to those single means, without which the end would be entirely unattainable. Such is the character of human language, that no word conveys to the mind, in all situations, one single definite idea; and nothing is more common than to use words in a figurative sense. Almost all compositions contain words, which, taken in their rigorous sense, would convey a meaning different from that which is obviously intended. It is essential to just construction, that many words which import something excessive should be understood in a more mitigated sense—in that sense which common usage justifies. The word "necessary" is of this description. It has not a fixed character peculiar to itself. It admits of all degrees of comparison. . . . A thing may be necessary, very necessary, absolutely or indispensably necessary. To no mind would the same idea be conveyed by these several phrases. . . . It is, we think, impossible to compare the sentence which prohibits a state from laying "imposts or duties on imports or exports, except what may be absolutely necessary for executing its inspection laws," [Art. I, sec. 10] with that which authorizes Congress "to make all laws which shall be necessary and proper for carrying into execution" the powers of the general government, without feeling a conviction that the convention understood itself to change materially the meaning of the word "necessary," by prefixing the word "absolutely." This word, then, like others, is used in various senses; and, in its construction, the subject, the context, the intention of the person using them, are all to be taken into view.

Let this be done in the case under consideration. The subject is the execution of those great powers on which the welfare of a nation essentially depends. It must have been the intention of those who gave these powers, to insure, as far as human prudence could insure, their beneficial execution. This could not be done by confining the choice of means to such narrow limits as not to leave it in the power of Congress to adopt any which might be appropriate, and which were conducive to the end. This provision is made in a constitution intended to endure for ages to come, and, consequently, to be adapted to the various *crises* of human affairs. To have prescribed the means by which government should, in all future time, execute its powers, would have been to change, entirely, the character of the instrument, and give it the properties of a legal code. It would have been an unwise attempt to provide, by immutable rules, for exigencies which, if foreseen at all, must have been seen dimly, and which can be best provided for as they occur. To have declared that the best means shall not be used, but those alone without which the power given would be nugatory, would have been to deprive the legislature of the capacity to avail itself of experience, to exercise its reason, and to accommodate its legislation to circumstances. If we apply this principle of construction to any of the powers of government, we shall find it so pernicious in its operation that we shall be compelled to discard it. . . .

In ascertaining the sense in which the word "necessary" is used in this clause of the constitution, we may derive some aid from that with which it is associated. Congress shall have power "to make all laws which shall be necessary and proper to carry into execution" the powers of the government. If the word "necessary" was used in that strict and rigorous sense for which the counsel for the state of Maryland contend, it would be an extraordinary departure from the usual course of the human mind, as exhibited in composition, to add a word, the only possible effect of which is to qualify that strict and rigorous meaning; to present to the mind the idea of some choice of means of legislation not straightened and compressed within the narrow limits for which gentlemen contend.

But the argument which most conclusively demonstrates the error of the construction contended for by the counsel for the state of Maryland, is founded on the intention of the convention, as manifested in the whole clause. To waste time and argument in proving that without it Congress might carry its powers into execution, would not be much less idle than to hold a lighted taper to the sun. As little can it be required to prove, that in the absence of this clause, Congress would have some choice of means. That it might employ those which, in its judgment, would most advantageously effect the object to be accomplished. That any means adapted to the end, any means which tended directly to the execution of the constitutional powers of the government, were in themselves constitutional. This clause, as construed by the state of Maryland, would abridge, and almost annihilate this useful and necessary right of the legislature to select its means. That this could not be intended, is, we should think, had it not been already controverted, too apparent for controversy. We think so for the following reasons:

1st. The clause is placed among the powers of Congress, not among the limitations on those powers.

2d. Its terms purport to enlarge, not to diminish the powers vested in the government. It purports to be an additional power, not a restriction on those already granted. No reason has been, or can be assigned for thus concealing an intention to narrow the discretion of the national legislature under words which purport to enlarge it. . . . If, then, their intention had been, by this clause, to restrain the free use of means which might otherwise have been implied, that intention would have been inserted in another place, and would have been expressed in terms resembling these. "In carrying into execution the foregoing powers, and all others," & c., "no laws shall be passed but such as are necessary and proper." . . .

We admit, as all must admit, that the powers of the government are limited, and that its limits are not to be transcended. But we think the sound construction of the constitution must allow to the national legislature that discretion, with respect to the means by which the powers it confers are to be carried into execution, which will enable that body to perform the high duties assigned to it, in the manner most beneficial to the people. Let the end be legitimate, let it be within the scope of the constitution, and all means which are appropriate, which are plainly adapted to that end, which are not prohibited, but consist with the letter and spirit of the constitution, are constitutional.

That a corporation must be considered as a means not less usual, not of higher dignity, not more requiring a particular specification than other means, has been sufficiently proved....

... Should Congress, in the execution of its powers, adopt measures which are prohibited by the constitution; or should Congress, under the pretext of executing its powers pass laws for the accomplishment of objects not intrusted to the government, it would become the painful duty of this tribunal, should a case requiring such a decision come before it, to say that such an act was not the law of the land. But where the law is not prohibited, and is really calculated to effect any of the objects entrusted to the government, to undertake here to inquire into the degree of its necessity, would be to pass the line which circumscribes the judicial department, and to tread on legislative ground. This court disclaims all pretensions to such a power....

It being the opinion of the court that the act incorporating the bank is constitutional, and that the power of establishing a branch in the state of Maryland might be properly exercised by the bank itself, we proceed to inquire:

2. Whether the state of Maryland may, without violating the constitution, tax that branch?

That the power of taxation is one of vital importance; that it is retained by the states; that it is not abridged by the grant of a similar power to the government of the Union; that it is to be concurrently exercised by the two governments: are truths which have never been denied. But, such is the paramount character of the constitution that its capacity to withdraw any subject from the action of even this power, is admitted. The states are expressly forbidden to lay any duties on imports or exports, except what may be absolutely necessary for executing their inspection laws. If the obligation of this prohibition must be conceded ... the same paramount character would seem to restrain ... a state from such other exercise of this power, as is in its nature incompatible with, and repugnant to, the constitutional laws of the Union. A law, absolutely repugnant to another, as entirely repeals that other as if express terms of repeal were used.

On this ground the counsel for the bank place its claim to be exempted from the power of a state to tax its operations. There is no express provision for the case, but the claim has been sustained on a principle which so entirely pervades the constitution, is so intermixed with the materials which compose it, so interwoven with its web, so blended with its texture, as to be incapable of being separated from it without rending it into shreds.

This great principle is, that the constitution and the laws made in pursuance thereof are supreme; that they control the constitution and laws of the respective states, and cannot be controlled by them. From this, which may be almost termed an axiom, other propositions are deduced as corollaries.... These are, 1st. That a power to create implies a power to preserve. 2d. That a power to destroy if wielded by a different hand, is hostile to, and incompatible with these powers to create and to preserve. 3d. That where this repugnancy exists, that authority which is supreme must control, not yield to that over which it is supreme. . . .

That the power of taxing it by the states may be exercised so as to destroy it, is too obvious to be denied. But taxation is said to be an absolute power, which acknowledges no other limits than those expressly prescribed in the constitution, and like sovereign power of every other description, is trusted to the discretion of those who use it. But the very terms of this argument admit that the sovereignty of the state, in the article of taxation itself, is subordinate to, and may be controlled by the constitution of the United States. How far it has been controlled by that instrument must be a question of construction. In making this construction, no principle not declared can be admissible, which would defeat the legitimate operations of a supreme government. It is of the very essence of supremacy to remove all obstacles to its action within its own sphere, and so to modify every power vested in subordinate governments as to exempt its own operations from their own influence. This effect need not be stated in terms. It is so involved in the declaration of supremacy, so necessarily implied in it, that the expression of it could not make it more certain. We must, therefore, keep it in view while construing the constitution. . . .

. . . It is admitted that the power of taxing the people and their property is essential to the very existence of government, and may be legitimately exercised on the objects to which it is applicable, to the utmost extent to which the government may choose to carry it. The only security against the abuse of this power is found in the structure of the government itself. In imposing a tax the legislature acts upon its constituents. This is in general a sufficient security against erroneous and oppressive taxation.

The people of a state, therefore, give to their government a right of taxing themselves and their property, and as the exigencies of government cannot be limited, they prescribe no limits to the exercise of this right, resting confidently on the interest of the legislator, and on the influence of the constituents over their representative, to guard them against its abuse. But the means employed by the government of the Union have no such security, nor is the right of a state to tax them sustained by the same theory. Those means are not given by the people of a particular state, not given by the constituents of the legislature, which claim the right to tax them, but by the people of all the states. They are given by all, for the benefit of all—and upon theory, should be subjected to that government only which belongs to all. . . .

If we measure the power of taxation residing in a state, by the extent of sovereignty which the people of a single state possess, and can confer on its government, we have an intelligible standard, applicable to every case to which the power may be applied. We have a principle which leaves the power of taxing the people and property of a state unimpaired; which leaves to a state the command of all its resources, and which places beyond its reach, all those powers which are conferred by the people of the United States on the government of the Union, and all those means which are given for the purpose of carrying those powers into execution. We have a principle which is safe for the states, and safe for the Union. . . . We are not driven to the perplexing inquiry, so unfit for the judicial department, what degree of taxation is the legitimate use, and what degree may amount to the abuse of the power. The attempt to use it on the means employed by the government of the Union, in pursuance of the constitution, is itself an abuse, because it is the usurpation of a power which the people of a single state cannot give. . . .

That the power to tax involves the power to destroy; that the power to destroy may defeat and render useless the power to create; that there is a plain repugnance, in conferring on one government a power to control the constitutional measures of another, which other, with respect to those very measures, is declared to be supreme over that which exerts the control, are propositions not to be denied. But all inconsistencies are to be reconciled by the magic of the word *confidence*. Taxation, it is said, does not necessarily and unavoidably destroy. To carry to the excess of destruction would be an abuse, to presume which, would banish that confidence which is essential to all government.

But is this a case of confidence? Would the people of any one state trust those of another with a power to control the most insignificant operations of their state government? We know they would not. Why, then, should we suppose that the people of any one state should be willing to trust those of another with a power to control the operations of a government to which they have confided the most important and most valuable interests? In the legislature of the Union alone, are all represented. The legislature of the Union alone, therefore, can be trusted by the people with the power of controlling measures which concern all, in the confidence that it will not be abused. This, then, is not a case of confidence, and we must consider it as it really is.

If we apply the principle for which the state of Maryland contends, to the constitution generally, we shall find it capable of changing totally the character of that instrument. We shall find it capable of arresting all the measures of the government, and of prostrating it at the foot of the states. The American people have declared their constitution, and the laws made in pursuance thereof, to be supreme; but this principle would transfer the supremacy, in fact, to the states.

If the states may tax one instrument, employed by the government in the execution of its powers, they may tax any and every other instrument. They may tax the mail; they may tax the mint; they may tax patent-rights; they may tax the papers of the custom-house; they may tax judicial process; they may tax all the means employed by the government, to an excess which would defeat all the ends of government. This was not intended by the American people. They did not design to make their government dependent on the states.

In the course of the argument, *The Federalist* has been quoted; and the opinions expressed by the authors of that work have been justly supposed to be entitled to great respect in expounding the constitution. No tribute can be paid to them which exceeds their merit; but in applying their opinions to the cases which may arise in the progress of our government, a right to judge of their correctness must be retained; and, to understand the argument, we must examine the proposition it maintains, and the objections against which it is directed. . . .

The objections to the constitution which are noticed in these numbers, were to the undefined power of the government to tax, not to the incidental privilege of exempting its own measures from state taxation. . . .

It has also been insisted, that, as the power of taxation in the general and state governments is acknowledged to be concurrent, every argument which would sustain the right of the general government to tax banks chartered by the states, will equally sustain the right of the states to tax banks chartered by the general government.

But the two cases are not on the same reason. The people of all the states have created the general government, and have conferred upon it the general power of taxation. The people of all the states, and the states themselves, are represented in Congress, and, by their representatives, exercise this power. When they tax the chartered institutions of the states, they tax their constituents; and these taxes must be uniform. But, when a state taxes the operations of the government of the United States, it acts upon institutions created, not by their own constituents, but by people over whom they claim no control. It acts upon the measures of a government created by others as well as themselves, for the benefit of others in common with themselves. The difference is that which always exists, and always must exist, between the action of the whole on a part, and the action of a part on the whole—between the laws of a government declared to be supreme, and those of a government which, when in opposition to those laws, is not supreme.

But if the full application of this argument could be admitted, it might bring into question the right of Congress to tax the state banks, and could not prove the right of the states to tax the Bank of the United States. . . .

We are unanimously of opinion that the law passed by the legislature of Maryland, imposing a tax on the Bank of the United States, is unconstitutional and void.

This opinion does not deprive the states of any resources which they originally possessed. It does not extend to a tax paid by the real property of the bank, in common with the other real property within the state, nor to a tax imposed on the interest which the citizens of Maryland may hold in this institution, in common with other property of the same description throughout the state. But this is a tax on the operations of the bank, and is, consequently, a tax on the operation of an instrument employed by the government of the Union to carry its powers into execution. Such a tax must be unconstitutional.

~ Case 3.2 ~

Chief Justice **MARSHALL:** "This power ... is complete in itself, may be exercised to its utmost extent, and acknowledges no limitations other than are prescribed in the constitution."

Gibbons v. Ogden
22 U.S. (9 Wh.) 1, 6 L. Ed. 23 (1824)

McCulloch *involved the scope of a set of federal powers that could only be implied from the Constitution.* Gibbons *concerned the reach of a power explicitly granted by the Constitution. Article I, sec. 8 reads: "The Congress shall have Power ... [t]o regulate Commerce with foreign Nations, and among the several States, and with the Indian Tribes. . . ." Yet these words leave many serious questions unresolved. State officials could claim, with considerable historical justification, that they had never surrendered authority to regulate commerce within their own states.*

The facts of Gibbons *posed a neat constitutional problem. New York state had given Robert Fulton and Robert Livingston a monopoly over navigation by steamship through the state's waters; they in turn had sold a license to Aaron Ogden, allowing him to share in their monopoly. Meanwhile, Thomas Gibbons, a former business partner of Ogden, had secured a federal coasting license and began operating a steamship between New Jersey and New York. Ogden then obtained from New York state courts an order forbidding Gibbons to do business within New York's waters. After losing on appeal in the state courts, Gibbons brought his case to the U.S. Supreme Court.*

Mr. Chief Justice **MARSHALL** delivered the opinion of the Court. . . .

This [constitution] contains an enumeration of powers expressly granted by the people to their government. It has been said that these powers ought to be construed strictly. But why ought they to be so construed? Is there one sentence in the constitution which gives countenance to this rule? In the 1st of the enumerated powers, that which grants, expressly, the means for carrying all others into execution, Congress is authorized "to make all laws which shall be necessary and proper" for the purpose. But this limitation on the means which may be used, is not extended to the powers which are conferred; nor is there one sentence in the constitution, which has been pointed out by the gentlemen of the bar, or which we have been able to discern, that prescribes this rule. We do not, therefore, think ourselves justified in adopting it. What do gentlemen mean by a strict construction? If they contend only against that enlarged construction which would extend words beyond their natural and obvious import, we might question the application of the term, but should not controvert the principle. If they contend for that narrow construction which, in support of some theory not to be found in the constitution, would deny to the government those powers which the words of the grant, as usually understood, import, and which are consistent with the general views and objects of the instrument; for that narrow construction, which would cripple the government and render it unequal to the objects for which it is declared to be instituted, and to which the powers given, as fairly understood, render it competent; then we cannot perceive the propriety of this strict construction, nor adopt it as the rule by which the constitution is to be expounded. As men, whose intentions require no concealment, generally employ the words which most directly and aptly express the ideas they intend to convey, the enlightened patriots who framed our constitution, and the people who adopted it, must be understood to have employed words in their natural sense, and to have intended what they have said. If, from the imperfection of human language, there should be serious doubts respecting the extent of any given power, it is a well-settled rule that the objects for which it was given, especially when those objects are expressed in the instrument itself, should have great influence in the construction. We know of no reason for excluding this rule from the present case. The [constitutional] grant does not convey power which might be beneficial to the grantor . . . but is an investment of power for the general advantage, in the hands of agents selected for that purpose; which power can never be exercised by the people themselves, but must be placed in the hands of agents or lie dormant. We know of no rule for construing the extent of such powers, other than is given by the language of the instrument which confers them, taken in connection with the purposes for which they were conferred.

The words are: "Congress shall have power to regulate commerce with foreign nations, and among the several states, and with the Indian tribes."

The subject to be regulated is commerce; and our constitution being, as was aptly said at the bar, one of enumeration, and not of definition, to ascertain the extent of the power it becomes necessary to settle the meaning of the word. The counsel for the appellee would limit it to traffic, to buying and selling, or the interchange of commodities, and do not admit that it comprehends navigation. This would restrict a general term, applicable to many objects, to one of its significations. Commerce, undoubtedly, is traffic, but it is something more; it is intercourse. It describes the commercial intercourse between nations, and parts of nations, in all its branches, and is regulated by prescribing rules for carrying on that intercourse. The mind can scarcely conceive a system for regulating commerce between nations, which shall exclude all laws concerning navigation, which shall be silent on the admission of the vessels of the one nation into the ports of the other, and be confined to prescribing rules for the conduct of individuals, in the actual employment of buying and selling, or of barter. . . .

. . . All America understands, and has uniformly understood, the word "commerce" to comprehend navigation. It was so understood, and must have been so understood, when the constitution was framed. The power over commerce, including navigation, was one of the primary objects for which the people of America adopted their government, and must have been contemplated in forming it. The convention must have used the word in that sense, because all have understood it in that sense, and the attempt to restrict it comes too late. . . .

The word used in the constitution, then, comprehends, and has been always understood to comprehend, navigation within its meaning; and a power to regulate navigation is as expressly granted as if that term had been added to the word "commerce."

To what commerce does this power extend? The constitution informs us, to commerce "with foreign nations, and among the several states, and with the Indian tribes." . . .

. . . The word "among" means intermingled with. A thing which is among others is intermingled with them. Commerce among the states cannot stop at the external boundary line of each state, but may be introduced into the interior.

It is not intended to say that these words comprehend that commerce which is completely internal, which is carried on between man and man in a state, or between different parts of the same state, and which does not extend to or affect other states. Such a power would be inconvenient, and is certainly unnecessary.

Comprehensive as the word "among" is, it may very properly be restricted to that commerce which concerns more states than one. . . . The completely internal commerce of a state, then, may be considered as reserved for the state itself.

But, in regulating commerce with foreign nations, the power of Congress does not stop at the jurisdictional lines of the several states. It would be a very useless power if it could not pass those lines. . . .

This principle is, if possible, still more clear when applied to commerce "among the several states." They either join each other, in which case they are separated by a mathematical line, or they are remote from each other, in which case other states lie between them. What is commerce "among" them; and how is it to be conducted? Can a trading expedition between two adjoining states commence and terminate outside of each? And if the trading intercourse be between two states remote from each other, must it not commence in one, terminate in the other, and probably pass through a third? Commerce among the states must, of necessity, be commerce with the states. In the regulation of trade with the Indian tribes, the action of the law, especially when the constitution was made, was chiefly within a state. The power of Congress, then, whatever it may be, must be exercised within the territorial jurisdiction of the several states. . . .

We are now arrived at the inquiry, What is this power?

It is the power to regulate; that is, to prescribe the rule by which commerce is to be governed. This power, like all others vested in Congress, is complete in itself, may be exercised to its utmost extent, and acknowledges no limitations other than are prescribed in the constitution. These are expressed in plain terms, and do not affect the questions which arise in this case. . . .

The power of Congress, then, comprehends navigation within the limits of every state in the Union; so far as that navigation may be, in any manner, connected with "commerce with foreign nations, or among the several states, or with the Indian tribes." It may, of consequence, pass the jurisdictional line of New York, and act upon the very waters to which the prohibition now under consideration applies.

But it has been urged with great earnestness, that, although the power of Congress to regulate commerce with foreign nations, and among the several states, be co-extensive with the subject itself, and have no other limits than are prescribed in the constitution, yet the states may severally exercise the same power within their respective jurisdictions. . . . [I]t is said that they possessed it as an inseparable attribute of sovereignty before the formation of the constitution, and still retain it, except so far as they have surrendered it by that instrument; that this principle results from the nature of the government, and is secured by the tenth amendment; that an affirmative grant of power is not exclusive, unless in its own nature it be such that the continued exercise of it by the former possessor is inconsistent with the grant, and that this is not of that description.

The appellant, conceding these postulates, except the last, contends that full power to regulate a particular subject implies the whole power, and leaves no residuum; that a grant of a whole is incompatible with the existence of a right in another to any part of it. . . .

In discussing the question, whether this power is still in the states . . . we may dismiss from it the inquiry, whether it is surrendered by the mere grant to Congress, or is retained until Congress shall exercise the power. We may dismiss that inquiry, because it has been exercised, and the regulations which Congress deemed it proper to make, are now in full operation. The sole question is, can a state regulate commerce with foreign nations and among the states, while Congress is regulating it? . . .

It has been contended by the counsel for the appellant, that, as the word "to regulate" implies in its nature full power over the thing to be regulated, it excludes, necessarily, the action of all others that would perform the same operation on the same thing. That regulation is designed for the entire result, applying, to those parts which remain as they were, as well as to those which are altered. It produces a uniform whole, which is as much disturbed and deranged by changing what the regulating power designs to leave untouched, as that on which it has operated.

There is great force in this argument, and the Court is not satisfied that it has been refuted.

Since, however, in exercising the power of regulating their own purely internal affairs, whether of trading or police, the states may sometimes enact laws, the validity of which depends on their interfering with, and being contrary to, an act of Congress passed in pursuance of the constitution, the Court will enter upon the inquiry, whether the laws of New York, as expounded by the highest tribunal of the state, have, in their application to this case, come into collision with an act of Congress, and deprived a citizen of a right to which that act entitles him. Should this collision exist, it will be immaterial whether those laws were passed in virtue of a concurrent power "to regulate commerce with foreign nations and among the several states," or in virtue of a power to regulate their domestic trade and police. In one case and the other, the acts of New York must yield to the law of Congress; and the decision sustaining the privilege they confer, against a right given by a law of the Union, must be erroneous. . . .

. . . This act authorizes a steamboat employed, or intended to be employed, only in a river or bay of the United States, owned wholly or in part by an alien, resident within the United States, to be enrolled and licensed as if the same belonged to a citizen of the United States.

This act demonstrates the opinion of Congress, that steamboats may be enrolled and licensed, in common with vessels using sails. They are, of course, entitled to the same privileges, and can no more be restrained from navigating waters, and entering ports which are free to such vessels, than if they were wafted on their voyage by the winds, instead of being propelled by the agency of fire. The one element may be as legitimately used as the other, for every commercial purpose authorized by the laws of the Union; and the act of a state inhibiting the use of either to any vessel having a license under the act of Congress, comes, we think, in direct collision with that act. . . .

[Justice **JOHNSON** concurred on the ground that the very grant of power to Congress over commerce "among the several states" automatically excluded states from passing any regulatory legislation in this field.]

～ Case 3.3 ～

Justice **STONE:** "Our conclusion is unaffected by the Tenth Amendment . . . [which] states but a truism that all is retained which has not been surrendered."

United States v. Darby Lumber Co.
312 U.S. 100, 61 S. Ct. 451, 85 L. Ed. 609 (1941)

Shortly after Marshall's death in 1835, the Supreme Court began to develop a doctrine that Edward S. Corwin called dual federalism. This new jurisprudence modified Marshall's view of national supremacy and visualized the nation and the states as equals. Thus, in determining the constitutionality of legislation, judges were supposed to weigh national powers against similar powers of the states.

In articulating this doctrine, the Court often held valid state regulation of business practices. (There was almost no federal regulatory legislation enacted until the 1880s.) These circumstances were ironic because when the justices revitalized dual federalism during the period 1890-1937, they typically used it to strike down federal statutes regulating business (especially corporate) activities.

That forty-seven year span was one in which a majority of the justices typically believed in economic laissez faire, that is, that both the Constitution and the public welfare would best be served by government's letting businessmen alone to go as the profit motive urged them. The Great Depression during the decade following 1929 was the product of dog-eat-dog economic policies, and Franklin D. Roosevelt's New Deal was a politically powerful, if ideologically uncertain, effort to control big business. During the first few years of FDR's administration, especially 1934-1936, the Court, often by a slim majority, struck down many federal regulatory efforts on the grounds that they infringed on state power.

After Roosevelt's landslide electoral victory in 1936, several of the justices began to see new economic light. National Labor Relations Board v. Jones & Laughlin, 301 U.S. 2 (1937) and West Coast Hotel v. Parrish (1937; see Case 4.2) revealed a reversal of judicial attitudes. There, and in companion cases, the Court sustained a federal statutory scheme regulating some of the conditions of labor in industries like those engaging in the manufacture of steel, production of large trucks, and making of clothing.

Darby involved a challenge by a lumber company to a different federal statute, the Fair Labor Standards Act of 1938, which set

*minimum wages and maximum hours and forbade child labor in certain
industries, including manufacturing. In the act, Congress decreed that
goods produced in violation of the FLSA's terms could not be shipped
across state lines.*

Mr. Justice **STONE** delivered the opinion of the Court. . . .

While the manufacture is not of itself interstate commerce, the shipment
of manufactured goods interstate is such commerce and the prohibition of
such shipment by Congress is indubitably a regulation of the commerce. The
power to regulate commerce is the power "to prescribe the rule by which
commerce is governed." Gibbons v. Ogden. . . .

It extends not only to those regulations which aid, foster and protect the
commerce, but embraces those which prohibit it. . . .

[Mr. Justice Stone next cites several cases in which the Court had upheld
national authority to ban certain objects from interstate commerce—such as
lottery tickets, impure foods, stolen cars, kidnapped persons, intoxicating
liquor.]

But it is said that the present prohibition falls within the scope of none of
these categories; that while the prohibition is nominally a regulation of the
commerce its motive or purpose is regulation of wages and hours of persons
engaged in manufacture, the control of which has been reserved to the
states. . . .

The power of Congress over interstate commerce is "complete in itself,
may be exercised to its utmost extent, and acknowledges no limitations other
than are prescribed in the Constitution." Gibbons v. Ogden. That power can
neither be enlarged nor diminished by the exercise or nonexercise of state
power. Congress, following its own conception of public policy concerning
the restrictions which may appropriately be imposed on interstate commerce,
is free to exclude from the commerce articles whose use in the states for
which they are destined it may conceive to be injurious to the public health,
morals or welfare, even though the state has not sought to regulate their
use. . . .

Such regulation is not a forbidden invasion of state power merely
because either its motive or its consequence is to restrict the use of articles of
commerce within the states of destination; and is not prohibited unless by
other Constitutional provisions. It is no objection to the assertion of the power
to regulate interstate commerce that its exercise is attended by the same
incidents which attend the exercise of the police power of the states. . . .

. . . The motive and purpose of a regulation of interstate commerce are
matters for the legislative judgment upon the exercise of which the Constitution places no restriction and over which the courts are given no control.
McCray v. United States (1904); Sonzinsky v. United States (1937).

In the more than a century which has elapsed since the decision of

Gibbons v. Ogden, these principles of constitutional interpretation have been so long and repeatedly recognized by this Court as applicable to the Commerce Clause, that there would be little occasion for repeating them now were it not for the decision of this Court twenty-two years ago in Hammer v. Dagenhart (1918).

Hammer v. Dagenhart has not been followed. The distinction on which the decision was rested that Congressional power to prohibit interstate commerce is limited to articles which in themselves have some harmful or deleterious property—a distinction which was novel when made and unsupported by any provision of the Constitution—has long since been abandoned. . . .

The conclusion is inescapable that Hammer v. Dagenhart was a departure from the principles which have prevailed in the interpretation of the Commerce Clause both before and since the decision and that such vitality, as a precedent, as it then had has long since been exhausted. It should be and now is overruled.

Validity of the wage and hour requirements. . . .

. . . As the Government seeks to apply the statute . . . the phrase "produced for interstate commerce" . . . embraces at least the case where an employer engaged . . . in the manufacture and shipment of goods in filling orders of extrastate customers, manufactures his product with the intent or expectation that according to the normal course of his business all or some part of it will be selected for shipment to those customers.

Without attempting to define the precise limits of the phrase, we think the acts alleged in the indictment are within the sweep of the statute. The obvious purpose of the Act was not only to prevent the interstate transportation of the proscribed product, but to stop the initial step toward transportation, production with the purpose of so transporting it. . . .

There remains the question whether such restriction on the production of goods for commerce is a permissible exercise of the commerce power. The power of Congress over interstate commerce is not confined to the regulation of commerce among the states. It extends to those activities intrastate which so affect interstate commerce or the exercise of the power of Congress over it as to make regulation of them appropriate means to the attainment of a legitimate end, the exercise of the granted power of Congress to regulate interstate commerce. See McCulloch v. Maryland. . . .

Congress, having by the present Act adopted the policy of excluding from interstate commerce all goods produced for the commerce which do not conform to the specified labor standards, it may choose the means reasonably adapted to the attainment of the permitted end, even though they involve control of intrastate activities.

The means adopted . . . for the protection of interstate commerce by the suppression of the production of the condemned goods for interstate commerce is so related to the commerce and so affects it as to be within the reach of the commerce power....

Our conclusion is unaffected by the Tenth Amendment which provides: "The powers not delegated to the United States by the Constitution, nor prohibited by it to the States, are reserved to the States respectively, or to the people." The amendment states but a truism that all is retained which has not been surrendered. There is nothing in the history of its adoptions to suggest that it was more than declaratory of the relationship between the national and state government as it had been established by the Constitution before the amendment or that its purpose was other than to allay fears that the new national government might seek to exercise powers not granted, and that the states might not be able to exercise fully their reserved powers....

From the beginning and for many years the amendment has been construed as not depriving the national government of authority to resort to all means for the exercise of a granted power which are appropriate and plainly adapted to the permitted end....

Reversed.

∼ Case 3.4 ∼

Justice **BLACKMUN:** "[T]he principal means chosen by the Framers to ensure the role of the States in the federal system lies in the structure of the Federal Government itself."

Justice **POWELL:** "[T]oday's decision effectively reduces the Tenth Amendment to meaningless rhetoric when Congress acts pursuant to the Commerce Clause."

Garcia v. San Antonio Metropolitan Transit Authority
469 U.S. 528, 105 S. Ct. 1005, 83 L. Ed. 2d 1016 (1985)

Justice **BLACKMUN** delivered the opinion of the Court....

We revisit ... an issue raised in National League of Cities v. Usery (1976). In that litigation, this Court, by a sharply divided vote, ruled that the Commerce Clause does not empower Congress to enforce the minimum-wage and overtime provisions of the Fair Labor Standards Act (FLSA) against the States "in areas of traditional governmental functions." Although *National League of Cities* supplied some examples of "traditional governmental functions," it did not offer a general explanation of how a "traditional" function is to be distinguished from a "nontraditional" one. Since then, federal and state courts have struggled with the task, thus imposed, of identifying a traditional function for purposes of state immunity under the Commerce Clause. . . .

Our examination of this "function" standard applied in these and other cases over the last eight years now persuades us that the attempt to draw the boundaries of state regulatory immunity in terms of "traditional governmental function" is not only unworkable but is inconsistent with established principles of federalism and, indeed, with those very federalism principles on which *National League of Cities* purported to rest. That case, accordingly, is overruled. . . .

II

Appellees have not argued that SAMTA [San Antonio Metropolitan Transit Authority] is immune from regulation under the FLSA on the ground that it is a local transit system engaged in intrastate commercial activity. In a practical sense, SAMTA's operations might well be characterized as "local." Nonetheless, it long has been settled that Congress' authority under the Commerce Clause extends to intrastate economic activities that affect interstate commerce. . . . Were SAMTA a privately owned and operated enterprise, it could not credibly argue that Congress exceeded the bounds of its Commerce Clause powers in prescribing minimum wages and overtime rates for SAMTA's employees. Any constitutional exemption from the requirements of the FLSA therefore must rest on SAMTA's status as a governmental entity rather than on the "local" nature of its operations.

The prerequisites for governmental immunity under *National League of Cities* were summarized by this Court in Hodel [v. Virginia Surface Mining & Recl. Assn. (1981)]. Under that summary, four conditions must be satisfied before a state activity may be deemed immune from a particular federal regulation under the Commerce Clause. First . . . the federal statute at issue must regulate "the 'States as States.' " Second, the statute must "address matters that are indisputably 'attribute[s] of state sovereignty.' " Third, state compliance with federal obligations must "directly impair [the States'] ability to structure integral operations in areas of traditional governmental functions." Finally, the relation of state and federal interests must not be such that "the nature of the federal interest . . . justifies state submission."

The controversy in the present cases has focused on the third *Hodel* requirement—that the challenged federal statute trench on "traditional governmental functions." The District Court voiced a common concern: "Despite the abundance of adjectives, identifying which particular state functions are immune remains difficult." Just how troublesome the task has been is revealed by the results reached in other federal cases. Thus, courts have held that regulating ambulance services, licensing automobile drivers, operating a municipal airport, performing solid waste disposal, and operating a highway authority are functions *protected* under *National League of Cities*. At the same time, courts have held that issuance of industrial development bonds, regulation of intrastate natural gas sales, regulation of traffic on public roads, regulation of air transportation, operation of a telephone system, leasing and sale of natural gas, operation of a mental health facility, and provision of in-house domestic services for the handicapped are *not* entitled to immunity. We find it difficult, if not impossible, to identify an organizing principle that places each of the cases in the first group on one side of a line and each of the cases in the second group on the other side. The constitutional distinction between licensing drivers and regulating traffic, for example, or between operating a highway authority and operating a mental health facility, is elusive at best.

Thus far, this Court itself has made little headway in defining the scope of the governmental functions deemed protected under *National League of Cities*. In that case the Court set forth examples of protected and unprotected functions, but provided no explanation of how those examples were identified. The only other case in which the Court has had occasion to address the problem is [Transportation Union v.] Long Island (1982). We there observed: "The determination of whether a federal law impairs a state's authority with respect to 'areas of traditional [state] functions' may at times be a difficult one." The accuracy of that statement is demonstrated by this Court's own difficulties in *Long Island* in developing a workable standard for "traditional governmental functions." . . .

. . . Neither do any of the alternative standards that might be employed to distinguish between protected and unprotected governmental functions appear manageable. We rejected the possibility of making immunity turn on a purely historical standard of "tradition" in *Long Island*, and properly so. The most obvious defect of a historical approach to state immunity is that it prevents a court from accommodating changes in the historical functions of States, changes that have resulted in a number of once-private functions like education being assumed by the States and their subdivisions. . . .

A nonhistorical standard for selecting immune governmental functions is likely to be just as unworkable as is a historical standard. The goal of identifying "uniquely" governmental functions, for example, has been rejected by the Court in the field of government tort liability in part because the notion of "uniquely" governmental function is unmanageable.

We believe, however, that there is a more fundamental problem at work here, a problem that explains why the Court was never able to provide a basis for the governmental/proprietary distinction in the intergovernmental tax immunity cases and why an attempt to draw similar distinctions with respect to federal regulatory authority under *National League of Cities* is unlikely to succeed. . . . The problem is that neither the governmental/proprietary distinction nor any other that purports to separate out important governmental functions can be faithful to the role of federalism in a democratic society. The essence of our federal system is that within the realm of authority left open to them under the Constitution, the States must be equally free to engage in any activity that their citizens choose for the common weal, no matter how unorthodox or unnecessary anyone else—including the judiciary—deems state involvement to be. Any rule of state immunity that looks to the "traditional," "integral," or "necessary" nature of governmental functions inevitably invites an unelected federal judiciary to make decisions about which state policies it favors and which ones it dislikes. . . .

We therefore now reject, as unsound in principle and unworkable in practice, a rule of state immunity from federal regulation that turns on a judicial appraisal of whether a particular governmental function is "integral" or "traditional." Any such rule leads to inconsistent results at the same time that it disserves principles of democratic self-governance, and it breeds inconsistency precisely because it is divorced from those principles. . . .

III

The central theme of *National League of Cities* was that the States occupy a special position in our constitutional system and that the scope of Congress' authority under the Commerce Clause must reflect that position. Of course, the Commerce Clause by its specific language does not provide any special limitation on Congress' actions with respect to the States. It is equally true, however, that the text of the Constitution provides the beginning rather than the final answer to every inquiry into questions of federalism, for "[b]ehind the words of the constitutional provisions are postulates which limit and control." Monaco v. Mississippi (1934). *National League of Cities* reflected the general conviction that the Constitution precludes "the National Government [from] devour[ing] the essentials of state sovereignty." In order to be faithful to the underlying federal premises of the Constitution, courts must look for the "postulates which limit and control."

What has proved problematic is not the perception that the Constitution's federal structure imposes limitations on the Commerce Clause, but rather the nature and content of those limitations. . . .

We doubt that courts ultimately can identify principled constitutional limitations on the scope of Congress' Commerce Clause powers over the States merely by relying on *a priori* definitions of state sovereignty. In part, this is because of the elusiveness of objective criteria for "fundamental" elements of state sovereignty, a problem we have witnessed in the search for "traditional governmental functions." There is, however, a more fundamental reason: the sovereignty of the States is limited by the Constitution itself. A variety of sovereign powers, for example, are withdrawn from the States by Article I, § 10. Section 8 of the same Article works an equally sharp contraction of state sovereignty by authorizing Congress to exercise a wide range of legislative powers and (in conjunction with the Supremacy Clause of

Article VI) to displace contrary state legislation. By providing for final review of questions of federal law in this Court, Article III curtails the sovereign power of the States' judiciaries to make authoritative determinations of law. Finally, the developed application, through the Fourteenth Amendment, of the greater part of the Bill of Rights to the States limits the sovereign authority that States otherwise would possess to legislate with respect to their citizens and to conduct their own affairs.

The States unquestionably do "retai[n] a significant measure of sovereign authority." EEOC v. Wyoming (Powell, J., dissenting). They do so, however, only to the extent that the Constitution has not divested them of their original powers and transferred those powers to the Federal Government. In the words of James Madison to the Members of the First Congress: "Interference with the power of the States was no constitutional criterion of the power of Congress. If the power was not given, Congress could not exercise it; if given, they might exercise it, although it should interfere with the laws, or even the Constitution of the States." . . .

As a result, to say that the Constitution assumes the continued role of the States is to say little about the nature of that role. . . .

When we look for the States' "residuary and inviolable sovereignty," the *Federalist* No. 39 (J. Madison), in the shape of the constitutional scheme rather than in predetermined notions of sovereign power, a different measure of state sovereignty emerges. Apart from the limitation on federal authority inherent in the delegated nature of Congress' Article I powers, the principal means chosen by the Framers to ensure the role of the States in the federal system lies in the structure of the Federal Government itself. It is no novelty to observe that the composition of the Federal Government was designed in large part to protect the States from overreaching by Congress. The Framers thus gave the States a role in the selection both of the Executive and the Legislative Branches of the Federal Government. The States were vested with indirect influence over the House of Representatives and the Presidency by their control of electoral qualifications and their role in presidential elections. U.S. Const., Art. I, § 2, and Art. II, § 1. They were given more direct influence in the Senate, where each State received equal representation and each Senator was to be selected by the legislature of his State. Art. I, § 3. The significance attached to the States' equal representation in the Senate is underscored by the prohibition of any constitutional amendment divesting a State of equal representation without the State's consent. Art. V. . . .

. . . In short, the Framers chose to rely on a federal system in which special restraints on federal power over the States inhered principally in the workings of the National Government itself, rather than in discrete limitations on the objects of federal authority. State sovereign interests, then, are more properly protected by procedural safeguards inherent in the structure of the federal system than by judicially created limitations on federal power.

The effectiveness of the federal political process in preserving the States' interests is apparent even today in the course of federal legislation. On the one hand, the States have been able to direct a substantial proportion of federal revenues into their own treasuries in the form of general and program-specific grants in aid. The federal role in assisting state and local governments is a longstanding one; Congress provided federal land grants to finance state governments from the beginning of the Republic, and direct cash grants were awarded as early as 1887 under the Hatch Act. In the past quarter-century alone, federal grants to States and localities have grown from $7 billion to $96 billion. As a result, federal grants now account for about one-fifth of state and local government expenditures. . . . [A]t the same time that the States have exercised their influence to obtain federal support, they have been able to exempt themselves from a wide variety of obligations imposed by Congress under the Commerce Clause. For example, the Federal Power Act, the National Labor Relations Act, the Labor-Management Reporting and Disclosure Act, the Occupational Safety and Health Act, the Employee Retirement Insurance Security Act, and the Sherman Act all contain express or implied exemptions for States and their subdivisions. The fact that some federal statutes such as the FLSA extend general obligations to the States cannot obscure the extent to which the political position of the States in the federal system has served to minimize the burdens that the States bear under the Commerce Clause.

We realize that changes in the structure of the Federal Government have taken place since 1789, not the least of which has been the substitution of popular election of Senators by the adoption of the Seventeenth Amendment in 1913, and that these changes may work to alter the influence of the States in the federal political process. Nonetheless . . . we are convinced that the fundamental limitation that the constitutional scheme imposes on the Commerce Clause to protect the "States as States" is one of process rather than one of result. Any substantive restraint on the exercise of Commerce Clause powers must find its justification in the procedural nature of this basic limitation, and it must be tailored to compensate for possible failings in the national political process rather than to dictate a "sacred province of state autonomy." EEOC v. Wyoming.

Insofar as the present cases are concerned, then, we need go no further than to state that we perceive nothing in the overtime and minimum-wage requirements of the FLSA, as applied to SAMTA, that is destructive of state sovereignty or violative of any constitutional provision. . . .

IV

. . . Though the separate concurrence [of Justice Blackmun] providing the fifth vote in *National League of Cities* was "not untroubled by certain possible implications" of the decision, the Court in that case attempted to articulate affirmative limits on the Commerce Clause power in terms of core

95

governmental functions and fundamental attributes of state sovereignty. But the model of democratic decisionmaking the Court there identified underestimated, in our view, the solicitude of the national political process for the continued vitality of the States. Attempts by other courts since then to draw guidance from this model have proved it both impracticable and doctrinally barren. In sum, in *National League of Cities* the Court tried to repair what did not need repair.

We do not lightly overrule recent precedent. We have not hesitated, however, when it has become apparent that a prior decision has departed from a proper understanding of congressional power under the Commerce Clause. See United States v. Darby (1941). Due respect for the reach of congressional power within the federal system mandates that we do so now.

National League of Cities v. Usery is overruled. The judgment of the District Court is reversed, and these cases are remanded to that court for further proceedings consistent with this opinion.

It is so ordered.

Justice **POWELL,** with whom the Chief Justice [**BURGER**], Justice **REHNQUIST,** and Justice **O'CONNOR** join, dissenting. . . .

There are, of course, numerous examples over the history of this Court in which prior decisions have been reconsidered and overruled. There have been few cases, however, in which the principle of *stare decisis* and the rationale of recent decisions were ignored as abruptly as we now witness. The reasoning of the Court in *National League of Cities,* and the principle applied there, have been reiterated consistently over the past eight years. Since its decision in 1976, *National League of Cities* has been cited and quoted in opinions joined by every member of the present Court. Hodel v. Virginia Surface Mining & Recl. Assn. (1981); United Transportation Union v. Long Island R. Co. (1982); FERC v. Mississippi (1982). Less than three years ago, in *Long Island R. Co.,* a unanimous Court reaffirmed the principles of *National League of Cities* but found them inapplicable to the regulation of a railroad heavily engaged in interstate commerce. . . .

The court in that case recognized that the test "may at times be a difficult one," but it was considered in that unanimous decision as settled constitutional doctrine. . . .

Although the doctrine is not rigidly applied to constitutional questions, "any departure from the doctrine of *stare decisis* demands special justification." In the present case, the five Justices who compose the majority today participated in *National League of Cities* and the cases reaffirming it. The stability of judicial decision, and with it respect for the authority of this Court, are not served by the precipitous overruling of multiple precedents that we witness in this case.

Whatever effect the Court's decision may have in weakening the application of *stare decisis*, it is likely to be less important than what the Court has done to the Constitution itself. A unique feature of the United States is the *federal* system of government guaranteed by the Constitution and implicit in the very name of our country. Despite some genuflecting in [the] Court's opinion to the concept of federalism, today's decision effectively reduces the Tenth Amendment to meaningless rhetoric when Congress acts pursuant to the Commerce Clause. . . .

To leave no doubt about its intention, the Court renounces its decision in *National League of Cities* because it "inevitably invites an unelected federal judiciary to make decisions about which state policies it favors and which ones it dislikes." In other words, the extent to which the States may exercise their authority, when Congress purports to act under the Commerce Clause, henceforth is to be determined from time to time by political decisions made by members of the federal government, decisions the Court says will not be subject to judicial review. I note that it does not seem to have occurred to the Court that *it*—an unelected majority of five Justices—today rejects almost 200 years of the understanding of the constitutional status of federalism. In doing so, there is only a single passing reference to the Tenth Amendment. Nor is so much as a dictum of any court cited in support of the view that the role of the States in the federal system may depend upon the grace of elected federal officials, rather than on the Constitution as interpreted by this Court. . . .

The Court apparently thinks that the States' success at obtaining federal funds for various projects and exemptions from the obligations of some federal statutes is indicative of the "effectiveness of the federal political process in preserving the States' interests. . . ." But such political success is not relevant to the question whether the political *processes* are the proper means of enforcing constitutional limitations. The fact that Congress generally does not transgress constitutional limits on its power to reach State activities does not make judicial review any less necessary to rectify the cases in which it does do so. The States' role in our system of government is a matter of constitutional law, not of legislative grace. "The powers not delegated to the United States by the Constitution, nor prohibited by it to the States, are reserved to the States, respectively, or to the people." U.S. Const., Amend. 10.

More troubling than the logical infirmities in the Court's reasoning is the result · of its holding, i.e., that federal political officials, invoking the Commerce Clause, are the sole judges of the limits of their own power. This result is inconsistent with the fundamental principles of our constitutional system. See, e.g., The *Federalist* No. 78 (Hamilton). At least since Marbury v. Madison (1803) it has been the settled province of the federal judiciary "to say what the law is" with respect to the constitutionality of acts of Congress. In rejecting the role of the judiciary in protecting the States from federal overreaching, the Court's opinion offers no explanation for ignoring the teaching of the most famous case in our history. . . .

... [T]he Court today propounds a view of federalism that pays only lip service to the role of the States.... [I]t fails to recognize the broad, yet specific areas of sovereignty that the Framers intended the States to retain. Indeed, the Court barely acknowledges that the Tenth Amendment exists.... The Court recasts this language to say that the States retain their sovereign powers "only to the extent that the Constitution has not divested them of their original powers and transferred those powers to the Federal Government." This rephrasing is not a distinction without a difference; rather, it reflects the Court's unprecedented view that Congress is free under the Commerce Clause to assume a State's traditional sovereign power, and to do so without judicial review of its action. Indeed, the Court's view of federalism appears to relegate the States to precisely the trivial role that opponents of the Constitution feared they would occupy....

Justice **REHNQUIST** dissenting....

Justice **O'CONNOR,** with whom Justice **POWELL** and Justice **REHNQUIST** join, dissenting....

4. GOVERNMENTAL CONTROL
OF THE ECONOMY

O ne of the principal reasons for calling the Constitutional Convention of 1787 was to resolve the economic problems created by democratically elected state legislatures that were setting up trade barriers against other states, printing paper money that allowed debtors to pay off their debts in depreciated currency, and making it easy for debtors to get out of contracts by declaring themselves bankrupt. The new Constitution met these perceived evils by delegating to Congress in Article I, sec. 8 power to "regulate Commerce . . . among the several States"; "coin Money"; and "establish . . . uniform Laws on the subject of Bankruptcies." In addition, Article I, sec. 10 forbade states to: "coin Money; emit Bills of Credit; make any Thing but gold and silver Coin a Tender in Payment of Debts; [or] pass any . . . Law impairing the Obligation of Contracts. . . ."

But most of these provisions require interpretation. For instance, the question when commerce is "among the several States" and when it is purely local generated almost two centuries of heated debate. Decisions such as Gibbons v. Ogden (1824; see Case 3.2) and United States v. Darby Lumber Co. (1941; see Case 3.3) wrestled with this issue. Other questions have caused equally bitter divisions and provoked as many judicial decisions.

Under Chief Justice Marshall (1801-1836), the Court tended to protect commerce and property against state legislation—there were few relevant federal statutes of any significance. But Marshall's successors, reflecting their generally friendly attitude toward state authority, were more permissive.

And, ironically, emerging business groups in the early-nineteenth century urged judges to view property rights differently from Marshall and his colleagues. These people secured from legislatures power to override older forms of property rights, such as that to quiet enjoyment of land, in order to facilitate more dynamic uses, such as building railroads—which meant taking private land—and constructing mills—which meant diverting rivers. These new economic interest groups wanted judges to uphold the constitutionality of such redistributions of rights.

The great change came after 1877, when Munn v. Illinois[1] *sustained legislation that restricted the capacity of businesses to charge what prices they wanted. Groups of lawyers and businessmen immediately undertook a campaign to "educate" judges about the sacredness of private property. Available were an economic theory called laissez faire and a social philosophy known as social Darwinism. Under the former, government was supposed to stand aside and let people freely compete to secure the greatest economic good. The latter rationalized away the human costs of the first by arguing that life was a struggle in which only "the fittest" deserved to survive.*

After some hesitation, judges bought this dual theory. First, they read the word person *in the Fifth and Fourteenth amendments' due process clauses (neither Congress nor the states can "deprive any person of life, liberty, or property, without due process of law") to include corporations. Second, they assumed* liberty *included freedom to make most kinds of contracts except through fraud or obvious physical duress (hunger did not count as duress). Third, courts held that due process— which historically had meant "normal legal procedures"—had a substantive dimension; that is, government could not do some things no matter how normal the procedures it used. (At the same time, as Chapter 3 noted, when business groups challenged federal regulations, the Supreme Court took a broad view of the Tenth Amendment and a narrow view of the reach of the commerce clause.)*

Lochner v. New York (1905; see Case 4.1) was the great case restricting state power over economic affairs. For a decade after Lochner *the Court backed down a bit, persuaded by the arguments of a crusading lawyer (and future Supreme Court justice) named Louis D. Brandeis that capitalism was creating dire social harm that legislatures could try to ease. By the end of World War I, however, the justices were reasserting laissez faire and social Darwinism. As the Court said in 1923, "[F]reedom of contract is . . . the general rule and restraint the exception."* [2] *These two theories alone did not cause the stock market crash of 1929 and the Great Depression that followed, but the connections were both close and obvious.*

Franklin D. Roosevelt's New Deal of the 1930s was an attempt to install governmental regulation, both state and federal, as the norm. And the Supreme Court waged war on behalf of laissez faire and social Darwinism. In May 1936, Justice Harlan Stone, who, as had Justices Oliver Wendell Holmes and Brandeis, thought judicial imposition of economic and social theories on the nation was wrong, wrote his sister:

> Our latest exploit was holding by a divided vote that there was no power
> in a state to regulate minimum wages for women. Since the court last
> week said this could not be done by the national government, as the
> matter was local, and it is said that it cannot be done by local

government even though it is local, we have tied Uncle Sam up in a hard knot.

The knot, of course, did not stay tied. In the ensuing election of 1936, in large part a national referendum on the New Deal, Roosevelt won in forty-six of the then-forty-eight states. Within a few weeks of the election, the justices began changing their minds, as evidenced in West Coast Hotel v. Parrish (1937; see Case 4.2).

By and large, since 1937 the Court has allowed Congress and the states to set the limits of state constitutional power over economic affairs (except where state authority has clashed with federal authority). The justices have insisted that channels of political communication be open so that today's minorities can become tomorrow's majority—or ruling coalition of minorities.

Nevertheless, as we shall see in Chapter 6, the Court has not abandoned the notion of substantive due process. Rather, judges have transferred its application to noneconomic rights such as privacy.

---

1. *94 U.S. 113.*
2. *Adkins v. Children's Hospital, 261 U.S. 525 (1923).*

∼ Case 4.1 ∼

Justice **PECKHAM:** "Statutes of the nature of that under review . . . are mere meddlesome interferences with the rights of the individual. . . ."

Justice **HOLMES:** "[T]he word liberty in the Fourteenth Amendment is perverted when it is held to prevent the natural outcome of dominant opinion, unless it can be said that a rational and fair man would admit that the statute proposed would infringe fundamental principles as they have been understood by the traditions of our people and our law."

Lochner v. New York
195 U.S. 45, 25 S. Ct. 539, 49 L. Ed. 937 (1905)

Near the turn of the century, as part of a general political movement to improve working conditions, New York adopted a statute forbidding an employer to require or allow employees in bakeries to work more than ten hours a day or more than sixty hours a week. Lochner, a bakery shop owner, was indicted for having his employees work more than sixty hours a week. In defense, he challenged the constitutionality of the statute. He lost in the state courts, then appealed to the U.S. Supreme Court.

Mr. Justice **PECKHAM** . . . delivered the opinion of the Court. . . .

The statute necessarily interferes with the right of contract between the employer and employees, concerning the number of hours in which the latter may labor in the bakery of the employer. The general right to make a contract in relation to his business is part of the liberty of the individual protected by the Fourteenth Amendment of the Federal Constitution. Allgeyer v. Louisiana [1897]. Under that provision no State can deprive any person of life, liberty or property without due process of law. The right to purchase or to sell labor is part of the liberty protected by this amendment, unless there are circumstances which exclude the right. There are, however, certain powers, existing in the sovereignty of each State in the Union, somewhat vaguely termed police powers, the exact description and limitation of which have not been attempted by the courts. Those powers . . . relate to the safety, health, morals and general welfare of the public. Both property and liberty are held on such reasonable conditions as may be imposed by the governing power of the State in the exercise of those powers, and with such conditions the Fourteenth Amendment was not designed to interfere. Mugler

v. Kansas [1887], In re Kemmler [1890], Crowley v. Christensen [1890], In re Converse [1891].

The State, therefore, has power to prevent individuals from making certain kinds of contracts. . . . Contracts in violation of a statute, either of the Federal or state government, or a contract to let one's property for immoral purposes, or to do any other unlawful act, could obtain no protection from the Federal Constitution, as coming under the liberty of person or of free contract. Therefore, when the State . . . in the assumed exercise of its police powers, has passed an act which seriously limits the right to labor or the right of contract in regard to their means of livelihood between persons . . . it becomes of great importance to determine which shall prevail—the right of the individual to labor for such time as he may choose, or the right of the State to prevent the individual from laboring . . . beyond a certain time prescribed by the State.

This court has recognized the existence and upheld the exercise of the police powers of the States in many cases. . . .

It must, of course, be conceded that there is a limit to the valid exercise of the police power by the State. . . . Otherwise the Fourteenth Amendment would have no efficacy and the legislatures of the States would have unbounded power, and it would be enough to say that any piece of legislation was enacted to conserve the morals, the health or the safety of the people. . . . The claim of the police power would be a mere pretext—become another and delusive name for the supreme sovereignty of the State to be exercised free from constitutional restraint. . . . In every case that comes before this court, therefore, where legislation of this character is concerned and where the protection of the Federal Constitution is sought, the question necessarily arises: Is this a fair, reasonable and appropriate exercise of the police power of the State? . . . Of course the liberty of contract relating to labor includes both parties to it. The one has as much right to purchase as the other to sell labor.

This is not a question of substituting the judgment of the court for that of the legislature. If the act be within the power of the State it is valid, although the judgment of the court might be totally opposed to the enactment of such a law. But the question would still remain: Is it within the police power of the State? and that question must be answered by the court.

. . . There is no reasonable ground for interfering with the liberty of person or the right of free contract, by determining the hours of labor, in the occupation of a baker. There is no contention that bakers as a class are not equal in intelligence and capacity to men in other trades or manual occupations, or that they are not able to assert their rights and care for themselves without the protecting arm of the State, interfering with their independence of judgment and action. They are in no sense wards of the State. Viewed in the light of a purely labor law, with no reference whatever to the question of health, we think that a law like the one before us involves neither the safety, the morals nor the welfare of the public and that the interest of the public is not in the slightest degree affected by such an act. The law must be upheld, if at all, as a law pertaining to the health of the individual engaged in the occupation of a baker. . . . Clean and wholesome bread does not depend upon whether the baker work but ten hours per day or only sixty hours a week. The limitation of the hours of labor does not come within the police power on that ground. . . .

We think that there can be no fair doubt that the trade of a baker, in and of itself, is not an unhealthy one to that degree which would authorize the legislature to interfere with the right to labor, and with the right of free contract on the part of the individual, either as employer or employee. . . . It might be safely affirmed that almost all occupations more or less affect the health. . . . But are we all, on that account, at the mercy of legislative majorities? A printer, a tinsmith, a locksmith, a carpenter, a cabinetmaker, a dry goods clerk, a bank's, a lawyer's or a physician's clerk, or a clerk in almost any kind of business, would all come under the power of the legislature, on this assumption. No trade, no occupation, no mode of earning one's living, could escape this all-pervading power, and the acts of the legislature in limiting the hours of labor in all employments would be valid, although such limitation might seriously cripple the ability of the laborer to support himself and his family. . . .

It is also urged . . . that it is to the interest of the State that its population should be strong and robust, and therefore any legislation which may be said to tend to make people healthy must be valid as health laws, enacted under the police power. If this be a valid argument . . . it follows that the protection of the Federal Constitution from undue interference with liberty of person and freedom of contract is visionary. . . . Scarcely any law but might find shelter under such assumptions. . . . Not only the hours of employees but the hours of employers, could be regulated, and doctors, lawyers, scientists, all professional men, as well as athletes and artisans, could be forbidden to fatigue their brains and bodies by prolonged hours of exercise. . . . We do not believe in the soundness of views which uphold this law. On the contrary, we think that such a law as this, although passed in the assumed exercise of the police power, and as relating to the public health, or the health of the employees named, is not within the meaning of that power, and is invalid. The act is . . . an illegal interference with the rights of individuals, both employers and employees, to make such contracts regarding labor upon such terms as they may think best. . . . Statutes of the nature of that under review . . . are mere meddlesome interferences with the rights of the individual. . . .

This interference on the part of the legislatures of the several States with the ordinary trades and occupations of the people seems to be on the increase. . . .

It is impossible to shut our eyes to the fact that many of the laws of this character, while passed under what is claimed to be the police power for the purpose of protecting the public health or welfare, are, in reality, passed from other motives. . . . The purpose of a statute must be determined from the natural and legal effect of the language employed; and whether or not it is repugnant to the Constitution of the United States must be determined from the natural effect of such statutes when put into operation, and not from their proclaimed purpose. . . . The court looks beyond the mere letter of the law in such cases. Yick Wo v. Hopkins [1886].

It is manifest to us that . . . the real object and purpose were simply to regulate the hours of labor between the master and his employees . . . in a private business, not dangerous in any degree to morals or in any real and substantial degree, to the health of the employees. Under such circumstances the freedom of the master and employee to contract with each other . . . cannot be prohibited or interfered with, without violating the Federal Constitution. . . .

Mr. Justice **HARLAN,** with whom Mr. Justice **WHITE** and Mr. Justice **DAY** concurred, dissenting. . . .

Granting . . . that there is a liberty of contract which cannot be violated even under the sanction of direct legislative enactment, but assuming, as according to settled law we may assume, that such liberty of contract is subject to such regulations as the State may reasonably prescribe for the common good and the well-being of society, what are the conditions under which the judiciary may declare such regulations to be in excess of legislative authority and void? Upon this point there is no room for dispute; for, the rule is universal that a legislative enactment, Federal or state, is never to be disregarded or held invalid unless it be, beyond question, plainly and palpably in excess of legislative power. . . . If there be doubt as to the validity of the statute, that doubt must therefore be resolved in favor of its validity, and the courts must keep their hands off, leaving the legislature to meet the responsibility for unwise legislation. If the end which the legislature seeks to accomplish be one to which its power extends, and if the means employed to that end, although not the wisest or best, are yet not plainly and palpably unauthorized by law, then the court cannot interfere. In other words, when the validity of a statute is questioned, the burden of proof, so to speak, is upon those who assert it to be unconstitutional. McCulloch v. Maryland [1819].

Let these principles be applied to the present case. . . .

It is plain that this statute was enacted in order to protect the physical well-being of those who work in bakery and confectionery establishments. . . . [T]he statute must be taken as expressing the belief of the people of New York that, as a general rule, and in the case of the average man, labor in excess of sixty hours during a week in such establishments may endanger the health of those who thus labor. Whether or not this be wise legislation it is not the province of the court to inquire. Under our systems of government the courts are not concerned with the wisdom or policy of legislation. . . . I find it impossible, in view of common experience, to say that there is here no real or substantial relation between the means employed by the State and the end sought to be accomplished by its legislation. . . . Nor can I say that the statute has no appropriate or direct connection with that protection to health which each State owes to her citizens . . . or that it is not promotive of the health of the employees in question . . . or that the regulation prescribed by the State is utterly unreasonable and extravagant or wholly arbitrary. . . . Still less can I say that the statute is, beyond question, a plain, palpable invasion of rights secured by the fundamental law. . . . Therefore I submit that this court will transcend its functions if it assumes to annul the statute of New York. . . .

Mr. Justice **HOLMES** dissenting. . . .

This case is decided upon an economic theory which a large part of the country does not entertain. If it were a question whether I agreed with that theory, I should desire to study it further and long before making up my mind. But I do not conceive that to be my duty, because I strongly believe that my agreement or disagreement has nothing to do with the right of a majority to embody their opinions in law. It is settled by various decisions of this court that state constitutions and state laws may regulate life in many ways which we as legislators might think as injudicious or if you like as tyrannical as this, and which equally with this interfere with the liberty to contract. Sunday laws and usury laws are ancient examples. . . . The liberty of the citizen to do as he likes so long as he does not interfere with the liberty of others to do the same, which has been a shibboleth for some well-known writers, is interfered with by school laws, by the Post Office, by every state or municipal institution which takes his money for purposes thought desirable whether he likes it or not. The Fourteenth Amendment does not enact Mr. Herbert Spencer's Social Statics. The other day we sustained the Massachusetts vaccination law. Jacobson v. Massachusetts [1905]. . . . United States and state statutes and decisions cutting down the liberty to contract by way of combination are familiar to this court. . . . Two years ago we upheld the prohibition of sales of stock on margins or for future delivery in the constitution of California. . . . The decision sustaining an eight hour law for miners is still recent. . . . Some of those laws embody convictions or prejudices which judges are likely to share. Some may not. But a constitution is not intended to embody a particular economic theory, whether of paternalism and the organic relation of the citizen to the State or of *laissez faire*. It is made for people of fundamentally differing views, and the accident of our finding certain opinions natural and familiar or novel and even shocking ought not to conclude our judgment upon the question whether statutes embodying them conflict with the Constitution of the United States.

General propositions do not decide concrete cases. The decision will depend on a judgment or intuition more subtle than any articulate major premise. . . . Every opinion tends to become a law. I think that the word liberty in the Fourteenth Amendment is perverted when it is held to prevent the natural outcome of a dominant opinion, unless it can be said that a rational and fair man necessarily would admit that the statute proposed would infringe fundamental principles as they have been understood by the traditions of our people and our law. It does not need research to show that no such sweeping condemnations can be passed upon the statute before us. A reasonable man might think it a proper measure on the score of health. Men whom I certainly could not pronounce unreasonable would uphold it as a first installment of a general regulation of the hours of work. . . .

～ Case 4.2 ～

Chief Justice **HUGHES:** "Even if the wisdom of the policy be regarded as debatable and its effects uncertain, still the legislature is entitled to its judgment."

Justice **SUTHERLAND:** "[I]n passing upon the validity of a statute, [a judge] discharges a duty imposed upon *him*, which cannot be consummated justly by an automatic acceptance of the views of others which have neither convinced, nor created a reasonable doubt in, his mind."

West Coast Hotel v. Parrish
300 U.S. 379, 57 S. Ct. 578, 81 L. Ed. 703 (1937)

After Lochner, *reform groups decided to emulate big business and "re-educate" judges. One result was the "Brandeis Brief," named for Louis D. Brandeis, who first used it in the Supreme Court, though his research was done by the National Consumers League. Brandeis's strategy was simple.* Major premise: As *the Court conceded in* Lochner, *a legislature could try to eliminate great social evils.* Minor premise: *Unregulated economic activity produced great social evils. This much of the argument took only several pages. What followed provided detailed evidence of the harm done to the health and lives of people, especially women, who had to work twelve to fourteen hours a day six or even seven days a week. The conclusion followed smoothly: Statutes setting minimum wages and maximum hours were reasonable ways of coping with these great social evils.*

For a decade the Court's acceptance of the Brandeis Brief eroded
Lochner. By the closing years of World War I, however, the justices were
inching back; and, in 1923, Adkins v. Children's Hospital, 261 U.S. 525,
reaffirmed Lochner and struck down a minimum wage law for women.
Roosevelt's New Deal ran head-on against the philosophy of Lochner,
Adkins, and similar rulings restricting congressional control over com-
merce. In 1936, by a 5-4 vote, Morehead v. New York, 298 U.S. 587, in-
validated a state minimum wage law for women, while other decisions
held the federal government lacked the authority to set minimum wages
because of the Tenth Amendment.

A few weeks before the election of 1936, the Court denied a
petition to reconsider its decision in Morehead; *but a few weeks after*
Roosevelt's landslide victory the Court heard argument in a case
challenging a very similar law from the state of Washington. The state
asked the Court only to distinguish, not overrule, Lochner, Adkins *and*
Morehead; *but Justice Owen Roberts, who had supplied the fifth vote in*
Morehead, *changed his mind on the constitutional issue.*

Mr. Chief Justice **HUGHES** delivered the opinion of the Court. . . .

The appellant conducts a hotel. The appellee Elsie Parrish was employed
as a chambermaid and (with her husband) brought this suit to recover the
difference between the wages paid her and the minimum wage fixed
pursuant to the state law. The minimum wage was $14.50 per week of 48
hours. The appellant challenged the act as repugnant to the due process
clause of the Fourteenth Amendment of the Constitution of the United States.
The Supreme Court of the State, reversing the trial court, sustained the
statute and directed judgment for the plaintiffs. . . . This case is here on
appeal.

The appellant relies upon the decision of this Court in Adkins v.
Children's Hospital. . . . [C]ounsel for the appellees attempted to distinguish
the *Adkins* case. . . . That effort at distinction is obviously futile. . . .

. . . Morehead v. New York [1936] held the New York minimum wage
act for women to be invalid. A minority of this Court thought that the New
York statute was distinguishable in a material feature from that involved in
the *Adkins* case, and that for that and other reasons the New York statute
should be sustained. But the Court of Appeals of New York had said that it
found no material difference between the two statutes, and this Court held
that the "meaning of the statute" as fixed by the decision of the state court
"must be accepted here as if the meaning had been specifically expressed in
the enactment." . . . That view led to the affirmance by this Court of the
judgment in the *Morehead* case, as the Court considered that the only
question before it was whether the *Adkins* case was distinguishable and that
reconsideration of that decision had not been sought. . . .

. . . The Supreme Court of Washington has upheld that minimum wage statute of that State. It has decided that the statute is a reasonable exercise of the police power of the State. In reaching that conclusion the state court has invoked principles long established by this Court in the application of the Fourteenth Amendment. The state court has refused to regard the decision in the *Adkins* case as determinative and has pointed to our decisions both before and since that case as justifying its position. We are of the opinion that this ruling . . . demands . . . reexamination of the *Adkins* case. The importance of the question, in which many States have similar laws are concerned, the close division by which the decision in the *Adkins* case was reached, and the economic conditions which have supervened, and in the light of which the reasonableness of the exercise of the protective power of the State must be considered, make it not only appropriate, but . . . imperative, that . . . the subject receive fresh consideration. . . .

The principle which must control our decision is not in doubt. The constitutional provision invoked is the due process clause of the Fourteenth Amendment governing the States, as the due process clause invoked in the *Adkins* case governed Congress. In each case the violation alleged by those attacking minimum wage regulation for women is deprivation of freedom of contract. What is this freedom? The Constitution does not speak of freedom of contract. It speaks of liberty and prohibits the deprivation of liberty without due process of law. In prohibiting that deprivation the Constitution does not recognize an absolute and uncontrollable liberty. Liberty in each of its phases has its history and connotation. But the liberty safeguarded is liberty in a social organization which requires the protection of law against the evils which menace the health, safety, morals and welfare of the people. Liberty under the Constitution is thus necessarily subject to the restraints of due process, and regulation which is reasonable in relation to its subject and is adopted in the interests of the community is due process.

This essential limitation of liberty in general governs freedom of contract in particular. More than twenty-five years ago we set forth the applicable principle in these words: . . . "[f]reedom of contract is a qualified and not an absolute right. There is no absolute freedom to do as one wills or to contract as one chooses. . . . Liberty implies the absence of arbitrary restraint, not immunity from reasonable regulations and prohibitions imposed in the interests of the community." Chicago, B. & Q, R. Co. v. McGuire [1911].

This power under the Constitution to restrict freedom of contract has had many illustrations. . . . Thus statutes have been sustained limiting employment in underground mines and smelters to eight hours a day . . . in forbidding the payment of seamen's wages in advance . . . in prohibiting contracts limiting liability for injuries to employees . . . in limiting hours of work of employees in manufacturing establishments . . . and in maintaining workmen's compensation laws. . . . In dealing with the relation of employer and employed, the legislature has necessarily a wide field of discretion in order that there may be suitable protection of health and safety, and that peace and good order may be promoted through regulations designed to insure wholesome conditions of work and freedom from oppression. . . .

The point that has been strongly stressed that adult employees should be deemed competent to make their own contracts was decisively met nearly forty years ago in Holden v. Hardy [1898] where we pointed out the inequality in the footing of the parties: . . .

> "The legislature has also recognized . . . that the proprietors of these establishments and their operatives do not stand upon an equality, and that their interests are, to a certain extent, conflicting. The former naturally desire to obtain as much labor as possible from their employees, while the latter are often induced by the fear of discharge to conform to regulations which their judgment, fairly exercised, would pronounce to be detrimental to their health or strength. . . . In such cases self-interest is often an unsafe guide, and the legislature may properly interpose its authority."

And we added that the fact "that both parties are of full age and competent to contract does not necessarily deprive the State of the power to interfere where the parties do not stand upon an equality, or where the public health demands that one party to the contract shall be protected against himself." "The State still retains an interest in his welfare, however reckless he may be . . . when the individual health, safety and welfare are sacrificed or neglected, the State must suffer."

. . . This established principle is peculiarly applicable in relation to the employment of women in whose protection the State has a special interest. That phase of the subject received elaborate consideration in Muller v. Oregon [1908] . . . where the constitutional authority of the State to limit the working hours of women was sustained. We emphasized the consideration that "woman's physical structure and the performance of maternal functions place her at a disadvantage in the struggle for subsistence" and that her physical well being "becomes an object of public interest and care in order to preserve the strength and vigor of the race." We emphasized the need of protecting women against oppression despite her possession of contractual rights. . . .

This array of precedents and the principles they applied were thought by the dissenting Justices in the *Adkins* case to demand that the minimum wage statute be sustained. The validity of the distinction made by the Court between a minimum wage and a maximum of hours in limiting liberty of contract was especially challenged. . . . That challenge persists and is without any satisfactory answer. As Chief Justice Taft observed [dissenting in *Adkins*]: "In absolute freedom of contract the one term is as important as the other, for both enter equally into the consideration given and received, a restriction as to the one is not greater in essence than the other and is of the same kind. One is the multiplier and the other the multiplicand." . . .

The minimum wage ... under the Washington statute is fixed after full consideration by representatives of employers, employees and the public. It may be assumed that the minimum wage is fixed in consideration of the services that are performed in the particular occupations under normal conditions. ... The statement of Mr. Justice Holmes in the *Adkins* case is pertinent: "This statute does not compel anybody to pay anything. It simply forbids employment at rates below those fixed as the minimum requirement of health and right living. It is safe to assume that women will not be employed at even the lowest wages allowed unless they earn them, or unless the employer's business can sustain the burden. ..."

We think that the views thus expressed are sound and that the decision in the *Adkins* case was a departure from the true application of the principles governing the regulation by the State of the relation of employer and employed. Those principles have been reenforced by our subsequent decisions. Thus in Radice v. New York [1924] we sustained the New York statute which restricted the employment of women in restaurants at night. ... In Nebbia v. New York [1934] ... the general subject of the regulation of the use of private property and of the making of private contracts received an exhaustive examination and we again declared that if such laws "have a reasonable relation to a proper legislative purpose, and are neither arbitrary nor discriminatory, the requirements of due process are satisfied"; that "with the wisdom of the policy adopted, with the adequacy or practicability of the law enacted to forward it, the courts are both incompetent and unauthorized to deal"; ... that the legislature is primarily the judge of the necessity of such an enactment, that every possible presumption is in favor of its validity. ...

With full recognition of the earnestness and vigor which characterize the prevailing opinion in the *Adkins* case, we find it impossible to reconcile that ruling with these well-considered declarations. What can be closer to the public interest than the health of women and their protection from unscrupulous and overreaching employers? And if the protection of women is a legitimate end of the exercise of state power, how can it be said that the requirement of the payment of a minimum wage fairly fixed in order to meet the very necessities of existence is not an admissible means to that end? ...

[A]doption of similar requirements by many States evidences a deepseated conviction both as to the presence of the evil and as to the means adapted to check it. Legislative response to that conviction cannot be regarded as arbitrary or capricious, and that is all we have to decide. Even if the wisdom of the policy be regarded as debatable and its effects uncertain, still the legislature is entitled to its judgment.

There is an additional and compelling consideration which recent economic experience has brought into a strong light. The exploitation of a class of workers who are in an unequal position with respect to bargaining power and are thus relatively defenseless against the denial of a living wage is not only detrimental to their health and well being but casts a direct burden for their support upon the community. What these workers lose in wages the taxpayers are called upon to pay. The bare cost of living must be met. We may take judicial notice of the unparalleled demands for relief which arose during the recent period of depression and still continue to an alarming extent despite the degree of economic recovery which has been achieved. . . .

The community is not bound to provide what is in effect a subsidy for unconscionable employers. . . . The argument that the legislation in question constitutes an arbitrary discrimination, because it does not extend to men is unavailing. This Court has frequently held that the legislative authority . . . is not bound to extend its regulation to all cases which it might possibly reach. The legislature "is free to recognize degrees of harm and it may confine its restrictions to those classes of cases where the need is deemed to be clearest." . . .

. . . Adkins v. Children's Hospital . . . should be, and it is, overruled. The judgment of the Supreme Court of the State of Washington is

Affirmed.

Mr. Justice **SUTHERLAND,** dissenting. . . .

Mr. Justice **VAN DEVANTER,** Mr. Justice **McREYNOLDS,** Mr. Justice **BUTLER** and I think the judgment of the court below should be reversed. . . .

Under our form of government, where the written Constitution, by its own terms, is the supreme law, some agency, of necessity, must have the power to say the final word as to the validity of a statute assailed as unconstitutional. The Constitution makes it clear that the power has been intrusted to this court when the question arises in a controversy within its jurisdiction; and so long as the power remains there, its exercise cannot be avoided without betrayal of the trust.

It has been pointed out many times . . . that this judicial duty is one of gravity and delicacy; and that rational doubts must be resolved in favor of the constitutionality of the statute. But whose doubts, and by whom resolved? Undoubtedly it is the duty of a member of the court, in the process of reaching a right conclusion, to give due weight to the opposing views of his associates; but in the end, the question . . . is not whether such views seem sound to those who entertain them, but whether they convince him that the statute is constitutional or engender in his mind a rational doubt upon that issue. The oath which he takes as a judge is not a composite oath, but an individual one. And in passing upon the validity of a statute, he discharges a duty imposed upon *him,* which cannot be consummated justly by an automatic acceptance of the views of others which have neither convinced, nor created a reasonable doubt in, his mind. If upon a question so important he thus surrender his deliberate judgment, he stands forsworn. He cannot subordinate his convictions to that extent and keep faith with his oath or retain his judicial and moral independence.

The suggestion that the only check upon the exercise of the judicial power . . . is the judge's own faculty of self-restraint, is both ill considered and mischievous. Self-restraint belongs in the domain of will and not of judgment. The check upon the judge is that imposed by his oath of office, by the Constitution and by his own conscientious and informed convictions; and since he has the duty to make up his own mind and adjudge accordingly, it is hard to see how there could be any other restraint. . . .

It is urged that the question involved should now receive fresh consideration, among other reasons, because of "the economic conditions which have supervened"; but the meaning of the Constitution does not change with the ebb and flow of economic events. We frequently are told in more general words that the Constitution must be construed in the light of the present. If by that it is meant that the Constitution is made up of living words that apply to every new condition which they include, the statement is quite true. But to say . . . that the words of the Constitution mean today what they did not mean when written—that is, that they do not apply to a situation now to which they would have applied then—is to rob that instrument of the essential element which continues it in force as the people have made it until they, and not their official agents, have made it otherwise. . . .

The judicial function is that of interpretation; it does not include the power of amendment under the guise of interpretation. To miss the point of difference between the two is to miss all that the phrase "supreme law of the land" stands for. . . .

If the Constitution, intelligently and reasonably construed in the light of these principles, stands in the way of desirable legislation, the blame must rest upon that instrument, and not upon the court for enforcing it according to its terms. The remedy in that situation—and the only true remedy—is to amend the Constitution. . . .

The people by their Constitution created three separate, distinct, independent and coequal departments of government. The governmental structure rests, and was intended to rest, not upon any one or upon any two, but upon all three of these fundamental pillars. It seems unnecessary to repeat . . . that the powers of these departments are different and are to be exercised independently. . . . Each is answerable to its creator . . . not to another agent. The view, therefore, of the Executive and of Congress that an act is constitutional is persuasive in a high degree; but it is not controlling.

. . . [T]he Washington statute . . . is in every substantial respect identical with the statute involved in the *Adkins* case. . . . And if the *Adkins* case was properly decided, as we . . . think it was, it necessarily follows that the Washington statute is invalid.

In support of minimum-wage legislation it has been urged . . . that great benefits will result in favor of underpaid labor. . . .

But with these speculations we have nothing to do. We are concerned only with the question of constitutionality.

That the clause of the Fourteenth Amendment which forbids a state to deprive any person of life, liberty or property without due process of law includes freedom of contract is so well settled as to be no longer open to question. Nor reasonably can it be disputed that contracts of employment of labor are included in the rule. Adair v. United States [1908], Coppage v. Kansas (1915). In the first of these cases, Mr. Justice Harlan, speaking for the court, said, "The right of a person to sell his labor upon such terms as he deems proper is, in its essence, the same as the right of the purchaser of labor to prescribe the conditions upon which he will accept such labor. . . . In all such particulars the employers and employees have a quality of right, and any legislation that disturbs that equality is an arbitrary interference with the liberty of contract which no government can legally justify in a free land."

In the *Adkins* case we referred to this language, and said that while there was no such thing as absolute freedom of contract . . . freedom of contract was the general rule and restraint the exception; and that the power to abridge that freedom could only be justified by the existence of exceptional circumstances. This statement of the rule has been many times affirmed; and we do not understand that it is questioned by the present decision. . . .

Neither the statute involved in the *Adkins* case nor the Washington statute . . . has the slightest relation to the capacity or earning power of the employee, to the number of hours which constitute the day's work, the character of the place where the work is to be done, or the circumstances or surroundings of the employment. The sole basis upon which the question of validity rests is the assumption that the employee is entitled to receive a sum of money sufficient to provide a living for her, keep her in health and preserve her morals. . . . [T]he question thus presented for the determination of the board [that sets minimum wages] can not be solved by any general formula prescribed by a statutory bureau, since it is not a composite but an individual question to be answered for each individual, considered by herself. . . .

The Washington statute, like the one for the District of Columbia, fixes minimum wages for adult women. Adult men . . . are left free to bargain as they please. . . . The common-law rules restricting the power of women to make contracts have, under our system, long since practically disappeared. Women today stand upon a legal and political equality with men. . . .

An appeal to the principle that the legislature is free to recognize degrees of harm and confine its restrictions accordingly, is but to beg the question, which is: . . . does the legislation . . . create an arbitrary discrimination? We think it does. Difference of sex affords no reasonable ground for making a restriction applicable to the wage contracts of all working women from which like contracts of all working men are left free. . . .

. . . It is hard to see why the power to fix minimum wages does not con-

note a like power in respect of maximum wages. And yet, if both ¡ow   be
exercised in such a way that the minimum and the maximum   ly
approach each other as to become substantially the same, the right   e
any contract in respect of wages will have been completely abrogé ea.

Editors' Note: The justices decided Parrish *in December 19* *, ᴜ*
as usual, it took time to write and circulate among the justi *ᵒᵉ*
opinion of the Court and a dissent. As a result, the decision w
made public until March 1937, shortly after Roosevelt had launc *_*
head-on attack against the Court by asking Congress to nominatᵢ ᴏᵣ
new justice for every justice on the Court over the age of seventy.
timing of Parrish *took much of the impetus out of Roosevelt's attack*
caused it to be dubbed "the switch in time that saved nine."

~ Case 4.3 ~

Justice **BLACK**: "Whether the legislature takes for its textbook
Adam Smith, Herbert Spencer, Lord Keynes, or some other is no
concern of ours."

Ferguson v. Skrupa
372 U.S. 726, 83 S. Ct. 1028, 10 L. Ed. 2d 93 (1963)

*Kansas had a law forbidding the practice of "debt adjusting" by
anyone except a licensed attorney. Skrupa, barred from debt adjusting
by the state, sued, claiming he had been denied due process of law. The
lower court upheld Skrupa's claim and Kansas appealed to the Supreme
Court.*

Justice **BLACK** delivered the opinion of the Court....
    ... Under the system of government created by our Constitution, it is up
to legislatures, not courts, to decide on the wisdom and utility of legislation.
There was a time when the Due Process Clause was used by this Court to
strike down laws which were thought unreasonable, that is, unwise or
incompatible with some particular economic or social philosophy. In this
manner the Due Process Clause was used, for example, to nullify laws
prescribing maximum hours for work in bakeries, Lochner v. New York

(1905), outlawing "yellow dog" contracts, Coppage v. Kansas (1915), setting minimum wages for women, Adkins v. Children's Hospital (1923), and fixing the weight of loaves of bread, Jay Burns Baking Co. v. Bryan (1924). This intrusion by the judiciary into the realm of legislative value judgments was strongly objected to at the time particularly by Mr. Justice Holmes and Mr. Justice Brandeis. Dissenting from the Court's invalidating a state statute which regulated the resale price of theatre and other tickets, Mr. Justice Holmes said, "I think the proper course is to recognize that a state legislature can do whatever it sees fit to do unless it is restrained by some express prohibition in the Constitution of the United States or of the State, and that Courts should be careful not to extend such prohibitions beyond their obvious meaning by reading into them conceptions of public policy that the particular Court may happen to entertain."

And in an earlier case he had emphasized that, "The criterion of constitutionality is not whether we believe the law to be for the public good."

The doctrine that prevailed in *Lochner, Coppage, Adkins, Burns,* and like cases—that due process authorizes courts to hold laws unconstitutional when they believe the legislature has acted unwisely—has long since been discarded. We have returned to the original constitutional proposition that courts do not substitute their social and economic beliefs for the judgment of legislative bodies, who are elected to pass laws. As this Court stated in a unanimous opinion in 1941, "We are not concerned ... with the wisdom, need, or appropriateness of the legislation." Legislative bodies have broad scope to experiment with economic problems, and this Court does not sit to "subject the State to an intolerable supervision hostile to the basic principles of our Government and wholly beyond the protection which the general clause of the Fourteenth Amendment was intended to secure." It is now settled that States "have power to legislate against what are found to be injurious practices in their internal commercial and business affairs, so long as their laws do not run afoul of some specific federal constitutional prohibition, or of some valid federal law."

... We conclude that the Kansas Legislature was free to decide for itself that legislation was needed to deal with the business of debt adjusting. Unquestionably, there are arguments showing that the business of debt adjusting has social utility, but such arguments are properly addressed to the legislature, not to us. We refuse to sit as a "superlegislature to weigh the wisdom of legislation," and we emphatically refuse to go back to the time when courts used the Due Process Clause "to strike down state laws, regulatory of business and industrial conditions, because they may be unwise, improvident, or out of harmony with a particular school of thought." Nor are we able or willing to draw lines by calling a law "prohibitory" or "regulatory." Whether the legislature takes for its textbook Adam Smith, Herbert Spencer, Lord Keynes, or some other is no concern of ours. The Kansas debt adjusting statute may be wise or unwise. But relief, if any be needed, lies not with us but with the body constituted to pass laws for the State of Kansas. . . .

Reversed.

Mr. Justice **HARLAN** concurs in this judgment on the ground that this state measure bears a rational relationship to a constitutionally permissible objective. . . .

~ Case 4.4 ~

Justice **O'CONNOR**: "[T]he Court has made it clear that it will not substitute its judgment for a legislature's judgment as to what constitutes [taking property for] a public use 'unless the use be palpably without reasonable foundation.' "

Hawaii Housing Authority v. Midkiff
467 U.S. 229, 104 S. Ct. 2321, 81 L. Ed. 2d 186 (1984)

In the mid-1960s, an investigation by the Hawaiian legislature showed that seventy-two persons held more than 90 percent of the privately owned land in the state. These people leased land to those who wished to build their own homes. Claiming that this concentration of ownership was inflating real estate prices and contributing to public unrest, the legislature passed the Land Reform Act of 1967. This statute authorized the Hawaiian Housing Authority (HHA), when asked by people leasing the land on which they lived, to condemn large tracts of land occupied by single-family homes, pay the land owner(s) a fair price as determined either by negotiation between the lessors and the lessees or by arbitration, and resell the land to the home owners at the purchase price, though with the proviso that no person could so purchase more than one lot.

In 1977 the HHA began condemnation procedures under the Land Reform Act and ordered Frank E. Midkiff and others to negotiate with some of their lessees over the value of land occupied by those lessees. When those negotiations broke down, the HHA ordered arbitration. Midkiff et al. refused and sued in a federal district court for an injunction against enforcement of the act. The district judge upheld the statute as constitutional, but the Court of Appeals for the Ninth Circuit reversed, saying the act was "a naked attempt on the part of

Hawaii to take the private property of A and transfer it to B solely for B's private use and benefit." Hawaii then appealed to the Supreme Court.

Justice **O'CONNOR** delivered the opinion of the Court. . . .

III

The majority of the Court of Appeals ... determined that the Act violates the "public use" requirement of the Fifth and Fourteenth Amendments. . . .

A

The starting point for our analysis of the Act's constitutionality is the Court's decision in Berman v. Parker (1954). In *Berman,* the Court held constitutional the District of Columbia Redevelopment Act of 1945. That Act provided both for the comprehensive use of the eminent domain power to redevelop slum areas and for the possible sale or lease of the condemned lands to private interests. In discussing whether the takings authorized by that Act were for a "public use," the Court stated

> "We deal, in other words, with what traditionally has been known as the police power. An attempt to define its reach or trace its outer limits is fruitless, for each case must turn on its own facts. The definition is essentially the product of legislative determinations addressed to the purposes of government, purposes neither abstractly nor historically capable of complete definition. Subject to specific constitutional limitations, when the legislature has spoken, the public interest has been declared in terms well-nigh conclusive. In such cases the legislature, not the judiciary, is the main guardian of the public needs to be served by social legislation, whether it be Congress legislating concerning the District of Columbia ... or the States legislating concerning local affairs. . . . This principle admits of no exception merely because the power of eminent domain is involved."

The Court explicitly recognized the breadth of the principle it was announcing, noting:

> "Once the object is within the authority of Congress, the right to realize it through the exercise of eminent domain is clear. For the power of eminent domain is merely the means to the end. . . . Once the object is within the authority of Congress, the means by which it will be attained is also for Congress to determine. Here one of the means chosen is the use of private enterprise for redevelopment of the area. Appellants argue that this makes the project a taking from one businessman for the benefit of another businessman. But the means of executing the project

are for Congress and Congress alone to determine, once the public purpose has been established."

The "public use" requirement is thus coterminous with the scope of a sovereign's police powers.

There is, of course, a role for courts to play in reviewing a legislature's judgment of what constitutes a public use, even when the eminent domain power is equated with the police power. But the Court in *Berman* made clear that it is "an extremely narrow" one. The Court in *Berman* cited with approval the Court's decision in Old Dominion Co. v. United States (1925), which held that deference to the legislature's "public use" determination is required "until it is shown to involve an impossibility." . . . In short, the Court has made clear that it will not substitute its judgment for a legislature's judgment as to what constitutes a public use "unless the use be palpably without reasonable foundation." United States v. Gettysburg Electric R. Co. (1896).

To be sure, the Court's cases have repeatedly stated that "one person's property may not be taken for the benefit of another private person without a justifying public purpose, even though compensation be paid." Thompson v. Consolidated Gas Corp. (1937). Thus, in Missouri Pacific R. Co. v. Nebraska, where the "order in question was not, *and was not claimed to be,* . . . a taking of private property for a public use under the right of eminent domain," the Court invalidated a compensated taking of property for lack of a justifying public purpose. (1896) (Emphasis added). But where the exercise of the eminent domain power is rationally related to a conceivable public purpose, the Court has never held a compensated taking to be proscribed by the Public Use Clause. See *Berman;* Block v. Hirsh (1921).

On this basis, we have no trouble concluding that the Hawaii Act is constitutional. The people of Hawaii have attempted, much as the settlers of the original 13 Colonies did,° to reduce the perceived social and economic evils of a land oligopoly traceable to their monarchs. The land oligopoly has, according to the Hawaii Legislature, created artificial deterrents to the normal functioning of the State's residential land market and forced thousands of individual homeowners to lease, rather than buy, the land underneath their homes. Regulating oligopoly and the evils associated with it is a classic exercise of a State's police powers. See Exxon Corp. v. Governor of Maryland (1978); Block v. Hirsh. We cannot disapprove of Hawaii's exercise of this power.

Nor can we condemn as irrational the Act's approach to correcting the land oligopoly problem. The Act presumes that when a sufficiently large

---

° After the American Revolution, the colonists in several states took steps to eradicate the feudal incidents with which large proprietors had encumbered land in the colonies. . . . [Footnote by the Court.]

number of persons declare that they are willing but unable to buy lots at fair prices the land market is malfunctioning. When such a malfunction is signalled, the Act authorizes HHA to condemn lots in the relevant tract. The Act limits the number of lots any one tenant can purchase and authorizes HHA to use public funds to ensure that the market dilution goals will be achieved. This is a comprehensive and rational approach to identifying and correcting market failure.

Of course, this Act, like any other, may not be successful in achieving its intended goals. But "whether *in fact* the provision will accomplish its objectives is not the question: the [constitutional requirement] is satisfied if . . . the . . . [state] Legislature *rationally could have believed* that the [Act] would promote its objective." Western & Southern Life Ins. Co. v. State Bd. of Equalization (1981). . . . When the legislature's purpose is legitimate and its means are not irrational, our cases make clear that empirical debates over the wisdom of takings—no less than debates over the wisdom of other kinds of socioeconomic legislation—are not to be carried out in the federal courts. Redistribution of fees simple to correct deficiencies in the market determined by the state legislature to be attributable to land oligopoly is a rational exercise of the eminent domain power. Therefore, the Hawaii statute must pass the scrutiny of the Public Use Clause.

B

The Court of Appeals read . . . our "public use" cases, especially *Berman,* as requiring that government possess and use property at some point during a taking. Since Hawaiian lessees retain possession of the property for private use throughout the condemnation process, the court found that the Act exacted takings for private use. Second, it determined that these cases involved only "the review of . . . *congressional* determination[s] that there was a public use, *not* the review of . . . state legislative determination[s]." Because state legislative determinations are involved in the instant cases, the Court of Appeals decided that more rigorous judicial scrutiny of the public use determinations was appropriate. . . .

The mere fact that property taken outright by eminent domain is transferred in the first instance to private beneficiaries does not condemn that taking as having only a private purpose. The Court long ago rejected any literal requirement that condemned property be put into use for the general public. "It is not essential that the entire community, nor even any considerable portion, . . . directly enjoy or participate in any improvement in order [for it] to constitute a public use." Rindge Co. v. Los Angeles (1923). "[W]hat in its immediate aspect [is] only a private transaction may . . . be raised by its class or character to a public affair." *Block.* As the unique way titles were held in Hawaii skewed the land market, exercise of the power of eminent domain was justified. The Act advances its purposes without the

State taking actual possession of the land. In such cases, government does not itself have to use property to legitimate the taking; it is only the taking's purpose, and not its mechanics, that must pass scrutiny under the Public Use Clause.

Similarly, the fact that a state legislature, and not the Congress, made the public use determination does not mean that judicial deference is less appropriate.° Judicial deference is required because, in our system of government, legislatures are better able to assess what public purposes should be advanced by an exercise of the taking power. State legislatures are as capable as Congress of making such determinations within their respective spheres of authority. See *Berman*. Thus, if a legislature, state or federal, determines there are substantial reasons for an exercise of the taking power, courts must defer to its determination that the taking will serve a public use.

IV

The State of Hawaii has never denied that the Constitution forbids even a compensated taking of property when executed for no reason other than to confer a private benefit on a particular private party. A purely private taking could not withstand the scrutiny of the public use requirement; it would serve no legitimate purpose of government and would thus be void. But no purely private taking is involved in this case. The Hawaii Legislature enacted its Land Reform Act not to benefit a particular class of identifiable individuals but to attack certain perceived evils of concentrated property ownership in Hawaii—a legitimate public purpose. Use of the condemnation power to achieve this purpose is not irrational. Since we assume for purposes of this appeal that the weighty demand of just compensation has been met, the requirements of the Fifth and Fourteenth Amendments have been satisfied. . . .

Reversed.

Justice **MARSHALL** took no part in the consideration or decision of these cases.

° It is worth noting that the Fourteenth Amendment does not itself contain an independent "public use" requirement. Rather, that requirement is made binding on the states only by the incorporation of the Fifth Amendment's Eminent Domain Clause through the Fourteenth Amendment's Due Process Clause. See Chicago, Burlington & Quincy R. Co. v. Chicago (1897). It would be ironic to find that state legislation is subject to greater scrutiny under the incorporated "public use" requirement than is congressional legislation under the express mandate of the Fifth Amendment. [Footnote by the Court.]

5. THE RIGHTS TO SPEAK, WRITE, AND VOTE

For both democratic theory and constitutionalism the rights to speak, write, and vote are central. For democratic theory the reasons are obvious: to govern through representatives the people must be able to select their representatives and, periodically, to reconsider those choices. Further, for elections to be more than beauty contests citizens must have ample opportunity to obtain as much relevant political information as they wish and to exchange with each other and to hear candidates exchange ideas about current and projected public policies.

While conceding that a right to participate in governing one's community is essential to human dignity, constitutionalists see other values and other rights at stake. In general constitutionalists view the freedoms to speak and to write not only as instrumental rights but also as forms of self-expression. A government that bars its people from expressing their inner thoughts—about politics, art, religion, or any other topic—treats its citizens like children, not like free adults.

The First Amendment provides clear support for both democratic and constitutionalist theory:

> Congress shall make no law . . . abridging the freedom of speech, or of the press; or the right of the people peaceably to assemble, and to petition the Government for a redress of grievances.

Still, these very plain words limit only Congress, not the states. Yet in the last century the Supreme Court began to read into the due process clause of the Fourteenth Amendment a state obligation to respect various portions of the Bill of Rights.[1] By 1925 the justices had held that states were bound by the free-speech, assembly, and petition clauses of the First Amendment. (Since that time the Court has in effect incorporated almost all of the first nine amendments into the Fourteenth.)

With such an alliance of constitutional text, political theories, and ingenious judicial interpretation, one might expect to encounter few significant obstacles in today's United States to open debate and fair electoral processes. But these rights are not as readily enforced and interpreted as it might seem.

The thorniest problem is the question of whether one may use speech and press to preach violent overthrow of the government. Does democratic citizenship require that people pursue only peaceful means to change their system of government? One may answer yes, but still have qualms about how easy it is to mistake reform for sedition and dissent for disloyalty. One may also invoke a "slippery slope" argument to challenge the wisdom of putting people in jail for advocating—as distinguished from practicing—revolution. As Thomas Jefferson said in his first inaugural address:

> If there be any among us who would wish to dissolve this Union or to change its republican form, let them stand undisturbed as monuments of the safety with which error of opinion may be tolerated where reason is left free to combat it.

Dennis v. United States (1951), the opening case in this chapter, illustrates these problems. We can see their difficulty not only in the sharp divisions among the justices (they could not, after all, even agree on an opinion for the Court), but also in the fact that a half-dozen years later the Court retreated from Dennis by narrowly interpreting the Smith Act, the federal sedition statute.[2] Even taken together, these two rulings do not settle the question of when speech or writing crosses the line between incitement to violence and advocacy of revolutionary reform.

Among the other questions that issues of free speech and press present are the propriety of certain places for public debate. Most people would agree that colleges and universities should be forums for open discussion of all problems, but what about public streets? Courthouses? Public schools? Again, reasonable people may reasonably differ here, just as some unreasonable people may, under the guise of protecting public order, use governmental power to silence dissent and others may use public forums to foment violence. Bethel School District v. Fraser (1986; see Case 5.3) addresses some of these difficulties.

A related issue, the effect of one person's speech or writing on another's reputation, raises the possibility of a clash between democracy's goal of maximizing political participation and constitutionalism's respect for individual personhood and dignity. To what extent should freedom of political debate include the right to defame an opponent? Should it make a difference if one's opponent is a public official or a candidate for public office, on the one hand, or on the other a private citizen attending to his or her personal affairs? New York Times v. Sullivan (1964; see Case 5.2) is the first modern case to confront these matters, though it is by no means the last. Almost a quarter of a century and a dozen rulings since, the justices—and the nation—are still undecided about how far the First Amendment reaches.

Voting, in contrast, would seem on the surface to be a straightforward matter. The constitutional document, however, makes few explicit references to any right to vote. Article I says that people in the states who are eligible to vote for the most numerous house of their state legislature can vote for U.S. representatives; and the Seventeenth Amendment, adopted in 1913, acknowledges the same right with regard to U.S. senators. Otherwise, the Fifteenth, Nineteenth, Twenty-fourth, and Twenty-sixth amendments refer only to a citizen's rights not to be discriminated against in casting a ballot because of race, sex, failure to pay a tax, or age for those over eighteen—but not to a general right to vote. Moreover, no constitutional provision explicitly acknowledges a right to vote for presidential candidates, though the Twenty-fourth Amendment applies to all elections of federal officers. (The Fourteenth Amendment's ban against a state's denying any person "the equal protection of the laws" is also relevant to any discussion of voting restrictions, though its framers may not have so understood it.)

In any event, to advance democracy and control fraud, it seems reasonable for states to allow political parties to hold primary elections to choose the parties' candidates, to require voters to register in advance of an election to prove residency, and to require that voters be able to read and write so they can understand political debate and can read the ballot. But all of these devices can be used to prevent "undesirables" from voting. Southern states used all of these instruments and more to keep blacks from the polls. The "white primary" was especially invidious in that it seemed so legally pure: States authorized political parties to set their own qualifications for membership and thus for the right to vote in their primaries. Since at that time the Democratic party was the only real party in the South, that party's excluding blacks meant those people lost their right to cast a meaningful ballot. Not until 1944 did the Supreme Court invalidate this device.[3] And it took another two decades for Congress, in the Voting Rights Act of 1965, to outlaw most other discriminatory uses of related practices.

By and large, blacks now vote in the same proportion as whites; but other problems remain. Most notable is that of constructing electoral districts of approximately equal population with lines drawn so as not to give advantage to one party or set of political interests. Gerrymandering—drawing electoral lines to favor a party or group—is an ancient American practice. In fact, Elbridge Gerry, whose name the practice bears, was a member of the Constitutional Convention of 1787.

Until 1962 the justices insisted that the proper place to protest maldistricting was the legislature, not the courts. but that year Baker v. Carr[4] held that unequal legislative districting presents a constitutional question that federal judges should confront. Reynolds v. Sims (1964; see Case 5.4) announced the controlling doctrine of "one person, one vote." As is so often true, however, the issue has not lain down and died because of judicial decisions. Although since Baker *most states have redistricted at least twice (and some many more times) and the worst evils of the old system have disappeared, cases alleging abuse still come to the federal courts. The mobility of Americans prevents electoral districts from remaining equal in population, and clever legislators can still manipulate lines to their own partisan advantage.*

The final issue this chapter confronts is that of candidates' getting their names on the ballot. Again values conflict. Restricting the people's choice to candidates nominated by the two major parties not only limits popular freedom, but also encourages the corruption of monopolies. On the other hand, if anyone could simply put his or her name on a ballot, the ballot might be terribly long and there might be no clear winner in the election. Thus the community has a valid interest in curbing frivolous candidacies. Once more, how and where to draw the line and who should do the drawing are serious issues for a constitutional democracy. Anderson v. Celebrezze (1983; see Case 5.5) demonstrates the complexity and importance of these problems.

---

1. *That the plain words of the Fourteenth Amendment imply some limitations on the states like those of the Bill of Rights is by no means far-fetched. The most obvious clause is not "due process" but that which reads: "No State shall make or enforce any law which shall abridge the privileges or immunities of citizens of the United States. . . ." In its first interpretation of the Fourteenth Amendment, however, the Court held that clause to have little substantive content. The Slaughter-House Cases, 16 Wall. 36 (1873).*
2. *Yates v. United States, 354 U.S. 298 (1957).*
3. *Smith v. Allwright, 321 U.S. 699 (1944).*
4. *369 U.S. 186.*

~ Case 5.1 ~

Chief Justice **VINSON:** "Speech is not an absolute, above and beyond control by the legislature. . . ."

Justice **BLACK:** "I cannot agree that the First Amendment permits us to sustain laws suppressing freedom of speech and press on the basis of Congress' or our own notions of mere 'reasonableness.' "

Dennis v. United States
341 U.S. 494, 71 S. Ct. 857, 95 L. Ed. 1137 (1951)

In 1940, on the eve of American entry into World War II, Congress, fearing internal subversion by both Nazis and communists, adopted a statute that, because its chief sponsor was Rep. Howard Smith of Virginia, became popularly known as the Smith Act. It was a law against sedition, that is, against stirring up or encouraging rebellion. The government used the statute hardly at all during the war. Most of the few American Nazis had the prudence to keep silent or were arrested on charges relating to espionage or similar crimes involving deeds rather than words. And for its part the Communist party, after initially supporting Hitler, instantly switched sides in 1941, when the Germans invaded Russia, and supported the American government. In fact, as a gesture of good will, the party soon dissolved itself.

Once Germany and Japan surrendered in 1945, the grand alliance between the Soviet Union and the West disintegrated, first into suspicious rivalry, then into cold war. During the months after the surrender, the Russians, who had made themselves masters in Eastern and Central Europe, refused to withdraw their troops from Iran, and, through their support of guerrillas fighting in Greece, threatened to take over that nation as well. In the next few years there were several prominent incidents of communist espionage in the United States and Canada, the most notorious of which involved the theft of atomic secrets. At the same time, there were revelations in Congress and in the press that a number of prominent and lesser American officials had at one time been members of the Communist party. In sum, Soviet victories abroad and the fear of similar triumphs within the United States caused a fear for national security in America that sometimes verged on panic.

Within that context, the federal government in 1949 successfully prosecuted and convicted Eugene Dennis and ten other national leaders of the Communist party in the United States for violating the Smith Act. The U.S. Court of Appeals for the Second Circuit sustained the convictions, and Dennis and his colleagues sought and obtained review from the U.S. Supreme Court. The justices chose to limit their review to the question of the constitutionality of the Smith Act.

Sec. 2 of the statute made it a crime "to knowingly and willfully advocate, abet, advise or teach the duty, necessity, desirability, or propriety of overthrowing or destroying any government in the United States by force or violence, or by assassination of any officer of such government"; further, sec. 2 made it criminal for anyone, with intent to cause such overthrow, to publish or display written materials advocating violent overthrow or to organize or help organize a group to carry out such a policy. Sec. 3 made it a crime to attempt or to conspire to commit any of the actions described in sec. 2.

Mr. Chief Justice **VINSON** announced the judgment of the Court and an opinion in which Mr. Justice **REED**, Mr. Justice **BURTON** and Mr. Justice **MINTON** join. . . .

II

The obvious purpose of the statute is to protect existing Government, not from change by peaceable, lawful and constitutional means, but from change by violence, revolution and terrorism. That it is within the *power* of the Congress to protect the Government of the United States from armed rebellion is a proposition which requires little discussion. Whatever theoretical merit there may be to the argument that there is a "right" to rebellion against dictatorial governments is without force where the existing structure of the government provides for peaceful and orderly change. We reject any principle of governmental helplessness in the face of preparation for revolution, which principle . . . carried to its logical conclusion must lead to anarchy. . . . The question with which we are concerned here is not whether Congress has such *power*, but whether the *means* which it has employed conflict with the First and Fifth Amendments to the Constitution.

One of the bases for the contention that the means which Congress has employed are invalid takes the form of an attack on the face of the statute on the grounds that . . . it prohibits academic discussion of the merits of Marxism-Leninism, that it stifles ideas and is contrary to all concepts of a free speech and a free press. . . .

The very language of the Smith Act negates the interpretation which petitioners would have us impose on that Act. It is directed at advocacy, not discussion. Thus, the trial judge properly charged the jury that they could not convict if they found that petitioners did "no more than pursue peaceful

studies and discussions or teaching and advocacy in the realm of ideas." . . .
Such a charge is in strict accord with the statutory language, and illustrates
the meaning to be placed on those words. . . . Congress was concerned with
the very kind of activity in which the evidence showed these petitioners
engaged.

III . . .

No important case involving free speech was decided by this Court prior
to Schenck v. United States (1919). The question the Court faced was whether
the evidence was sufficient to sustain the conviction. Writing for a unanimous
Court, Justice Holmes stated that "question in every case is whether the
words used are used in such circumstances and are of such a nature as to create a clear and present danger that they will bring about the substantive evils
that Congress has a right to prevent." . . .

In several later cases involving convictions under the Criminal Espionage
Act, the nub of the evidence the Court held sufficient to meet the "clear and
present danger" test . . . was: . . . Frohwerk v. United States (1919)—
publication of twelve newspaper articles attacking the war; Debs v. United
States (1919)—one speech attacking United States' participation in the war;
Abrams v. United States (1920)—circulation of copies of two different
socialist circulars attacking the war; Schaefer v. United States (1920)—
publication of a German-language newspaper with allegedly false articles,
critical of capitalism and the war; Pierce v. United States (1920)—circulation
of copies of a four-page pamphlet written by a clergyman, attacking the
purposes of the war and United States' participation therein.

The rule we deduce from these cases is that where an offense is specified
by a statute in nonspeech or nonpress terms, a conviction relying upon speech
or press as evidence of violation may be sustained only when the speech or
publication created a "clear and present danger" of attempting or accomplishing the prohibited crime, e.g., interference with enlistment. . . .

The next important case before the Court in which free speech was the
crux of the conflict was Gitlow v. New York (1925). There New York had
made it a crime to "advocate . . . the necessity or propriety of overthrowing
. . . the government by force. . . ." The evidence of violation of the statute was
that the defendant had published a Manifesto attacking the Government and
capitalism. The convictions were sustained, Justices Holmes and Brandeis
dissenting. The majority refused to apply the "clear and present danger" test
to the specific utterance. . . . Justices Holmes and Brandeis refused to accept
this approach. . . . [I]n Whitney v. California (1927) . . . the Court was
confronted with a conviction under the California Criminal Syndicalist
statute. The Court sustained the conviction, Justices Brandeis and Holmes
concurring in the result. In their concurrence they repeated that even though
the legislature had designated certain speech as criminal, this could not

prevent the defendant from showing that there was no danger that the substantive evil would be brought about.

Although no case subsequent to *Whitney* and *Gitlow* has expressly overruled the majority opinions in those cases, there is little doubt that subsequent opinions have inclined toward the Holmes-Brandeis rationale. Speech is not an absolute, above and beyond control by the legislature when its judgment, subject to review here, is that certain kinds of speech are so undesirable as to warrant criminal sanction. Nothing is more certain in modern society than the principle that there are no absolutes, that a name, a phrase, a standard has meaning only when associated with the considerations which gave birth to the nomenclature. . . . To those who would paralyze our Government in the face of impending threat by encasing it in a semantic strait jacket we must reply that all concepts are relative.

In this case we are squarely presented with the application of the "clear and present danger" test, and must decide what that phrase imports. We first note that many of the cases in which this Court has reversed convictions by use of this or similar tests have been based on the fact that the interest which the State was attempting to protect was itself too insubstantial to warrant restriction of speech. . . . Overthrow of the Government by force and violence, however, is certainly a substantial enough interest for the Government to limit speech. Indeed this is the ultimate value of any society, for if a society cannot protect its very structure from armed internal attack, it must follow that no subordinate value can be protected. . . .

Obviously, the words cannot mean that before the Government may act, it must wait until the *putsch* is about to be executed, the plans have been laid and the signal is awaited. If Government is aware that a group aiming at its overthrow is attempting to indoctrinate its members and to commit them to a course whereby they will strike when the leaders feel the circumstances permit, action by the Government is required. . . . Certainly an attempt to overthrow the Government by force, even though doomed from the outset because of inadequate numbers or power of the revolutionists, is a sufficient evil for Congress to prevent. The damage which such attempts create both physically and politically to a nation makes it impossible to measure the validity in terms of the probability of success, or the immediacy of a successful attempt. In the instant case the trial judge charged the jury that they could not convict unless they found that petitioners intended to overthrow the Government "as speedily as circumstances would permit." This does not mean, and could not properly mean, that they would not strike until there was certainty of success. What was meant was that the revolutionists would strike when they thought the time was ripe. We must therefore reject the contention that success or probability of success is the criterion.

The situation with which Justice Holmes and Brandeis were concerned in *Gitlow* was a comparatively isolated event, bearing little relation in their minds to any substantial threat to the safety of the community. . . . They were not confronted with any situation comparable to the instant one—the development of an apparatus designed and dedicated to the overthrow of the Government in the context of world crisis after crisis.

Chief Judge Learned Hand, writing for the majority below, interpreted the phrase as follows: "In each case [courts] must ask whether the gravity of the 'evil,' discounted by its improbability, justifies such invasion of free speech as is necessary to avoid the danger." . . . We adopt this statement of the rule. . . .

The formation by petitioners of such a highly organized conspiracy, with rigidly disciplined members subject to call when the leaders, these petitioners, felt that the time had come for action, coupled with the inflammable nature of world conditions, similar uprisings in other countries, and the touch-and-go nature of our relations with countries with whom petitioners were in the very least ideologically attuned, convince us that their convictions were justified on this score. And this analysis disposes of the contention that a conspiracy to advocate, as distinguished from the advocacy itself, cannot be constitutionally restrained, because it comprises only the preparation. It is the existence of the conspiracy which creates the danger. . . . If the ingredients of the reaction are present, we cannot bind the Government to wait until the catalyst is added. . . .

Affirmed.

Mr. Justice **CLARK** took no part in the consideration or decision of this case.

Mr. Justice **FRANKFURTER** concurring in affirmance of the judgment. . . .

The demands of free speech in a democratic society as well as the interest in national security are better served by candid and informed weighing of the competing interests, within the confines of the judicial process, than by announcing dogmas too inflexible for the non-Euclidian problems to be solved.

But how are competing interests to be assessed? Since they are not subject to quantitative ascertainment, the issue necessarily resolves itself into asking who is to make the adjustment?—who is to balance the relevant factors and ascertain which interest is in the circumstances to prevail? Full responsibility for the choice cannot be given to the courts. Courts are not representative bodies. They are not designed to be a good reflex of a democratic society. Their judgment is best informed, and therefore most dependable, within narrow limits. Their essential quality is detachment, founded on independence. History teaches that the independence of the judiciary is jeopardized when courts become embroiled in the passions of the day and assume primary responsibility in choosing between competing political, economic and social pressures.

Primary responsibility for adjusting the interests which compete in the situation before us of necessity belongs to the Congress. . . . We are to set aside the judgment of those whose duty it is to legislate only if there is no reasonable basis for it. . . . We are to determine whether a statute is sufficiently definite to meet the constitutional requirements of due process, and whether it respects the safeguards against undue concentration of authority secured by separation of power. . . . We must assure fairness of procedure. . . . And, of course, the proceedings in a particular case before us must have the warrant of substantial proof. Beyond these powers we must not go. . . . Above all we must remember that this Court's power of judicial review is not "an exercise of the powers of a super-legislature." . . .

Some members of the Court—and at times a majority—have done more. They have suggested that our function in reviewing statutes restricting freedom of expression differs sharply from our normal duty in sitting in judgment on legislation. . . . It has been suggested, with the casualness of a footnote, that such legislation is not presumptively valid . . . and it has been weightily reiterated that freedom of speech has a "preferred position" among constitutional safeguards. . . .°

Free speech cases are not an exception to the principle that we are not legislators, that direct policy-making is not our province. How best to reconcile competing interests is the business of legislatures, and the balance they strike is a judgment not to be displaced by ours, but to be respected unless outside the pale of fair judgment. . . .

On the one hand is the interest in security. The Communist Party was not designed by these defendants as an ordinary political party. . . .

° *Frankfurter was referring to United States v. Carolene Products Co., 304 U.S. 144 (1938). That case was decided shortly after the Court's unsuccessful war with Franklin D. Roosevelt. There the justices had tried to carve out for themselves a new set of roles. In that footnote, partially written by Chief Justice Charles Evans Hughes, Justice Harlan Stone said for the Court that the justices would, as a general rule, presume that social or economic legislation adopted by a legislature was constitutional. Stone, however, questioned whether that general rule of presumption should hold under any of three circumstances: where a specific provision of the Bill of Rights was involved; where the democratic integrity of the political processes themselves was involved; or where a law was aimed at a small and insular minority who lacked power in political processes. Taking its name from the last of these possible exceptions, a doctrine grew up that American constitutional structure accorded a "preferred position" to freedom of speech, press, assembly, and association—as rights necessary to the functioning of democratic political process—over other claims of government or private citizens. At one time Frankfurter accepted Stone's distinctions, but later he changed his mind. Much of the Court's history since 1938 can be seen as a chronicle of disputes among the justices about the meaning and force of Stone's philosophy.—Eds.*

In 1947 . . . at least 60,000 members were enrolled in the Party. Evidence was introduced in this case that the membership was organized in small units, linked by an intricate chain of command, and protected by elaborate precautions designed to prevent disclosure of individual identity. There are no reliable data tracing acts of sabotage or espionage directly to these defendants. But a Canadian Royal Commission appointed in 1946 to investigate espionage reported that it was "overwhelmingly established" that "the Communist movement was the principal base within which the espionage network was recruited." The most notorious spy in recent history was led into the service of the Soviet Union through Communist indoctrination. Evidence supports the conclusion that members of the Party seek and occupy positions of importance in political and labor organizations. Congress was not barred by the Constitution from believing that indifference to such experience would be an exercise not of freedom but of irresponsibility.

On the other hand is the interest in free speech. The right to exert all governmental powers in aid of maintaining our institutions and resisting their physical overthrow does not include intolerance of opinions and speech that cannot do harm although opposed and perhaps alien to dominant, traditional opinion. The treatment of its minorities, especially their legal position, is among the most searching tests of the level of civilization attained by a society. It is better for those who have almost unlimited power of government in their hands to err on the side of freedom. We have enjoyed so much freedom for so long that we are perhaps in danger of forgetting how much blood it cost to establish the Bill of Rights. . . .

. . . Suppressing advocates of overthrow inevitably will also silence critics who do not advocate overthrow but fear that their criticism may be so construed. . . . It is a sobering fact that in sustaining the conviction before us we can hardly escape restriction on the interchange of ideas.

. . . Freedom of expression is the well-spring of our civilization—the civilization we seek to maintain and further by recognizing the right of Congress to put some limitation upon expression. Such are the paradoxes of life. . . .

It is not for us to decide how we would adjust the clash of interests which this case presents were the primary responsibility for reconciling it ours. Congress has determined that the danger created by advocacy of overthrow justifies the ensuing restriction on freedom of speech. The determination was made after due deliberation, and the seriousness of the congressional purpose is attested by the volume of legislation passed to effectuate the same ends.

Can we then say that the judgment Congress exercised was denied it by the Constitution? Can we establish a constitutional doctrine which forbids the elected representatives of the people to make this choice? Can we hold that the First Amendment deprives Congress of what it deemed necessary for the Government's protection?

To make validity of legislation depend on judicial reading of events still in the womb of time—a forecast, that is, of the outcome of forces at best appreciated only with knowledge of the topmost secrets of nations—is to charge the judiciary with duties beyond its equipment. . . .

Civil liberties draw at best only limited strength from legal guaranties. Preoccupation by our people with the constitutionality, instead of with the wisdom, of legislation or of executive action is preoccupation with a false value. . . . Focusing attention on constitutionality tends to make constitutionality synonymous with wisdom. When legislation touches freedom of thought and freedom of speech, such a tendency is a formidable enemy of the free spirit. Much that should be rejected as illiberal, because repressive and envenoming, may well be not unconstitutional. The ultimate reliance for the deepest needs of civilization must be found outside their vindication in courts of law; apart from all else, judges, howsoever they may conscientiously seek to discipline themselves against it, unconsciously are too apt to be moved by the deep undercurrents of public feeling. A persistent, positive translation of the liberating faith into the feelings and thoughts and actions of men and women is the real protection against attempts to straitjacket the human mind. Such temptations will have their way, if fear and hatred are not exorcised. The mark of a truly civilized man is confidence in the strength and security derived from the inquiring mind. . . . Without open minds there can be no open society. And if society be not open the spirit of man is mutilated and becomes enslaved. . . .

Mr. Justice **JACKSON**, concurring. . . .

This prosecution is the latest of never-ending, because never successful, quests for some legal formula that will secure an existing order against revolutionary radicalism. It requires us to reappraise, in the light of our own times and conditions, constitutional doctrines devised under other circumstances to strike a balance between authority and liberty. . . .

The highest degree of constitutional protection is due to the individual acting without conspiracy. But even an individual cannot claim that the Constitution protects him in advocating or teaching overthrow of government by force or violence. I should suppose no one would doubt that Congress has power to make such attempted overthrow a crime. But the contention is that one has the constitutional right to work up a public desire and a will to do what it is a crime to attempt. I think direct incitement by speech or writing can be made a crime, and I think there can be a conviction without also proving that the odds favored its success by 99 to 1, or some other extremely high ratio. . . .

Mr. Justice **BLACK**, dissenting. . . .

At the outset I want to emphasize what the crime involved in this case is, and what it is not. These petitioners were not charged with an attempt to overthrow the Government. They were not charged with overt acts of any kind designed to overthrow the Government. They were not even charged with saying anything or writing anything designed to overthrow the Government. The charge was that they agreed to assemble and to talk and publish certain ideas at a later date: The indictment is that they conspired to organize the Communist Party and to use speech or newspapers and other publications in the future to teach and advocate the forcible overthrow of the Government. No matter how it is worded, this is a virulent form of prior censorship of speech and press, which I believe the First Amendment forbids. . . .

So long as this Court exercises the power of judicial review . . . I cannot agree that the First Amendment permits us to sustain laws suppressing freedom of speech and press on the basis of Congress' or our own notions of mere "reasonableness." Such a doctrine waters down the First Amendment so that it amounts to little more than an admonition to Congress. The Amendment as so construed is not likely to protect any but those "safe" or orthodox views which rarely need its protection. . . .

Public opinion being what it now is, few will protest the conviction of these Communist petitioners. There is hope, however, that in calmer times when present pressures, passions and fears subside, this or some later Court will restore the First Amendment liberties to the high preferred place where they belong in a free society.

Mr. Justice **DOUGLAS,** dissenting.

If this were a case where those who claimed protection under the First Amendment were teaching the techniques of sabotage, the assassination of the President, the filching of documents from public files, the planting of bombs, the art of street warfare, and the like, I would have no doubts. The freedom to speak is not absolute; the teaching of methods of terror and other seditious conduct should be beyond the pale along with obscenity and immorality. This case was argued as if those were the facts. . . .

So far as the present record is concerned, what petitioners did was to organize people to teach and themselves teach the Marxist-Leninist doctrine contained chiefly in four books: *Foundations of Leninism* by Stalin (1924), *The Communist Manifesto* by Marx and Engels (1848), *State and Revolution* by Lenin (1917), *History of the Communist Party of the Soviet Union* (B) (1939). . . .

How it can be said that there is a clear and present danger that this advocacy will succeed is, therefore, a mystery. Some nations less resilient than the United States, where illiteracy is high and where democratic traditions are only budding, might have to take drastic steps and jail these men for merely speaking their creed. But in America they are miserable merchants of unwanted ideas. . . . The fact that their ideas are abhorrent does not make them powerful. . . .

The First Amendment provides that "Congress shall make no law ... abridging the freedom of speech." The Constitution provides no exception. This does not mean, however, that the Nation need hold its hand until it is in such weakened condition that there is no time to protect itself from incitement to revolution. Seditious conduct can always be punished. But the command of the First Amendment is so clear that we should not allow Congress to call a halt to free speech except in the extreme case of peril from the speech itself. The First Amendment makes confidence in the common sense of our people and in their maturity of judgment the great postulate of our democracy. . . . The First Amendment reflects the philosophy of Jefferson "that it is time enough for the rightful purposes of civil government for its officers to interfere when principles break out into overt acts against peace and good order." The political censor has no place in our public debates. . . .

Editors' Notes: In Dennis *there was no opinion of the Court. Eight justices participated (Clark had been attorney general when the prosecutions began and so did not sit on the case), but two (Black and Douglas) dissented and two others (Frankfurter and Jackson) refused to join in Vinson's opinion. Thus Vinson spoke not for the Supreme Court but for only four of its nine members.*

Despite references in Vinson's opinion to the evidence introduced at the trial and allusions in other opinions to that evidence, the justices, when they agreed to hear the case, had excluded from their examination the question of the sufficiency of the evidence. When, in calmer times, the Court did review the evidence in a similar case, it found that evidence—similar to that used against Dennis et al.—insufficient to convict. Yates v. United States, *354 U.S. 298 (1957).*

Yates *also gave a much narrower definition of the scope of the Smith Act, and the government has not again prosecuted under the statute.*

~ Case 5.2 ~

Justice **BRENNAN:** "The constitutional guarantees require . . . a federal rule that prohibits a public official from recovering damages for a defamatory falsehood relating to his official conduct unless he proves that the statement was made with 'actual malice'—that is, with knowledge that it was false or with reckless disregard of whether it was false or not."

Justice **BLACK:** "I base my vote to reverse on the belief that the First and Fourteenth Amendments not merely 'delimit' a State's power to award damages to 'public officials against critics of their official conduct' but completely prohibit a State from exercising such a power."

New York Times v. Sullivan
376 U.S. 254, 84 S. Ct. 710, 11 L. Ed. 2d 686 (1964)

In 1960, when the civil rights movement in the South was gaining momentum, the New York Times *printed an advertisement, "Heed Their Rising Voices," which sought financial support and described the brutal reaction of police in Montgomery, Alabama, and Orangeburg, South Carolina, to peaceful protests by black students seeking to affirm "human dignity" protected by the Constitution. Peaceful efforts at reform, the advertisement claimed, were "being met by an unprecedented wave of terror by those who would deny and negate that document. . . ." L. B. Sullivan, a city commissioner of Montgomery, whose work included supervision of police, sued the* Times *and four persons whose names had appeared (without their permission) as sponsoring the advertisement. The* Times *conceded that the ad was inaccurate in some of its details, but noted that it had not named any individual as responsible for the violence. The jury awarded damages of $500,000. The Alabama supreme court affirmed, holding the advertisement was libelous* per se *and not privileged under the First and Fourteenth amendments. By the time the* Times *had sought and obtained review and presented oral argument, eleven other suits by local officials, asking for $5.6 million, were pending against it.*

Mr. Justice **BRENNAN** delivered the opinion of the Court.

We are required in this case to determine for the first time the extent to which the constitutional protections for speech and press limit a State's power to award damages in a libel action brought by a public official against critics of his official conduct. . . .

I

We may dispose at the outset of two grounds asserted to insulate the judgment of the Alabama courts from constitutional scrutiny. The first is the proposition relied on by the State Supreme Court—that "The Fourteenth Amendment is directed against State action and not private action." That proposition has no application to this case. Although this is a civil lawsuit between private parties, the Alabama courts have applied a state rule of law which petitioners claim to impose invalid restrictions on their constitutional freedoms of speech and press. . . .

The second contention is that the constitutional guarantees of freedom of speech and of the press are inapplicable here, at least so far as the *Times* is concerned, because the allegedly libelous statements were published as part of a paid, "commercial" advertisement. . . .

The publication here . . . communicated information, expressed opinion, recited grievances, protested claimed abuses, and sought financial support on behalf of a movement whose existence and objectives are matters of the highest public interest and concern. . . . That the *Times* was paid for publishing the advertisement is as immaterial in this connection as is the fact that newspapers and books are sold. . . . Any other conclusion would discourage newspapers from carrying "editorial advertisements" of this type, and so might shut off an important outlet for the promulgation of information and ideas by persons who do not themselves have access to publishing facilities—who wish to exercise their freedom of speech even though they are not members of the press. . . .

II . . .

Respondent relies heavily, as did the Alabama courts, on statements of this Court to the effect that the Constitution does not protect libelous publications. Those statements do not foreclose our inquiry here. None of the cases sustained the use of libel laws to impose sanctions upon expression critical of the official conduct of public officials. . . .

. . . Like insurrection, contempt, advocacy of unlawful acts, breach of the peace, obscenity, solicitation of legal business, and the various other formulae for the repression of expression that have been challenged in this Court, libel can claim no talismanic immunity from constitutional limitations. It must be measured by standards that satisfy the First Amendment.

The general proposition that freedom of expression upon public questions is secured by the First Amendment has long been settled by our decisions. The constitutional safeguard, we have said, "was fashioned to assure unfettered interchange of ideas for the bringing about of political and social changes desired by the people." Roth v. United States (1957). "The maintenance of the opportunity for free political discussion to the end that government may be responsive to the will of the people and that changes may be obtained by lawful means, an opportunity essential to the security of the Republic, is a fundamental principle of our constitutional system." Stromberg v. California (1931). "[I]t is a prized American privilege to speak one's mind, although not always with perfect good taste, on all public institutions," Bridges v. California (1941), and this opportunity is to be afforded for "vigorous advocacy" no less than "abstract discussion." N.A.A.C.P. v. Button (1963). . . .

Thus we consider this case against the background of a profound national commitment to the principle that debate on public issues should be uninhibited, robust, and wide-open, and that it may well include vehement, caustic, and sometimes unpleasantly sharp attacks on government and public officials. The present advertisement, as an expression of grievance and protest on one of the major public issues of our time, would seem clearly to qualify for the constitutional protection. The question is whether it forfeits that protection by the falsity of some of its factual statements and by its alleged defamation of respondent.

Authoritative interpretations of the First Amendment guarantees have consistently refused to recognize an exception for any test of truth—whether administered by judges, juries, or administrative officials—and especially one that puts the burden of proving truth on the speaker. Cf. Speiser v. Randall (1958). The constitutional protection does not turn upon "the truth, popularity, or social utility of the ideas and beliefs which are offered." *Button.* . . . As Madison said, "Some degree of abuse is inseparable from the proper use of every thing; and in no instance is this more true than in that of the press." . . .

Injury to official reputation affords no more warrant for repressing speech that would otherwise be free than does factual error. Where judicial officers are involved, this Court has held that concern for the dignity and reputation of the courts does not justify the punishment as criminal contempt of criticism of the judge or his decision. *Bridges.* . . . This is true even though the utterance contains "half-truths" and "misinformation." Pennekamp v. Florida (1946). Such repression can be justified, if at all, only by a clear and present danger of the obstruction of justice. . . . If judges are to be treated as "men of fortitude, able to thrive in a hardy climate," Craig v. Harney (1947), surely the same must be true of other government officials, such as elected city commissioners. Criticism of their official conduct does not lose its constitutional protection merely because it is effective criticism and hence diminishes their official reputations.

If neither factual error nor defamatory content suffices to remove the constitutional shield from criticism of official conduct, the combination of the two elements is no less inadequate. This is the lesson to be drawn from the great controversy over the Sedition Act of 1798, . . . which first crystallized a national awareness of the central meaning of the First Amendment. . . .

Madison prepared the Report [of the Virginia legislature against the

Alien and Sedition laws] in support of the protest. His premise was that the Constitution created a form of government under which "The people, not the government, possess the absolute sovereignty." The structure of the government dispersed power in reflection of the people's distrust of concentrated power, and of power itself at all levels. . . . Earlier, in a debate in the House of Representatives, Madison had said: "If we advert to the nature of Republican Government, we shall find that the censorial power is in the people over the Government, and not in the Government over the people." . . . The right of free public discussion of the stewardship of public officials was thus, in Madison's view, a fundamental principle of the American form of government. . . .

The state rule of law is not saved by its allowance of the defense of truth. . . . Allowance of the defense of truth, with the burden of proving it on the defendant, does not mean that only false speech will be deterred. . . . Under such a rule, would-be critics of official conduct may be deterred from voicing their criticism, even though it is believed to be true and even though it is in fact true, because of doubt whether it can be proved in court or fear of the expense of having to do so. They tend to make only statements which "steer far wider of the unlawful zone." *Speiser*. The rule thus dampens the vigor and limits the variety of public debate. It is inconsistent with the First and Fourteenth Amendments.

The constitutional guarantees require, we think, a federal rule that prohibits a public official from recovering damages for a defamatory falsehood relating to his official conduct unless he proves that the statement was made with "actual malice"—that is, with knowledge that it was false or with reckless disregard of whether it was false or not. . . .

Such a privilege for criticism of official conduct is appropriately analogous to the protection accorded a public official when *he* is sued for libel by a private citizen. . . . The reason for the official privilege is said to be that the threat of damage suits would otherwise "inhibit the fearless, vigorous, and effective administration of policies of government" and "dampen the ardor of all but the most resolute, or the most irresponsible, in the unflinching discharge of their duties." Barr v. Matteo (1959). Analogous considerations support the privilege for the citizen-critic of government. It is as much his duty to criticize as it is the official's duty to administer. . . . It would give public servants an unjustified preference over the public they serve, if critics of official conduct did not have a fair equivalent of the immunity granted to the officials themselves.

We conclude that such a privilege is required by the First and Fourteenth Amendments.

III

We hold today that the Constitution delimits a State's power to award damages for libel in actions brought by public officials against critics of their official conduct. Since this is such an action, the rule requiring proof of actual malice is applicable. . . .

Since respondent may seek a new trial, we deem that considerations of effective judicial administration require us to review the evidence in the present record to determine whether it could constitutionally support a judgment for respondent. This Court's duty is not limited to the elaboration of constitutional principles; we must also in proper cases review the evidence to make certain that those principles have been constitutionally applied. This is such a case, particularly since the question is one of alleged trespass across "the line between speech unconditionally guaranteed and speech which may legitimately be regulated." *Speiser.* . . . In cases where that line must be drawn, the rule is that we "examine for ourselves the statements in issue and the circumstances under which they were made to see . . . whether they are of a character which the principles of the First Amendment, as adopted by the Due Process Clause of the Fourteenth Amendment, protect." *Pennekamp.* . . .

Applying these standards, we consider that the proof presented to show actual malice lacks the convincing clarity which the constitutional standard demands, and hence that it would not constitutionally sustain the judgment for respondent under the proper rule of law. The case of the individual petitioners requires little discussion. Even assuming that they could constitutionally be found to have authorized the use of their names on the advertisement, there was no evidence whatever that they were aware of any erroneous statements or were in any way reckless in that regard. . . .

As to the *Times,* we similarly conclude that the facts do not support a finding of actual malice. . . . We think the evidence against the *Times* supports at most a finding of negligence in failing to discover the misstatements, and is constitutionally insufficient to show the recklessness that is required for a finding of actual malice. . . .

We also think the evidence was constitutionally defective in another respect: it was incapable of supporting the jury's finding that the allegedly libelous statements were made "of and concerning" respondent. . . .

There was no reference to respondent in the advertisement, either by name or official position. . . . Although the statements may be taken as referring to the police, they did not on their face make even an oblique reference to respondent as an individual.

. . . For good reason, "no court of last resort in this country has ever held, or even suggested, that prosecutions for libel on government have any place in the American system of jurisprudence." City of Chicago v. Tribune Co. (1923 [Supreme Court of Illinois]). The present proposition would sidestep this obstacle by transmuting criticism of government, however impersonal it may seem on its face, into personal criticism, and hence potential libel, of the officials of whom the government is composed. There is no legal alchemy by which a State may thus create the cause of action that would otherwise be denied.... Raising as it does the possibility that a good-faith critic of government will be penalized for his criticism, the proposition relied on by the Alabama courts strikes at the very center of the constitutionally protected area of free expression....

Reversed and remanded.

Mr. Justice **BLACK,** with whom Mr. Justice **DOUGLAS** joins, concurring.

... I base my vote to reverse on the belief that the First and Fourteenth Amendments not merely "delimit" a State's power to award damages to "public officials against critics of their official conduct" but completely prohibit a State from exercising such a power. The Court goes on to hold that a State can subject such critics to damages if "actual malice" can be proved against them. "Malice," even as defined by the Court, is an elusive, abstract concept, hard to prove and hard to disprove. The requirement that malice be proved provides at best an evanescent protection for the right critically to discuss public affairs and certainly does not measure up to the sturdy safeguard embodied in the First Amendment....

In my opinion the Federal Constitution has dealt with this deadly danger to the press in the only way possible without leaving the free press open to destruction—by granting the press an absolute immunity for criticism of the way public officials do their public duty.... Stopgap measures like those the Court adopts are in my judgment not enough. This record certainly does not indicate that any different verdict would have been rendered here whatever the Court had charged the jury about "malice," "truth," "good motives," "justifiable ends," or any other legal formulas which in theory would protect the press. Nor does the record indicate that any of these legalistic words would have caused the courts below to set aside or to reduce the half-million-dollar verdict in any amount....

We would, I think, more faithfully interpret the First Amendment by holding that at the very least it leaves the people and the press free to criticize officials and discuss public affairs with impunity.... While our Court has held that some kinds of speech and writings, such as "obscenity," Roth v. United States (1957), and "fighting words," Chaplinsky v. New Hampshire (1942), are not expression within the protection of the First Amendment, freedom to discuss public affairs and public officials is unquestionably, as the Court today holds, the kind of speech the First Amendment was primarily designed to keep within the area of free discussion. To punish the exercise of this right to discuss public affairs or to penalize it through libel judgments is to abridge or shut off discussion of the very kind most needed. This Nation, I suspect, can live in peace without libel suits based on public discussions of public affairs and public officials. But I doubt that a country can live in freedom where its people can be made to suffer physically or financially for criticizing their government, its actions, or its officials. "For a representative democracy ceases to exist the moment that the public functionaries are by any means absolved from their responsibility to their constituents; and this happens whenever the constituent can be restrained in any manner from speaking, writing, or publishing his opinions upon any public measure, or upon the conduct of those who may advise or execute it." ° An unconditional right to say what one pleases about public affairs is what I consider to be the minimum guarantee of the First Amendment. . . .

Mr. Justice **GOLDBERG** with whom Mr. Justice **DOUGLAS** joins, concurring in the result. . . .

In my view, the First and Fourteenth Amendments to the Constitution afford to the citizen and to the press an absolute, unconditional privilege to criticize official conduct despite the harm which may flow from excesses and abuses. . . . The right should not depend upon a probing by the jury of the motivation of the citizen or press. The theory of our Constitution is that every citizen may speak his mind and every newspaper express its view on matters of public concern and may not be barred from speaking or publishing because those in control of government think that what is said or written is unwise, unfair, false, or malicious. . . .

. . . It may be urged that deliberately and maliciously false statements have no conceivable value as free speech. That argument, however, is not responsive to the real issue presented by this case, which is whether that freedom of speech which all agree is constitutionally protected can be effectively safeguarded by a rule allowing the imposition of liability upon a jury's evaluation of the speaker's state of mind. If individual citizens may be held liable in damages for strong words, which a jury finds false and maliciously motivated, there can be little doubt that public debate and advocacy will be constrained. And if newspapers, publishing advertisements dealing with public issues, thereby risk liability, there can also be little doubt that the ability of minority groups to secure publication of their views on public affairs and to seek support for their causes will be greatly diminished. . . .

This is not to say that the Constitution protects defamatory statements directed against the private conduct of a public official or private citizen. Freedom of press and of speech insures that government will respond to the will of the people and that changes may be obtained by peaceful means. Purely private defamation has little to do with the political ends of a self-governing society. The imposition of liability for private defamation does not

---

° 1 Tucker, *Blackstone's Commentaries* (1803), 297 [editor's appendix]. [Footnote by Justice Black.]

abridge the freedom of public speech or any other freedom protected by the First Amendment. . . .

The conclusion that the Constitution affords the citizen and the press an absolute privilege for criticism of official conduct does not leave the public official without defenses against unsubstantiated opinions or deliberate misstatements. "Under our system of government, counterargument and education are the weapons available to expose these matters, not abridgment . . . of free speech. . . ." Wood v. Georgia (1962). The public official certainly has equal if not greater access than most private citizens to media of communication. In any event, despite the possibility that some excesses and abuses may go unremedied, we must recognize that "the people of this nation have ordained in the light of history, that, in spite of the probability of excesses and abuses, [certain] liberties are, in the long view, essential to enlightened opinion and right conduct on the part of the citizens of a democracy." Cantwell v. Connecticut (1940). As Mr. Justice Brandeis correctly observed, "sunlight is the most powerful of all disinfectants." . . .

~ Case 5.3 ~

Chief Justice **BURGER:** "The First Amendment does not prevent the school officials from determining that to permit a vulgar and lewd speech such as respondent's would undermine the school's mission."

Justice **STEVENS:** "[A] strong presumption in favor of free expression should apply whenever an issue of this kind is arguable. . . . [T]his Court should defer to the views of the district and circuit judges who are in a much better position to evaluate this speech than we are."

Bethel School District v. Fraser
478 U.S. ___, 106 S. Ct. 3159, 92 L. Ed. 2d 549 (1986)

Problems of free speech range far beyond efforts to change governmental policies by rational persuasion. During the Vietnam War, for instance, Cohen v. California, 403 U.S. 15 (1971), held that the First Amendment protected the emotive content of communication and reversed the conviction of a young man who had walked around a courthouse with the words "Fuck the Draft" on his jacket. There are also

*problems about the proper places in which to conduct debate. In 1969
Tinker v. Des Moines, 393 U.S. 503, sustained the right of students in a
public high school to wear black armbands to protest the Vietnam War,
even though school officials had forbidden such demonstrations because
of fear they might disrupt educational activities.*

*This case involved questions of emotive content and of propriety of
language as well as place. Matthew N. Fraser, a student in a public high
school, delivered a speech nominating a friend for student office. The
audience was an assembly of 600 students, ranging in age from fourteen
to eighteen, all of whom were required to attend. Fraser used a parade
of graphic sexual metaphors to praise the nominee. In part he said:*

> I know a man who is firm—he's firm in his pants, he's firm in his shirt,
> his character is firm—but most . . . of all, his belief in you, the students
> of Bethel, is firm.
>
> [He] is a man who takes his point and pounds it in. If necessary,
> he'll take an issue and nail it to the wall. He doesn't attack things in
> spurts—he drives hard, pushing and pushing until finally—he succeeds.
>
> Jeff is a man who will go to the very end—even the climax, for
> each and every one of you. . . .

*Some students were confused, and others responded with shouts
and gestures depicting the sexual metaphors. School officials had
warned Fraser that the sort of speech he planned to give might have "severe consequences," and after the speech—and a hearing—they suspended him for three days and removed his name from the list of
students eligible to speak at graduation exercises. The specific rule he
was charged with violating read: "Conduct which materially and
substantially interferes with the educational process is prohibited,
including the use of obscene, profane language or gestures."*

*Fraser appealed through the school's disciplinary system, but the
hearing officer held that the speech had been obscene. Fraser then sued
in a U.S. District Court, alleging that the school had violated rights
protected by the First and Fourteenth amendments. That court decided
in his favor; school officials appealed to the U.S. Court of Appeals for
the Ninth Circuit, which sustained the decision. Fraser then sought and
obtained review by the Supreme Court.*

Chief Justice **BURGER** delivered the opinion of the Court. . . .

II

This Court acknowledged in Tinker v. Des Moines Independent Community School Dist. (1969) that students do not "shed their constitutional
rights to freedom of speech or expression at the schoolhouse gate." The Court

of Appeals read that case as precluding any discipline of Fraser for indecent speech and lewd conduct in the school assembly. That court appears to have proceeded on the theory that the use of lewd and obscene speech in order to make what the speaker considered to be a point in a nominating speech for a fellow student was essentially the same as the wearing of an armband in *Tinker* as a form of protest or the expression of a political position.

The marked distinction between the political "message" of the armbands in *Tinker* and the sexual content of respondent's speech in this case seems to have been given little weight by the Court of Appeals. In upholding the students' right to engage in a nondisruptive, passive expression of a political viewpoint in *Tinker*, this Court was careful to note that the case did "not concern speech or action that intrudes upon the work of the schools or the rights of other students."

It is against this background that we turn to consider the level of First Amendment protection accorded to Fraser's utterances and actions before an official high school assembly attended by 600 students.

III

The role and purpose of the American public school system was well described by two historians, saying "public education must prepare pupils for citizenship in the Republic. . . . It must inculcate the habits and manners of civility as values in themselves conducive to happiness and as indispensable to the practice of self-government in the community and the nation." C. Beard & M. Beard, *New Basic History of the United States* 228 (1968). In Ambach v. Norwick (1979), we echoed the essence of this statement of the objectives of public education as the "inculcat[ion of] fundamental values necessary to the maintenance of a democratic political system."

These fundamental values of "habits and manners of civility" essential to a democratic society must, of course, include tolerance of divergent political and religious views, even when the views expressed may be unpopular. But these "fundamental values" must also take into account consideration of the sensibilities of others, and, in the case of a school, the sensibilities of fellow students. The undoubted freedom to advocate unpopular and controversial views in schools and classrooms must be balanced against the society's countervailing interest in teaching students the boundaries of socially appropriate behavior. Even the most heated political discourse in a democratic society requires consideration for the personal sensibilities of the other participants and audiences. . . .

The First Amendment guarantees wide freedom in matters of adult public discourse. A sharply divided Court upheld the right to express an antidraft viewpoint in a public place, albeit in terms highly offensive to most citizens. See Cohen v. California (1971). It does not follow, however, that simply because the use of an offensive form of expression may not be prohibited to adults making what the speaker considers a political point, that the same latitude must be permitted to children in a public school. In New Jersey v. T. L. O. (1985), we reaffirmed that the constitutional rights of students in public school are not automatically coextensive with the rights of adults in other settings. . . .

Surely it is a highly appropriate function of public school education to prohibit the use of vulgar and offensive terms in public discourse. Indeed, the "fundamental values necessary to the maintenance of a democratic political system" disfavor the use of terms of debate highly offensive or highly threatening to others. Nothing in the Constitution prohibits the states from insisting that certain modes of expression are inappropriate and subject to sanctions. The inculcation of these values is truly the "work of the schools." *Tinker.* The determination of what manner of speech in the classroom or in school assembly is inappropriate properly rests with the school board.

The process of educating our youth for citizenship in public schools is not confined to books, the curriculum, and the civics class; schools must teach by example the shared values of a civilized social order. . . . The schools, as instruments of the state, may determine that the essential lessons of civil, mature conduct cannot be conveyed in a school that tolerates lewd, indecent, or offensive speech and conduct such as that indulged in by this confused boy.

The pervasive sexual innuendo in Fraser's speech was plainly offensive to both teachers and students—indeed to any mature person. By glorifying male sexuality, and in its verbal content, the speech was acutely insulting to teenage girl students. The speech could well be seriously damaging to its less mature audience, many of whom were only 14 years old and on the threshold of awareness of human sexuality. Some students were reported as bewildered by the speech and the reaction of mimicry it provoked.

This Court's First Amendment jurisprudence has acknowledged limitations on the otherwise absolute interest of the speaker in reaching an unlimited audience where the speech is sexually explicit and the audience may include children. In Ginsberg v. New York (1968) this Court upheld a New York statute banning the sale of sexually oriented material to minors, even though the material in question was entitled to First Amendment protection with respect to adults. And in addressing the question whether the First Amendment places any limit on the authority of public schools to remove books from a public school library, all Members of the Court, otherwise sharply divided, acknowledged that the school board has the authority to remove books that are vulgar. Board of Education v. Pico (1982). These cases recognize the obvious concern on the part of parents, and school authorities acting *in loco parentis* to protect children—especially in a captive audience—from exposure to sexually explicit, indecent, or lewd speech. . . .

The judgment of the Court of Appeals for the Ninth Circuit is

Reversed.

Justice **BLACKMUN** concurs in the result.

Justice **BRENNAN,** concurring in the judgment.

. . . The Court, referring to [Fraser's] remarks as "obscene," "vulgar," "lewd," and "offensively lewd," concludes that school officials properly punished respondent for uttering the speech. Having read the full text of respondent's remarks, I find it difficult to believe that it is the same speech the Court describes. To my mind, the most that can be said about respondent's speech—and all that need be said—is that in light of the discretion school officials have to teach high school students how to conduct civil and effective public discourse, and to prevent disruption of school educational activities, it was not unconstitutional for school officials to conclude, under the circumstances of this case, that respondent's remarks exceeded permissible limits. Thus, while I concur in the Court's judgment, I write separately to express my understanding of the breadth of the Court's holding.

The Court today reaffirms the unimpeachable proposition that students do not " 'shed their constitutional rights to freedom of speech or expression at the schoolhouse gate.' " If respondent had given the same speech outside of the school environment, he could not have been penalized simply because government officials considered his language to be inappropriate, see Cohen v. California (1971); the Court's opinion does not suggest otherwise. Moreover, despite the Court's characterizations, the language respondent used is far removed from the very narrow class of "obscene" speech which the Court has held is not protected by the First Amendment. It is true, however, that the State has interests in teaching high school students how to conduct civil and effective public discourse and in avoiding disruption of educational school activities. Thus, the Court holds that under certain circumstances, high school students may properly be reprimanded for giving a speech at a high school assembly which school officials conclude disrupted the school's educational mission. Respondent's speech may well have been protected had he given it in school but under different circumstances, where the school's legitimate interests in teaching and maintaining civil public discourse were less weighty.

In the present case, school officials sought only to ensure that a high school assembly proceed in an orderly manner. There is no suggestion that school officials attempted to regulate respondent's speech because they disagreed with the views he sought to express. Cf. *Tinker.* Nor does this case involve an attempt by school officials to ban written materials they consider "inappropriate" for high school students, or to limit what students should hear, read, or learn about. Thus, the Court's holding concerns only the authority that school officials have to restrict a high school student's use of disruptive language in a speech given to a high school assembly.

The authority school officials have to regulate such speech by high school students is not limitless. " . . . Courts have a First Amendment responsibility to insure that robust rhetoric . . . is not suppressed by prudish failures to distinguish the vigorous from the vulgar." Under the circumstances of this case, however, I believe that school officials did not violate the First Amendment in determining that respondent should be disciplined for the disruptive language he used while addressing a high school assembly. . . .

Justice' **MARSHALL** dissenting. . . .

Justice **STEVENS,** dissenting.
"Frankly, my dear, I don't give a damn."
When I was a high school student, the use of those words in a public forum shocked the Nation. Today Clark Gable's four-letter expletive is less offensive than it was then. Nevertheless, I assume that high school administrators may prohibit the use of that word in classroom discussion and even in extracurricular activities that are sponsored by the school and held on school premises. For I believe a school faculty must regulate the content as well as the style of student speech in carrying out its educational mission. It does seem to me, however, that if a student is to be punished for using offensive speech, he is entitled to fair notice of the scope of the prohibition and the consequences of its violation. The interest in free speech protected by the First Amendment and the interest in fair procedure protected by the Due Process Clause of the Fourteenth Amendment combine to require this conclusion. . . .

Justice Sutherland taught us that a "nuisance may be merely a right thing in the wrong place,—like a pig in the parlor instead of the barnyard." Euclid v. Ambler Realty Co. (1926). Vulgar language, like vulgar animals, may be acceptable in some contexts and intolerable in others. See FCC v. Pacifica Foundation (1978). Indeed, even ordinary, inoffensive speech may be wholly unacceptable in some settings. See Schenck v. United States (1919).

It seems fairly obvious that respondent's speech would be inappropriate in certain classroom and formal social settings. On the other hand, in a locker room or perhaps in a school corridor the metaphor in the speech might be regarded as rather routine comment. If this be true, and if respondent's audience consisted almost entirely of young people with whom he conversed on a daily basis, can we—at this distance—confidently assert that he must have known that the school administration would punish him for delivering it?

For three reasons, I think not. First, it seems highly unlikely that he would have decided to deliver the speech if he had known that it would result in his suspension and disqualification from delivering the school commencement address. Second, I believe a strong presumption in favor of free expression should apply whenever an issue of this kind is arguable. Third, because the Court has adopted the policy of applying contemporary community standards in evaluating expression with sexual connotations, this Court should defer to the views of the district and circuit judges who are in a much better position to evaluate this speech than we are. . . .

~ Case 5.4 ~

Chief Justice **WARREN:** "To the extent that a citizen's right to vote is debased, he is that much less a citizen. The fact that an individual lives here or there is not a legitimate reason for overweighting or diluting the efficacy of his vote."

Justice **HARLAN:** "[T]he Equal Protection Clause was never intended to inhibit the States in choosing any democratic method they pleased for the apportionment of their legislatures."

Reynolds v. Sims
377 U.S. 533, 84 S. Ct. 1361, 12 L. Ed. 2d 506 (1964)

In most states, the legislature had historically drawn the lines of districts from which voters would choose members of the state legislature as well as of the U.S. House of Representatives so as to maximize the power of voters whose interests and party dominated that particular legislature. There were several earlier challenges to such gerrymandering, but the first serious case, Colegrove v. Green, 328 U.S. 549, reached the Supreme Court in 1946. At issue was the validity under the Fourteenth Amendment's equal protection clause of the action of the state of Illinois, which set the population of some urban congressional districts at six to nine times the population of some rural districts. (The obvious result, of course, was to make the vote of a person living in Chicago worth one-sixth or even one-ninth of the vote of a farmer or other rural resident—a useful way of insuring that, as a group, the Illinois congressional delegation would remain hypersensitive to agricultural interests; it was also a means for Republicans to combat the political power of the Democratic machine that controlled Chicago.)

With only seven justices participating (Justice Jackson was at Nuremberg as the chief American prosecutor in the war crimes trials, and Chief Justice Stone died shortly after oral argument), the Court divided 3-1-3. The first three justices thought that the case presented a question that the Constitution left for Congress to resolve, a so-called "political question." The other three justices thought that the question was "justiciable," that is, proper for a court to decide. The seventh justice, Wiley Rutledge, voted with the first three because he thought that the timing of the suit made it highly improbable that the legislature could redistrict the state in time for the elections of November 1946, and thus all members of Congress from Illinois would have to be elected from the entire state—a cure, he thought, that was worse than the disease.

Because a majority of the justices hearing the case could not agree on an opinion, Colegrove v. Green laid down no official doctrine. But, because later decisions refusing to review other districting plans cited Colegrove as an authority, most judges and commentators thought it was settled constitutional law that legislative districting, no matter how unfair, raised "political" rather than "justiciable" questions. In 1962, however, the Warren Court decided Baker v. Carr, 369 U.S. 186, a challenge to Tennessee's gerrymandering. Black and Douglas, who had dissented in Colegrove (the third dissenter died in 1949), were able to pick up four more votes from among younger justices to form a solid majority holding that districting presented a constitutional question that courts should decide under the equal protection clause. Very quickly, hundreds of suits all over the country were filed, challenging a bevy of schemes that accorded extra voting power to special groups.

Reynolds v. Sims involved an attack on Alabama's system of representation in both houses of the state legislature. Electoral districts for the lower house of the legislature ranged in population from 6,700 to 104,000. Clearly that apportionment was doomed, but Alabama (and several other states with similar arrangements) argued that if districts for the lower house were made equal, a state could apportion seats for the upper house so as to give added weight to certain kinds of geographic areas and social interests that might otherwise be drowned in a system based purely on numbers. The U.S. Senate provided an obvious analogy. After losing in a special three-judge federal district court, Alabama (and for very different reasons those who challenged the apportionment) appealed to the U.S. Supreme Court.

Mr. Chief Justice **WARREN** delivered the opinion of the Court. . . .

. . . A consistent line of decisions by this Court . . . has . . . repeatedly recognized that all qualified voters have a constitutionally protected right to vote, Ex parte Yarbrough (1884) and to have their votes counted, United States v. Mosley (1915). The right to vote can neither be denied outright, Guinn v. United States (1915) nor destroyed by alteration of ballots, see

United States v. Classic (1941) nor diluted by ballot-box stuffing, Ex parte Siebold (1880). The right to vote freely for the candidate of one's choice is of the essence of a democratic society, and any restrictions on that right strike at the heart of representative government. And the right of suffrage can be denied by a debasement or dilution of the weight of a citizen's vote just as effectively as by wholly prohibiting the free exercise of the franchise.

In Baker v. Carr (1962) we held that a claim asserted under the Equal Protection Clause challenging the constitutionality of a State's apportionment of seats in its legislature, on the ground that the right to vote of certain citizens was effectively impaired since debased and diluted, in effect presented a justiciable controversy subject to adjudication by federal courts. . . .

In Gray v. Sanders (1963) we held that the Georgia county unit system . . . was unconstitutional since it resulted in a dilution of the weight of the votes of certain Georgia voters merely because of where they resided. After indicating that the Fifteenth and Nineteenth Amendments prohibit a State from overweighting or diluting votes on the basis of race or sex, we stated:

> "How then can one person be given twice or ten times the voting power of another person in a statewide election merely because he lives in a rural area or because he lives in the smallest rural county? Once the geographical unit for which a representative is to be chosen is designated, all who participate in the election are to have an equal vote— whatever their race, whatever their sex, whatever their occupation, whatever their income, and wherever their home may be in that geographical unit. This is required by the Equal Protection Clause of the Fourteenth Amendment. The concept of 'we the people' under the Constitution visualizes no preferred class of voters but equality among those who meet the basic qualifications. . . ."

In Wesberry v. Sanders (1964) we held that . . . the constitutional test for the validity of congressional districting schemes was one of the substantial equality of population among the various districts established by a state legislature for the election of members of the Federal House of Representatives.

. . . We concluded that the constitutional prescription for election of members of the House of Representatives "by the People," construed in its historical context, "means that as nearly as is practicable one man's vote in a congressional election is to be worth as much as another's." We further stated: . . .

> "No right is more precious in a free country than that of having a voice in the election of those who make the laws under which, as good citizens, we must live. Other rights, even the most basic, are illusory if the right to vote is undermined. Our Constitution leaves no room for classification of people in a way that unnecessarily abridges this right. . . ."

Legislators represent people, not trees or acres. Legislators are elected by voters, not farms or cities or economic interests. As long as ours is a representative form of government and our legislatures are those instruments of government elected directly by and directly representative of the people, the right to elect legislators in a free and unimpaired fashion is a bedrock of our political system. . . . And, if a State should provide that the votes of citizens in one part of the State should be given two times, or five times, or ten times the weight of votes of citizens in another part of the State, it could hardly be contended that the right to vote of those residing in the disfavored areas had not been effectively diluted. . . . Of course, the effect of state legislative districting schemes which give the same number of representatives to unequal numbers of constituents is identical. . . . One must be ever aware that the Constitution forbids "sophisticated as well as simple-minded modes of discrimination." Lane v. Wilson (1939).

. . . Since legislatures are responsible for enacting laws by which all citizens are to be governed, they should be bodies which are collectively responsive to the popular will. And the concept of equal protection has been traditionally viewed as requiring the uniform treatment of persons standing in the same relation to the governmental action questioned or challenged. With respect to the allocation of legislative representation, all voters, as citizens of a State, stand in the same relation regardless of where they live. . . . Since the achieving of fair and effective representation for all citizens is concededly the basic aim of legislative apportionment, we conclude that the Equal Protection Clause guarantees the opportunity for equal participation by all voters in the election of state legislators. . . . Our constitutional system amply provides for the protection of minorities by means other than giving them majority control of state legislatures. . . .

We are told that the matter of apportioning representation in a state legislature is a complex and many-faceted one. We are advised that States can rationally consider factors other than population in approaching legislative representation. We are admonished not to restrict the power of the States to impose differing views as to political philosophy on their citizens. We are cautioned about the dangers of entering into political thickets and mathematical quagmires. Our answer is this: a denial of constitutionally protected rights demands judicial protection; our oath and our office require no less of us. . . .

To the extent that a citizen's right to vote is debased, he is that much less a citizen. The fact that an individual lives here or there is not a legitimate reason for overweighting or diluting the efficacy of his vote. . . .

We hold that, as a basic constitutional standard, the Equal Protection Clause requires that the seats in both houses of a bicameral state legislature must be apportioned on a population basis. . . .

The system of representation in the two Houses of the Federal Congress is one ingrained in our Constitution, as part of the law of the land. It is one conceived out of compromise and concession indispensable to the establishment of our federal republic. Arising from unique historical circumstances, it is based on the consideration that in establishing our type of federalism a group of formerly independent States bound themselves together under one national government. . . .

Political subdivisions of States—counties, cities, or whatever—never were and never have been considered as sovereign entities. Rather, they have been traditionally regarded as subordinate governmental instrumentalities created by the State to assist in the carrying out of state governmental functions. . . .

We do not believe that the concept of bicameralism is rendered anachronistic and meaningless when the predominant basis of representation in the two state legislative bodies is required to be the same—population. A prime reason for bicameralism, modernly considered, is to insure mature and deliberate consideration of, and to prevent precipitate action on, proposed legislative measures. Simply because the controlling criterion for apportioning representation is required to be the same in both houses does not mean that there will be no differences in the composition and complexion of the two bodies. Different constituencies can be represented in the two houses. One body could be composed of single-member districts while the other could have at least some multimember districts. The length of terms of the legislators in the separate bodies could differ. The numerical size of the two bodies could be made to differ, even significantly, and the geographical size of districts from which legislators are elected could also be made to differ. And apportionment in one house could be arranged so as to balance off minor inequities in the representation of certain areas in the other house. . . .

By holding that as a federal constitutional requisite both houses of a state legislature must be apportioned on a population basis, we mean that the Equal Protection Clause requires that a State make an honest and good faith effort to construct districts, in both houses of its legislature, as nearly of equal population as is practicable. We realize that it is a practical impossibility to arrange legislative districts so that each one has an identical number of residents, or citizens, or voters. Mathematical exactness of precision is hardly a workable constitutional requirement.

. . . .[W]e affirm the judgment below and remand the cases for further proceedings consistent with the views stated in this opinion.

It is so ordered.

Mr. Justice **CLARK,** concurring in the affirmance. . . .

Mr. Justice **STEWART.** . . .
I would affirm the judgment of the District Court holding that this apportionment violated the Equal Protection Clause. . . .

Mr. Justice **HARLAN**, dissenting. . . .

Had the Court paused to probe more deeply into the matter, it would have found that the Equal Protection Clause was never intended to inhibit the States in choosing any democratic method they pleased for the apportionment of their legislatures. This is shown by the language of the Fourteenth Amendment taken as a whole, by the understanding of those who proposed and ratified it, and by the political practices of the States at the time the Amendment was adopted. It is confirmed by numerous state and congressional actions since the adoption of the Fourteenth Amendment, and by the common understanding of the Amendment as evidenced by subsequent constitutional amendments and decisions of this Court before Baker v. Carr made an abrupt break with the past in 1962.

The failure of the Court to consider any of these matters cannot be excused or explained by any concept of "developing" constitutionalism. It is meaningless to speak of constitutional "development" when both the language and history of the controlling provisions of the Constitution are wholly ignored. Since it can, I think, be shown beyond doubt that state legislative apportionments, as such, are wholly free of constitutional limitations, save such as may be imposed by the Republican Form of Government Clause (Const., Art. IV, § 4), the Court's action now bringing them within the purview of the Fourteenth Amendment amounts to nothing less than an exercise of the amending power by this Court.

So far as the Federal Constitution is concerned, the complaints in these cases should all have been dismissed below for failure to state a cause of action, because what has been alleged or proved shows no violation of any constitutional right. . . .

The Court's elaboration of its new "constitutional" doctrine indicates how far—and how unwisely—it has strayed from the appropriate bounds of its authority. The consequence of today's decision is that in all but the handful of States which may already satisfy the new requirements the local District Court or, it may be, the state courts, are given blanket authority and the constitutional duty to supervise apportionment of the State Legislatures. It is difficult to imagine a more intolerable and inappropriate interference by the judiciary with the independent legislatures of the States. . . .

With these cases the Court approaches the end of the third round set in motion by the complaint filed in Baker v. Carr. What is done today deepens my conviction that judicial entry into this realm is profoundly ill-advised and constitutionally impermissible. . . . I believe that the vitality of our political system, on which in the last analysis all else depends, is weakened by reliance on the judiciary for political reform; in time a complacent body politic may result.

These decisions also cut deeply into the fabric of our federalism. What must follow from them may eventually appear to be the product of state legislatures. Nevertheless, no thinking person can fail to recognize that the aftermath of these cases, however desirable it may be thought in itself, will have been achieved at the cost of a radical alteration in the relationship between the States and the Federal Government, more particularly the Federal Judiciary. . . .

Finally, these decisions give support to a current mistaken view of the Constitution and the constitutional function of this Court. This view, in a nutshell, is that every major social ill in this country can find its cure in some constitutional "principle," and that this Court should "take the lead" in promoting reform when other branches of government fail to act. The Constitution is not a panacea for every blot upon the public welfare, nor should this Court, ordained as a judicial body, be thought of as a general haven for reform movements. The Constitution is an instrument of government, fundamental to which is the premise that in a diffusion of governmental authority lies the greatest promise that this Nation will realize liberty for all its citizens. This Court, limited in function in accordance with the premise, does not serve its high purpose when it exceeds its authority, even to satisfy justified impatience with the slow workings of the political process. For when, in the name of constitutional interpretation, the Court *adds* something to the Constitution that was deliberately excluded from it, the Court in reality substitutes its view of what should be so for the amending process. . . .

~ **Case 5.5** ~

Justice **STEVENS:** "A State's claim that it is enhancing the ability of its citizenry to make wise decisions by restricting the flow of information to them must be viewed with some skepticism."

Justice **REHNQUIST:** "[T]he Constitution does not require that a State allow any particular Presidential candidate to be on its ballot. . . ."

Anderson v. Celebrezze
460 U.S. 780, 103 S. Ct. 1564, 75 L. Ed. 2d 547 (1983)

Ohio required independent candidates for the presidency to file a statement and nominating petition signed by 5,000 qualified voters 75 days before the primary election (229 days before the general election). In 1980 John Anderson did not file the necessary papers until May, two months after the deadline but some weeks before the state primary elections and well before the national nominating conventions had met. Ohio officials denied him a place on the ballot, and he filed suit in a U.S. district court. The judge ordered the state to place Anderson's name on the ballot, but the Court of Appeals for the Sixth Circuit reversed. Noting that the courts of appeals for the First and Fourth circuits had sustained orders against enforcement of similar laws in Maine and Maryland, the Supreme Court granted review.

Justice **STEVENS** delivered the opinion of the Court. . . .

I

. . . "[T]he rights of voters and the rights of candidates do not lend themselves to neat separation; laws that affect candidates always have at least some theoretical, correlative effect on voters." Bullock v. Carter (1972). Our primary concern is with the tendency of ballot access restrictions "to limit the field of candidates from which voters might choose." Therefore, "[i]n approaching candidate restrictions, it is essential to examine in a realistic light the extent and nature of their impact on voters."

The impact of candidate eligibility requirements on voters implicates basic constitutional rights.° Writing for a unanimous Court in NAACP v. Alabama (1958), Justice Harlan stated that it "is beyond debate that freedom to engage in association for the advancement of beliefs and ideas is an inseparable aspect of the 'liberty' assured by the Due Process Clause of the Fourteenth Amendment, which embraces freedom of speech." In our first review of Ohio's electoral scheme, Williams v. Rhodes (1968), this Court explained the interwoven strands of "liberty" affected by ballot access restrictions:

"... [T]he state laws place burdens on two different, although overlapping, kinds of rights—the right of individuals to associate for the advancement of political beliefs, and the right of qualified voters,

---

° In this case, we base our conclusions directly on the First and Fourteenth Amendments and do not engage in a separate Equal Protection Clause analysis. We rely, however, on the analysis in a number of our prior election cases resting on the Equal Protection Clause of the Fourteenth Amendment. These cases, applying the "fundamental rights" strand of equal protection analysis, have identified the First and Fourteenth Amendment rights implicated by restrictions on the eligibility of voters and candidates, and have considered the degree to which the State's restrictions further legitimate state interests. [Footnote by the Court.]

regardless of their political persuasion, to cast their votes effectively. Both of these rights, of course, rank among our most precious
freedoms."

As we have repeatedly recognized, voters can assert their preferences only
through candidates or parties or both. . . . The right to vote is "heavily
burdened" if that vote may be cast only for major-party candidates at a time
when other parties or other candidates are "clamoring for a place on the
ballot." *Williams*. The exclusion of candidates also burdens voters' freedom
of association, because an election campaign is an effective platform for the
expression of views on the issues of the day, and a candidate serves as a
rallying-point for like-minded citizens.

Although these rights of voters are fundamental, not all restrictions
imposed by the States on candidates' eligibility for the ballot impose
constitutionally-suspect burdens on voters' rights to associate or to choose
among candidates. We have recognized that, "as a practical matter, there
must be a substantial regulation of elections if they are to be fair and honest
and if some sort of order, rather than chaos, is to accompany the democratic
processes." Storer v. Brown (1974). To achieve these necessary objectives,
States have enacted comprehensive and sometimes complex election codes.
Each provision of these schemes, whether it governs the registration and
qualification of voters, the selection and eligibility of candidates, or the voting
process itself, inevitably affects . . . the individual's right to vote and his right
to associate with others for political ends. Nevertheless, the state's important
regulatory interests are generally sufficient to justify reasonable, nondiscrimi-
natory restrictions.

Constitutional challenges to specific provisions of a State's election laws
therefore cannot be resolved by any "litmus-paper test" that will separate
valid from invalid restrictions. *Storer*. Instead, a court must resolve such a
challenge by an analytical process that parallels its work in ordinary litigation.
It must first consider the character and magnitude of the asserted injury to
the rights protected by the First and Fourteenth Amendments. . . . It then
must identify and evaluate the precise interests put forward by the State as
justifications for the burden imposed by its rule. In passing judgment, the
Court must not only determine the legitimacy and strength of each of those
interests; it also must consider the extent to which those interests make it
necessary to burden the plaintiff's rights. Only after weighing all these factors
is the reviewing court in a position to decide whether the challenged
provision is unconstitutional. . . .

II

An early filing deadline may have a substantial impact on independent-
minded voters. In election campaigns, particularly those which are national in
scope, the candidates and the issues simply do not remain static over time. . . .

Such developments will certainly affect the strategies of candidates who have already entered the race; they may also create opportunities for new candidacies. Yet Ohio's filing deadline prevents persons who wish to be independent candidates from entering the significant political arena established in the State by a Presidential election campaign—and creating new political coalitions of Ohio voters—at any time after mid-to-late March. At this point developments in campaigns for the major-party nominations have only begun, and the major parties will not adopt their nominees and platforms for another five months. . . .

[The statute] also burdens the signature-gathering efforts of independents who decide to run in time to meet the deadline. When the primary campaigns are far in the future and the election itself is even more remote, the obstacles facing an independent candidate's organizing efforts are compounded. Volunteers are more difficult to recruit and retain, media publicity and campaign contributions are more difficult to secure, and voters are less interested in the campaign.

. . . [I]t is especially difficult for the State to justify a restriction that limits political participation by an identifiable political group whose members share a particular viewpoint, associational preference, or economic status. "Our ballot access cases . . . focus on the degree to which the challenged restrictions operate as a mechanism to exclude certain classes of candidates from the electoral process. The inquiry is whether the challenged restriction unfairly or unnecessarily burdens 'the availability of political opportunity.' " Clements v. Fashing (1982) (plurality opinion), quoting Lubin v. Panish (1974).°

A burden that falls unequally on new or small political parties or on independent candidates impinges, by its very nature, on associational choices protected by the First Amendment. It discriminates against those candidates and—of particular importance—against those voters whose political preferences lie outside the existing political parties. By limiting the opportunities of independent-minded voters to associate in the electoral arena to enhance their political effectiveness as a group, such restrictions threaten to reduce diversity and competition in the marketplace of ideas. In short, the primary values protected by the First Amendment—"a profound national commitment to the principle that debate on public issues should be uninhibited, robust, and wide-open," New York Times Co. v. Sullivan (1964)—are served

---

° In addition, because the interests of minor parties and independent candidates are not well represented in state legislatures, the risk that the First Amendment rights of those groups will be ignored in legislative decisionmaking may warrant more careful judicial scrutiny. [S]ee generally United States v. Carolene Products Co. (1938); J. Ely, *Democracy and Distrust: A Theory of Judicial Review* 73-88 (1980). [Footnote by the Court.]

when election campaigns are not monopolized by the existing political parties.

Furthermore, in the context of a Presidential election, state-imposed restrictions implicate a uniquely important national interest. For the President and the Vice President of the United States are the only elected officials who represent all the voters in the Nation. Moreover, the impact of the votes cast in each State is affected by the votes cast for the various candidates in other States. Thus in a Presidential election a State's enforcement of more stringent ballot access requirements, including filing deadlines, has an impact beyond its own borders. Similarly, the State has a less important interest in regulating Presidential elections than statewide or local elections, because the outcome of the former will be largely determined by voters beyond the State's boundaries. . . . The Ohio filing deadline challenged in this case does more than burden the associational rights of independent voters and candidates. It places a significant state-imposed restriction on a nationwide electoral process.

III

The State identifies three separate interests that it seeks to further by its early filing deadline for independent Presidential candidates. . . .

Voter Education

There can be no question about the legitimacy of the State's interest in fostering informed and educated expressions of the popular will in a general election. Moreover, the Court of Appeals correctly identified that interest as one of the concerns that motivated the Framers' decision not to provide for direct popular election of the President. We are persuaded, however, that the State's important and legitimate interest in voter education does not justify the specific restriction on participation in a Presidential election that is at issue in this case.

The passage of time since the Constitutional Convention in 1787 has brought about two changes that are relevant to the reasonableness of Ohio's statutory requirement that independents formally declare their candidacy at least seven months in advance of a general election. First . . . today even trivial details about national candidates are instantaneously communicated nationwide in both verbal and visual form. Second . . . today the vast majority of the electorate not only is literate but is informed on a day-to-day basis about events and issues that affect election choices. . . . [I]t is somewhat unrealistic to suggest that it takes more than seven months to inform the electorate about the qualifications of a particular candidate simply because he lacks a partisan label.

Our cases reflect a greater faith in the ability of individual voters to inform themselves about campaign issues. . . .

It is also by no means self-evident that the interest in voter education is served at all by a requirement that independent candidates must declare their candidacy before the end of March. . . . Had the requirement been enforced in Ohio, petitioner Anderson might well have determined that it would be futile for him to allocate any of his time and money to campaigning in that State. The Ohio electorate might thereby have been denied whatever benefits his participation in local debates could have contributed to an understanding of the issues. A State's claim that it is enhancing the ability of its citizenry to make wise decisions by restricting the flow of information to them must be viewed with some skepticism. As we observed in another First Amendment context, it is often true "that the best means to that end is to open the channels of communication rather than to close them." Virginia Pharmacy Board v. Virginia Consumer Council (1976).

Equal Treatment

We also find no merit in the State's claim that the early filing deadline serves the interest of treating all candidates alike. . . .

The consequences of failing to meet the statutory deadline are entirely different for party primary participants and independents. The name of the nominees of the Democratic and Republican parties will appear on the Ohio ballot in November even if they did not decide to run until after Ohio's March deadline had passed, but the independent is simply denied a position on the ballot if he waits too long.° Thus, under Ohio's scheme, the major parties may include all events preceding their national conventions in the calculus that produces their respective nominees and campaign platforms, but the independent's judgment must be based on a history that ends in March. . . .

Political Stability

. . . The State's brief explains that the State has a substantial interest in protecting the two major political parties from "damaging intraparty feuding." . . .

Ohio's asserted interest in political stability amounts to a desire to protect existing political parties from competition. . . .

° It is true, of course, that Ohio permits "write-in" votes for independents. We have previously noted that this opportunity is not an adequate substitute for having the candidate's name appear on the printed ballot. . . . [Citing Lubin v. Panish (1974).] [Footnote by the Court.]

In *Williams* we squarely held that protecting the Republican and Democratic parties from external competition cannot justify the virtual exclusion of other political aspirants from the political arena. Addressing Ohio's claim that it "may validly promote a two-party system in order to encourage compromise and political stability," we wrote:

> "The fact is, however, that the Ohio system does not merely favor a 'two-party system'; it favors two particular parties—the Republicans and the Democrats—and in effect tends to give them a complete monopoly. There is, of course, no reason why two parties should retain a permanent monopoly on the right to have people vote for or against them. Competition in ideas and governmental policies is at the core of our electoral process and of the First Amendment freedoms. . . ."

. . . [*Storer*] recognized the legitimacy of the State's interest in preventing "splintered parties and unrestrained factionalism." But we did not suggest that a political party could invoke the powers of the State to assure monolithic control over its own members and supporters. Political competition that draws resources away from the major parties cannot, for that reason alone, be condemned as "unrestrained factionalism." . . . Moreover, we pointed out that the policy [upheld in *Storer*] "involves no discrimination against independents."

Ohio's challenged restriction is substantially different from the California provisions upheld in *Storer*. . . . [T]he early filing deadline does discriminate against independents. And the deadline is neither a "sore loser" provision nor a disaffiliation statute. Furthermore, it is important to recognize that *Storer* upheld the State's interest in avoiding political fragmentation in the context of elections wholly within the boundaries of California. The State's interest in regulating a nationwide Presidential election is not nearly as strong; no State could singlehandedly assure "political stability" in the Presidential context. The Ohio deadline does not serve any state interest in "maintaining the integrity of the various routes to the ballot" for the Presidency, because Ohio's Presidential preference primary does not serve to narrow the field for the general election. A major party candidate who loses the Ohio primary, or who does not even run in Ohio, may nonetheless appear on the November general election ballot as the party's nominee. In addition, the national scope of the competition for delegates at the Presidential nominating conventions assures that "intraparty feuding" will continue until August. . . .

IV

. . . Under any realistic appraisal, the "extent and nature" of the burdens Ohio has placed on the voters' freedom of choice and freedom of association, in an election of nationwide importance, unquestionably outweigh the State's minimal interest in imposing a March deadline.

Reversed.

Justice **REHNQUIST,** with whom Justice **WHITE,** Justice **POWELL,** and Justice **O'CONNOR** join, dissenting.

Article II of the Constitution provides that "[e]ach State shall appoint, in such Manner as the Legislature thereof may direct, a Number of Electors" who shall select the President of the United States. This provision, one of few in the Constitution that grants an express plenary power to the States, conveys "the broadest power of determination" and "[i]t recognizes that [in the election of a President] the people act through their representatives in the legislature, and *leaves it to the legislature exclusively to define the method of effecting the object.*" McPherson v. Blacker (1892) (emphasis added). . . .

. . . [T]he Constitution does not require that a State allow any particular Presidential candidate to be on its ballot, and so long as the Ohio ballot access laws are rational and allow nonparty candidates reasonable access to the general election ballot,° this Court should not interfere with Ohio's exercise of its Article II, § 1, cl 2 power. . . .

Anderson makes no claim, and thus has offered no evidence to show, that the early filing deadline impeded his "signature-gathering efforts." That alone should be enough to prevent the Court from finding that the deadline has such an impact. A statute "is not to be upset upon hypothetical and unreal possibilities, if it would be good upon the facts as they are." Pullman Co. v. Knott (1914). What information the record does contain on this point leads to a contrary conclusion. The record shows that in 1980 five independent candidates submitted nominating petitions with the necessary 5,000 signatures by the March 20 deadline and thus qualified for the general election ballot in Ohio. . . .

The Court's intimation that the Ohio filing deadline infringes on a nonparty candidate who makes the decision to run for President after the March deadline is similarly without support in the record. . . . Anderson was not such a candidate. Anderson formally announced his candidacy for the Presidency on June 8, 1979—over nine months before Ohio's March 20 deadline. . . .

Finally, there is nothing in the record to indicate that this is a case where "independent-minded voters" are prevented from rallying behind a candidate selected later in the election year so as to guaranty "major parties" a monopoly on the election process. Like-minded voters who do not want to

---

° Anderson would not have been totally excluded from participating in the general election since Ohio allows for "write-in" candidacies. The Court suggests, however, that this is of no relevance because a write-in procedure "is not an adequate substitute for having the candidate's name appear on the printed ballot." Until today the Court had not squarely so held and in fact in earlier decisions the Court had treated the availability of write-in candidacies as quite relevant. See *Storer.* [Footnote by Justice Rehnquist.]

participate in an existing political party are at complete liberty to form a new political party. . . . It is true that Ohio provides this benefit only where a group of voters acts with some foresight and shows a degree of support among the electorate, but this case presents no challenge to these requirements.

. . . [T]he effect of the Ohio filing deadline is quite easily summarized: it requires that a candidate, who has already decided to run for President, decide by March 20 which route his candidacy will take. . . . Anderson . . . submitted in a timely fashion his nominating petition for Ohio's Republican Primary. Then, realizing that he had no chance for the Republican nomination, Anderson sought to change the form of this candidacy. The Ohio filing deadline prevented him from making this change. Quite clearly, rather than prohibiting him from seeking the Presidency, the filing deadline only prevented Anderson from having two shots at it in the same election year.

Thus, Ohio's filing deadline does not create a restriction "denying the franchise to citizens." Likewise, Ohio's filing deadline does not create a restriction that makes it "virtually impossible" for new-party candidates or nonparty candidates to qualify for the ballot, such as those addressed in *Williams, Bullock,* and *Lubin.* Yet in deciding this case, we are not without guidance from prior decisions by this Court.

In *Storer,* the Court was faced with a California statute prohibiting an independent candidate from affiliating with a political party for 12 months preceding the primary election. This required a prospective candidate to decide on the form of his candidacy at a date some eight months earlier than Ohio requires. In upholding, in the face of a First Amendment challenge, this disaffiliation statute and a statute preventing candidates who had lost a primary from running as independents, the Court determined that the laws were "expressive of a general state policy aimed at maintaining the integrity of various routes to the ballot," and that the statutes furthered "the State's interest," described by the Court as "compelling," "in the stability of its political system." . . . The similarities between the effect of the Ohio filing deadline and the California disaffiliation statute are obvious.

Refusing to own up to the conflict its opinion creates with *Storer,* the Court tries to distinguish it, saying that it "did not suggest that a political party could invoke the powers of the State to assure monolithic control over its own members and supporters." The Court asserts that the Ohio filing deadline is more like the statutory scheme in *Williams,* which was designed to protect " 'two particular parties—the Republicans and the Democrats—and in effect tends to give them a complete monopoly.' " . . . But this simply is not the case. The Ohio filing deadline in no way makes it "virtually impossible" . . . for new parties or nonparty candidates to secure a position on the general election ballot. It does require early decisions. But once a decision is made, there is no claim that the additional requirements for new parties and nonparty candidates are too burdensome. In fact, past experience has shown otherwise. What the Ohio filing deadline prevents is a candidate such as Anderson from seeking a party nomination and then, finding that he is rejected by the party, bolting from the party to form an independent candidacy. This is precisely the same behavior that California sought to prevent by the disaffiliation statute this Court upheld in *Storer*. . . .

The point the Court misses is that in cases like this and *Storer*, we have never required that States meet some kind of "narrowly tailored" standard in order to pass constitutional muster. In reviewing election laws like Ohio's filing deadline, we have said before that a court's job is to ensure that the State "in no way freezes the status quo, but implicitly recognizes the potential fluidity of American political life." Jenness v. Fortson (1971). If it does not freeze the status quo, then the State's laws will be upheld if they are "tied to a particularized legitimate purpose, and [are] in no sense invidious or arbitrary." Rosario v. Rockefeller (1973). The Court tries to avoid the rules set forth in some of these cases, saying that such rules were "applicable only to party primaries" and that "this case involves restrictions on access to the general election ballot." The fallacy in this reasoning is quite apparent: one cannot restrict access to the primary ballot without also restricting access to the general election ballot. . . .

The Ohio filing deadline easily meets the test described above. [T]he interest of the "stability of its political system," *Storer*, . . . alone is sufficient to support Ohio ballot access laws. . . . But this is not the only interest furthered by Ohio's laws.

Ohio maintains that requiring an early declaration of candidacy gives its voters a better opportunity to take a careful look at the candidates and see how they withstand the close scrutiny of a political campaign. . . . But the Court finds that "the State's important and legitimate interest in voter education does not justify the specific restriction on participation in a Presidential election that is at issue in this case." . . .

I cannot agree with the suggestion that the early deadline reflects a lack of "faith" in the voters. That Ohio wants to give its voters as much time as possible to gather information on the potential candidates would seem to lead to the contrary conclusion. There is nothing improper about wanting as much time as possible in which to evaluate all available information when making an important decision. Besides, the Court's assertion that it does not take seven months to inform the electorate is difficult to explain in light of the fact that Anderson allowed himself some 19 months to complete this task; and we are all well aware that Anderson's decision to make an early go of it is not atypical. . . .

6. THE RIGHT TO PRIVACY

T*he word* privacy *does not appear in the constitutional document, but there is more than a hint of a "right to be let alone." The Preamble begins by listing "the Blessings of Liberty" as among the new Union's basic purposes. The First Amendment protects "the free exercise" of religion and forbids government to establish religion; the Third Amendment bans quartering of troops in civilian homes in time of peace; the Fourth speaks of "the right of the people to be secure in their persons, houses, papers, and effects, against unreasonable searches and seizures"; the Fifth forbids government to compel anyone "in any criminal case to be a witness against himself"; and the broadest amendment, the Ninth, reads:*

> The enumeration in the Constitution, of certain rights, shall not be construed to deny or disparage others retained by the people.

This amendment is imperative in mood, that is, it commands. It says, in language reminiscent of the Ten Commandments, "shall not," not "may not be," or "might not be," or "should not be." That a constitution should protect unlisted rights is a basic tenet of constitutionalism, which holds that governmental powers are like islands floating in "an ocean of rights." [1] *It is government that must justify its actions by pointing to authority delegated by the Constitution, not citizens who must prove the legitimacy of their rights. And over the years, courts have recognized as fundamental such unlisted rights as*

to be free from bodily restraint except in accordance with law;
to marry;
to have or not have children and to educate one's children as long as one meets certain minimum standards set by the state;
to "acquire useful knowledge";
to vote, subject only to reasonable restrictions to prevent fraud, and to cast a ballot equal in weight to every other person's ballot;
to associate with others for peaceful purposes;
to privacy;
to travel within the United States;
to retain American citizenship;

167

> to receive equal protection of the laws not only from the states but
>   also from the federal government;
> to use the federal courts; and
> to enjoy a presumption of innocence when accused of crime.

These are rights we all might wish for ourselves. Yet the notion of unlisted rights can bring harm as well as good: witness the unhappy history of the Court's treatment of the right to property, discussed in Chapter 4, and its creation of a right called "freedom of contract," to which judges gave precedence over governmental authority to curb the evils of unrestricted economic competition. There is another caution here: Even ardent constitutionalists would concede that, as members of a community, individuals have obligations toward their fellow human beings, including the obligation not to trample on others' rights to enjoy autonomy, privacy, and dignity. No thoughtful person would defend a man who kills people in the basement of his own home as being protected by a right to privacy or absolve a rapist on grounds that he has a right to use his own body as he sees fit.

Thus, even a "pure constitutionalist" would recognize the legitimacy of government's imposing limits on privacy and autonomy. Moreover, the United States is not a pure constitutionalist state, but a constitutional democracy in which the people exercise a large degree of self-government. To what extent should judges defer to the judgment of popularly elected officials in drawing lines between permissible and impermissible governmental restrictions on unlisted rights?

If a constitutional interpreter, whoever he or she may be, decides that certain rights, such as privacy, are more fundamental than other rights or governmental powers, how does that interpreter justify those choices by general principles rather than as matters of personal taste?

Until 1965 the Supreme Court danced around the issue of privacy. Then, in the birth control case—Griswold v. Connecticut[2]—a majority of the Court found a right to privacy in the Constitution. Connecticut had a law that made it a crime to use, advise, or abet the use of "any drug, medicinal article or instrument for the purpose of preventing conception." The state had arrested and convicted several people for instructing married couples on how to practice birth control. For the majority, Justice William O. Douglas looked at the Bill of Rights as a whole and found a right to privacy in "the penumbras" of the clauses listed above. But Douglas's opinion had two themes, one that the state law violated a more general right to privacy and a second that the state violated a more specific right of marital privacy. (It was not until a few years later that the Court accepted the broader avenue of Douglas's argument and struck down a state law that allowed contraceptives to be sold only to married couples.)[3]

In Griswold, *Justice Arthur Goldberg wrote a concurring opinion stressing that "the Ninth Amendment ... lends strong support to the view that the 'liberty' protected by the Fifth and Fourteenth Amendments ... is not restricted to rights specifically mentioned in the first eight amendments." Justice John Marshall Harlan II also concurred, but he based his decision squarely on the due process clause (as containing substantive, not merely procedural, meaning) of the Fourteenth Amendment. He referred to his reasoning in an earlier dissent:*

> [T]hrough the course of this Court's decisions [due process] has represented the balance which our Nation, built upon postulates of respect for the liberty of the individual, has struck between that liberty and the demands of organized society. . . . The balance of which I speak is the balance struck by this country, having regard to what history teaches are the traditions from which it developed as well as the traditions from which it broke. That tradition is a living thing.

Dissenting, Justices Hugo L. Black and Potter Stewart denied that the Constitution included any general right to privacy. Moreover, they claimed that Goldberg's reliance on the Ninth Amendment and Harlan's use of due process were only smokescreens for judges' preferring their own personal opinions over the views of the people's elected representatives. If the plain words of the Constitution are not good enough, they said, "Amendments suggested by the people's elected representatives can be submitted to the people or their selected agents for ratification."

Despite this protest, a right to privacy now seems solidly entrenched in the Constitution, but battles over its scope continue. Roe v. Wade *(1973; see Case 6.1) extended privacy to include a woman's decision to have an abortion, at least during the first three months of pregnancy.* Akron v. Akron Center for Reproductive Health *(1985; see Case 6.2) and a bevy of rulings in between confirmed that right, though divisions within the Court have become even sharper. If President Reagan succeeds in selecting enough federal judges who disagree with* Roe, *it is probable that the decision will one day be overturned.*

What about the rights of consenting adult homosexuals to engage in intimate relations? Or of consenting married couples to engage in certain sexual acts? Does a right to privacy protect such acts when performed in the home? Bowers v. Hardwick *(1986; see Case 6.3) answers those questions with a firm no. At the very least these issues will return to haunt legislators, executive officials, and judges.*

---

1. *Edward S. Corwin, "The Basic Doctrine of American Constitutional Law,"* 12 Michigan Law Review 247 (1914).
2. *381 U.S. 479.*
3. *Eisenstadt v. Baird, 405 U.S. 438 (1972).*

~ Case 6.1 ~

Justice **BLACKMUN:** "The right of privacy ... whether it is to be found in the Fourteenth Amendment's concept of personal liberty ... or ... in the Ninth Amendment's reservation of rights to the people, is broad enough to encompass a woman's decision whether or not to terminate her pregnancy."

Justice **WHITE:** "I find nothing in the language or history of the Constitution to support the Court's judgment. ... This issue, for the most part, should be left with the people and the political processes the people have devised to govern their affairs."

Roe v. Wade
410 U.S. 113, 93 S. Ct. 705, 35 L. Ed. 2d 147 (1973)

Mr. Justice **BLACKMUN** delivered the opinion of the Court. ...

We forthwith acknowledge our awareness of the sensitive and emotional nature of the abortion controversy, of the vigorous opposing views, even among physicians, and of the deep and seemingly absolute convictions that the subject inspires. One's philosophy, one's experiences, one's exposure to the raw edges of human existence, one's religious training, one's attitudes toward life and family and their values, and the moral standards one establishes and seeks to observe, are all likely to influence and to color one's thinking and conclusions about abortion.

In addition, population growth, pollution, poverty, and racial overtones tend to complicate and not to simplify the problem.

Our task, of course, is to resolve the issue by constitutional measurement free of emotion and of predilection. We seek earnestly to do this, and, because we do, we have inquired into, and in this opinion place some emphasis upon, medical and medical-legal history and what that history reveals about man's attitudes toward the abortive procedure over the centuries. We bear in mind, too, Mr. Justice Holmes' admonition in his now vindicated dissent in Lochner v. New York (1905):

> "It [the Constitution] is made for people of fundamentally differing views, and the accident of our finding certain opinions natural and familiar or novel and even shocking ought not to conclude our judgment upon the question whether statutes embodying them conflict with the Constitution of the United States."

I

The Texas statutes ... make it a crime to "procure an abortion," as therein defined, or to attempt one, except with respect to "an abortion procured or attempted by medical advice for the purpose of saving the life of the mother." Similar statutes are in existence in a majority of the States. . . .

VI

It perhaps is not generally appreciated that the restrictive criminal abortion laws in effect in a majority of States today are of relatively recent vintage. Those laws . . . are not of ancient or even of common law origin. Instead, they derive from statutory changes effected, for the most part, in the latter half of the nineteenth century.

1. *Ancient attitudes.* . . . We are told that at the time of the Persian Empire abortifacients were known and that criminal abortions were severely punished. We are also told, however, that abortion was practiced in Greek times as well as in the Roman Era, and that "it was resorted to without scruple." The Ephesian, Soranos, often described as the greatest of the ancient gynecologists, appears to have been generally opposed to Rome's prevailing free-abortion practices. . . . Greek and Roman law afforded little protection to the unborn. If abortion was prosecuted in some places, it seems to have been based on a concept of a violation of the father's right to his offspring. Ancient religion did not bar abortion.

2. *The Hippocratic Oath.* What then of the famous Oath that has stood so long as the ethical guide of the medical profession and bears the name of the Great Greek (460(?)-377(?) B.C.), who has been described as the Father of Medicine? . . . The Oath varies somewhat according to the particular translation, but in any translation the content is clear: "I will give no deadly medicine to anyone if asked, nor suggest any such counsel: and in like manner I will not give to a woman a pessary to produce abortion. . . ."

. . . [T]he Oath . . . represents the apex of development of strict ethical concepts in medicine, and its influence endures to this day. Why did not the authority of Hippocrates dissuade abortion practice in his time and that of Rome? The late Dr. Edelstein provides us with a theory: The Oath was not uncontested even in Hippocrates' day; only the Pythagorean school of philosophers frowned upon the related act of suicide. Most Greek thinkers, on the other hand, commended abortion, at least prior to viability. See Plato, Republic, V, 46a; Aristotle, Politics, VII, 1335 b 25. For the Pythagoreans, however, it was a matter of dogma. For them the embryo was animate from the moment of conception, and abortion meant destruction of a living being. . . .

Edelstein then concludes that the Oath originated in a group representing only a small segment of Greek opinion and that it certainly was not accepted by all ancient physicians. . . .

3. *The common law.* It is undisputed that at the common law, abortion performed before "quickening"—the first recognizable movement of the fetus in utero, appearing usually from the sixteenth to the eighteenth week of

pregnancy—was not an indictable offense. The absence of a common law crime for pre-quickening abortion appears to have developed from a confluence of earlier philosophical, theological, and civil and canon law concepts of when life begins. These disciplines variously approached the question in terms of the point at which the embryo or fetus became "formed" or recognizably human, or in terms of when a "person" came into being, that is, infused with a "soul" or "animated." A loose consensus evolved in early English law that these events occurred at some point between conception and live birth.... Although Christian theology and the canon law came to fix the point of animation at 40 days for a male and 80 days for a female, a view that persisted until the nineteenth century, there was otherwise little agreement about the precise time of formation or animation. There was agreement, however, that prior to this point the fetus was to be regarded as part of the mother and its destruction, therefore, was not homicide....

Whether abortion of a quick fetus was a felony at common law, or even a lesser crime, is still disputed. Bracton, writing early in the thirteenth century, thought it homicide. But the later and predominant view, following the great common law scholars, has been that it was at most a lesser offense. In a frequently cited passage, Coke took the position that abortion of a woman "quick with childe" is "a great misprision and no murder." Blackstone followed, saying that while abortion after quickening had once been considered manslaughter (though not murder), "modern law" took a less severe view. A recent review of the common law precedents argues, however, that those precedents contradict Coke and that even post-quickening abortion was never established as a common law crime. This is of some importance because while most American courts ruled ... that abortion of an unquickened fetus was not criminal under their received common law, others followed Coke in stating that abortion of a quick fetus was a "misprision," a term they translated to mean "misdemeanor." That their reliance on Coke on this aspect of the law was uncritical and, apparently in all the reported cases, dictum ... makes it now appear doubtful that abortion was ever firmly established as a common law crime even with respect to the destruction of a quick fetus.

4. *The English statutory law.* England's first criminal abortion statute ... came in 1803. It made abortion of a quick fetus, § 1, a capital crime but in § 2 it provided lesser penalties for the felony of abortion before quickening.... This contrast was continued in the general revision of 1828.... It disappeared, however, together with the death penalty in 1837....

Recently [1967] Parliament enacted a new abortion law.... The Act permits a licensed physician to perform an abortion where two other licensed physicians agree (a) "that the continuance of the pregnancy would involve risk to the life of the pregnant woman, or of injury to the physical or mental health of the pregnant woman or any existing children of her family, greater than if the pregnancy were terminated," or (b) "that there is a substantial risk that if the child were born it would suffer from such physical or mental abnormalities as to be seriously handicapped." The Act also provides that, in making this determination, "account may be taken of the pregnant woman's actual or reasonably foreseeable environment." It also permits a physician, without the concurrence of others, to terminate a pregnancy where he is of the good faith opinion that the abortion "is immediately necessary to save the life or to prevent grave permanent injury to the physical or mental health of the pregnant woman."

5. *The American law.* In this country the law in effect in all but a few States until mid-nineteenth century was the pre-existing English common law. . . . It was not until after the War Between the States that legislation began generally to replace the common law. Most of these initial statutes dealt severely with abortion after quickening but were lenient with it before quickening. . . .

Gradually, in the middle and late 19th century the quickening distinction disappeared from the statutory law of most States and the degree of the offense and the penalties were increased. By the end of the 1950's a large majority of the States banned abortion, however and whenever performed, unless done to save or preserve the life of the mother. . . . In the past several years, however, a trend toward liberalization of abortion statutes has resulted in adoption, by about one-third of the States, of less stringent laws. . . .

It is thus apparent that at common law, at the time of the adoption of our Constitution, and throughout the major portion of the nineteenth century, abortion was viewed with less disfavor than under most American statutes currently in effect. Phrasing it another way, a woman enjoyed a substantially broader right to terminate a pregnancy than she does in most States today. . . .

6. *The position of the American Medical Association.* The anti-abortion mood prevalent in this country in the late nineteenth century was shared by the medical profession. Indeed, the attitude of the profession may have played a significant role in the enactment of stringent criminal abortion legislation during that period. . . .

An AMA Committee on Criminal Abortion was appointed in May 1857. It presented its report in [1859]. . . . The Committee then offered, and the Association adopted, resolutions protesting "against such unwarrantable destruction of human life," calling upon state legislatures to revise their abortion laws, and requesting the cooperation of state medical societies "in pressing the subject." . . .

Except for periodic condemnation of the criminal abortionist, no further formal AMA action took place until 1967. In that year the Committee on Human Reproduction urged the adoption of a stated policy of opposition to induced abortion, except when there is "documented medical evidence" of a threat to the health or life of the mother, or that the child "may be born with incapacitating physical deformity or mental deficiency," or that a pregnancy "resulting from legally established statutory or forcible rape or incest may constitute a threat to the mental or physical health of the patient," and two other physicians "chosen because of their recognized professional competence have examined the patient and have concurred in writing," and the procedure "is performed in a hospital accredited by the Joint Commission on Accreditation of Hospitals." . . . This recommendation was adopted by the House of Delegates. . . .

In 1970 . . . a reference committee noted "polarization of the medical profession on this controversial issue." . . . On June 25, 1970, the House of Delegates adopted preambles and most of the resolutions proposed by the reference committee. The preambles emphasized "the best interests of the patient," "sound clinical judgment," and "informed patient consent," in contrast to "mere acquiescence to the patient's demand." The resolutions asserted that abortion is a medical procedure that should be performed by a licensed physician in an accredited hospital only after consultation with two other physicians and in conformity with state law, and that no party to the procedure should be required to violate personally held moral principles. . . .

VII

Three reasons have been advanced to explain historically the enactment of criminal abortion laws in the nineteenth century and to justify their continued existence.

It has been argued occasionally that these laws were the product of a Victorian social concern to discourage illicit sexual conduct. Texas, however, does not advance this justification . . . and it appears that no court or commentator has taken the argument seriously. . . .

A second reason is concerned with abortion as a medical procedure. When most criminal abortion laws were first enacted, the procedure was a hazardous one for the woman. This was particularly true prior to the development of antisepsis. . . . Abortion mortality was high. Even after 1900, and perhaps until as late as the development of antibiotics in the 1940's, standard modern techniques such as dilation and curettage were not nearly so safe as they are today. Thus it has been argued that a State's real concern in enacting a criminal abortion law was to protect the pregnant woman, that is, to restrain her from submitting to a procedure that placed her life in serious jeopardy.

Modern medical techniques have altered this situation. . . . Mortality rates for women undergoing early abortions, where the procedure is legal, appear to be as low as or lower than the rates for normal childbirth. Consequently, any interest of the State in protecting the woman from an inherently hazardous procedure, except when it would be equally dangerous for her to forgo it, has largely disappeared. Of course, important state interests in the area of health and medical standards do remain. The State has a legitimate interest in seeing to it that abortion, like any other medical procedure, is performed under circumstances that insure maximum safety for the patient. . . . The prevalence of high mortality rates at illegal "abortion mills" strengthens, rather than weakens, the State's interest in regulating the conditions under which abortions are performed. Moreover, the risk to the woman increases as her pregnancy continues. Thus the State retains a definite interest in protecting the woman's own health and safety when an abortion is proposed at a late stage of pregnancy.

The third reason is the State's interest—some phrase it in terms of duty—in protecting prenatal life. Some of the argument for this justification rests on the theory that a new human life is present from the moment of conception. The State's interest and general obligation to protect life then extends, it is argued, to prenatal life. Only when the life of the pregnant mother herself is at stake, balanced against the life she carries within her, should the interest of the embryo or fetus not prevail. Logically, of course, a legitimate state interest in this area need not stand or fall on acceptance of the belief that life begins at conception or at some other point prior to live birth. In assessing the State's interest, recognition may be given to the less rigid claim that as long as at least potential life is involved, the State may assert interests beyond the protection of the pregnant woman alone. . . .

VIII

The Constitution does not explicitly mention any right of privacy. In a line of decisions, however . . . the Court has recognized that a right of personal privacy, or a guarantee of certain areas or zones of privacy, does exist under the Constitution. In varying contexts the Court or individual Justices have indeed found at least the roots of that right in the First Amendment, Stanley v. Georgia (1969); in the Fourth and Fifth Amendments, Terry v. Ohio (1968), Katz v. United States (1967), Boyd v. United States (1886), see Olmstead v. United States (1928) (Brandeis, J. dissenting); in the penumbras of the Bill of Rights, Griswold v. Connecticut (1965); in the Ninth Amendment, *id.* (Goldberg, J. concurring); or in the concept of liberty guaranteed by the first section of the Fourteenth Amendment, see Meyer v. Nebraska (1923). These decisions make it clear that only personal rights that can be deemed "fundamental" or "implicit in the concept of ordered liberty," Palko v. Connecticut (1937), are included in this guarantee of personal privacy. They also make it clear that the right has some extensions to activities relating to marriage, Loving v. Virginia (1967); procreation, Skinner v. Oklahoma (1942); contraception, Eisenstadt v. Baird (1942); family relationships, Prince v. Massachusetts (1944); and child rearing and education, Pierce v. Society of Sisters (1925), Meyer v. Nebraska (1923).

This right of privacy . . . whether it be found in the Fourteenth Amendment's concept of personal liberty and restrictions upon state action, as we feel it is, or, as the District Court determined, in the Ninth Amendment's reservation of rights to the people, is broad enough to encompass a woman's decision whether or not to terminate her pregnancy. The detriment that the State would impose upon the pregnant woman by denying this choice altogether is apparent. Specific and direct harm medically diagnosable even in early pregnancy may be involved. Maternity, or additional offspring, may force upon the woman a distressful life and future. Psychological harm may be imminent. Mental and physical health may be taxed by child care. There is also the distress, for all concerned, associated with the unwanted child, and there is the problem of bringing a child into a family already unable, psychologically and otherwise, to care for it. In other cases, as in this one, the additional difficulties and continuing stigma of unwed motherhood may be involved. All these are factors the woman and her responsible physician necessarily will consider in consultation.

. . . [A]ppellant and some amici° argue that the woman's right is absolute. . . . With this we do not agree. . . . The Court's decisions recognizing a right of privacy also acknowledge that some state regulation in areas protected by that right is appropriate. As noted above, a state may properly assert important interests in safe-guarding health, in maintaining medical standards, and in protecting potential life. At some point in pregnancy, these respective interests become sufficiently compelling to sustain regulation of the factors that govern the abortion decision. . . .

We therefore conclude that the right of personal privacy includes the abortion decision, but that this right is not unqualified and must be considered against important state interests in regulation. . . .

IX

A

The appellee and certain *amici* argue that the fetus is a "person" within the language and meaning of the Fourteenth Amendment. In support of this they outline at length and in detail the well-known facts of fetal development. If this suggestion of personhood is established, the appellant's case, of course, collapses, for the fetus' right to life is then guaranteed specifically by the amendment. . . . On the other hand, the appellee conceded on reargument that no case could be cited that holds that a fetus is a person within the meaning of the Fourteenth Amendment.

The Constitution does not define "person" in so many words. Sec. I of the Fourteenth Amendment contains three references to "person." . . .

° *The term* amici *means "friends of court"* (amici curiae *in Latin), parties whom a court permits to file briefs in a case although they are not directly involved.—Eds.*

"Person" is used in other places in the Constitution. . . . But in nearly all these instances, the use of the word is such that it has application only postnatally. None indicates, with any assurance, that it has any possible pre-natal application.

All this, together with our observation . . . that throughout the major portion of the nineteenth century prevailing legal abortion practices were far freer than they are today, persuades us that the word "person," as used in the Fourteenth Amendment, does not include the unborn. . . .

This conclusion, however, does not of itself fully answer the contentions raised by Texas, and we pass on to other considerations.

B

The pregnant woman cannot be isolated in her privacy. She carries an embryo and, later, a fetus. . . . The situation therefore is inherently different from marital intimacy, or bedroom possession of obscene material, or marriage, or procreation, or education. . . . [I]t is reasonable and appropriate for a State to decide that at some point in time another interest, that of health of the mother or that of potential human life, becomes significantly involved. The woman's privacy is no longer sole and any right of privacy she possesses must be measured accordingly.

Texas urges that, apart from the Fourteenth Amendment, life begins at conception and is present throughout pregnancy, and that, therefore, the State has a compelling interest in protecting that life from and after conception. We need not resolve the difficult question of when life begins. When those trained in the respective disciplines of medicine, philosophy, and theology are unable to arrive at any consensus, the judiciary, at this point in the development of man's knowledge, is not in a position to speculate as to the answer.

It should be sufficient to note briefly the wide divergence of thinking on this most sensitive and difficult question. There has always been strong support for the view that life does not begin until live birth. . . .

In the areas other than criminal abortion the law has been reluctant to endorse any theory that life, as we recognize it, begins before live birth or to accord legal rights to the unborn except in narrowly defined situations and except when the rights are contingent upon live birth. . . . In most States recovery is said to be permitted only if the fetus was viable or at least quick when the injuries were sustained, though few courts have squarely so held. In a recent development, generally opposed by the commentators, some States permit the parents of a stillborn child to maintain an action for wrongful death because of prenatal injuries. Such an action, however, would appear to be one to vindicate the parents' interest and is thus consistent with the view that the fetus, at most, represents only the potentiality of life. Similarly, unborn children have been recognized as acquiring rights or interests by way of inheritance or other devolution of property, and have been represented by guardians ad litem. Perfection of the interests involved, again, has generally been contingent upon live birth. In short, the unborn have never been recognized in the law as persons in the whole sense.

In view of all this, we do not agree that, by adopting one theory of life, Texas may override the rights of the pregnant woman. . . .

With respect to the State's important and legitimate interest in the health of the mother, the "compelling" point, in the light of present medical knowledge, is at approximately the end of the first trimester. This is so because of the now established medical fact . . . that until the end of the first trimester mortality in abortion may be less than mortality in normal childbirth. It follows that, from and after this point, a state may regulate the abortion procedure to the extent that the regulation reasonably relates to the preservation and protection of maternal health. . . .

This means, on the one hand, that, for the period of pregnancy prior to this "compelling" point, the attending physician, in consultation with his patient, is free to determine, without regulation by the State, that in his judgment the patient's pregnancy should be terminated. If that decision is reached, the judgment may be effectuated by an abortion free of interference by the State.

With respect to the State's important and legitimate interest in potential life, the "compelling" point is at viability. This is so because the fetus then presumably has the capability of meaningful life outside the mother's womb. State regulation protective of fetal life after viability thus has both logical and biological justifications. If the State is interested in protecting fetal life after viability, it may go so far as to proscribe abortion during that period except when it is necessary to preserve the life or health of the mother.

Measured against these standards, Art. 1196 of the Texas Penal Code . . . sweeps too broadly. The statute makes no distinction between abortions performed early in pregnancy and those performed later, and it limits to a single reason, "saving" the mother's life, the legal justification for the procedure. The statute, therefore, cannot survive the constitutional attack made upon it here. . . .

Mr. Chief Justice **BURGER**, concurring. . . .

Mr. Justice **DOUGLAS**, concurring. . . .

Mr. Justice **STEWART**, concurring. . . .

Mr. Justice **WHITE** with whom Mr. Justice **REHNQUIST** joins, dissenting. . . .

. . . I find nothing in the language or history of the Constitution to support the Court's judgment. The Court simply fashions and announces a new constitutional right for pregnant mothers and, with scarcely any reason or authority its action, invests that right with sufficient substance to override most existing state abortion statutes. The upshot is that the people and the legislatures of the fifty States are constitutionally disentitled to weigh the relative importance of the continued existence and development of the fetus on the one hand against a spectrum of possible impacts on the mother on the other hand. As an exercise of raw judicial power, the Court perhaps has authority to do what it does today; but in my view its judgment is an improvident and extravagant exercise of the power of judicial review that the Constitution extends to this Court.

The Court apparently values the convenience of the pregnant mother more than the continued existence and development of the life or potential life which she carries. Whether or not I might agree with that marshalling of values, I can in no event join the Court's judgment because I find no constitutional warrant for imposing such an order of priorities on the people and legislatures of the States. In a sensitive area such as this, involving as it does issues over which reasonable men may easily and heatedly differ, I cannot accept the Court's exercise of its clear power of choice by interposing a constitutional barrier to state efforts to protect human life and by investing mothers and doctors with the constitutionally protected right to exterminate it. This issue, for the most part, should be left with the people and to the political processes the people have devised to govern their affairs. . . .

Mr. Justice **REHNQUIST**, dissenting. . . .

. . . I have difficulty in concluding, as the Court does, that the right of "privacy" is involved in this case. Texas . . . bars the performance of a medical abortion by a licensed physician on a plaintiff such as Roe. A transaction resulting in an operation such as this is not "private" in the ordinary usage of that word. Nor is the "privacy" which the Court finds here even a distant relative of the freedom from searches and seizures protected by the Fourth Amendment to the Constitution which the Court has referred to as embodying a right to privacy. . . .

If the Court means by the term "privacy" not more than that the claim of a person to be free from unwanted state regulation of consensual transactions may be a form of "liberty" protected by the Fourteenth Amendment, there is no doubt that similar claims have been upheld in our earlier decisions on the basis of that liberty. I agree . . . that the "liberty," against deprivation of which without due process the Fourteenth Amendment protects, embraces more than the rights found in the Bill of Rights. But that liberty is not guaranteed absolutely against deprivation, but only against deprivation without due process of law. The test traditionally applied in the area of social and economic legislation is whether or not a law such as that challenged has a rational relation to a valid state objective. Williamson v. Lee Optical Co. (1955). If the Texas statute were to prohibit an abortion even where the mother's life is in jeopardy, I have little doubt that such a statute would lack a rational relation to a valid state objective. . . . But the Court's sweeping invalidation of any restriction on abortion during the first trimester is impossible to justify under that standard, and the conscious weighing of competing factors which the Court's opinion apparently substitutes for the established test is far more appropriate to a legislative judgment than to a judicial one. . . .

While the Court's opinion quotes from the dissent of Mr. Justice Holmes in Lochner v. New York (1905) the result it reaches is more closely attuned to the majority opinion of Mr. Justice Peckham in that case. As in *Lochner* and similar cases applying substantive due process standards . . . adoption of the compelling state interest standard will inevitably require this Court to examine the legislative policies and pass on the wisdom of these policies in the very process of deciding whether a particular state interest put forward may or may not be "compelling." The decision here to break the term of pregnancy into three distinct terms and to outline the permissible restrictions the State may impose in each one, for example, partakes more of judicial legislation than it does of a determination of the intent of the drafters of the Fourteenth Amendment.

The fact that a majority of the States, reflecting, after all, the majority sentiment in those States, have had restrictions on abortions for at least a century, it seems to me, is a strong indication that the asserted right to an abortion is not "so rooted in the traditions and conscience of our people as to be ranked as fundamental." . . . Even today, when society's views on abortion are changing, the very existence of the debate is evidence that the "right" to an abortion is not so universally accepted. . . .

To reach its result the Court necessarily has had to find within the scope of the Fourteenth Amendment a right that was apparently completely unknown to the drafters of the Amendment. . . . By the time of the adoption of the Fourteenth Amendment in 1868 there were at least thirty-six laws enacted by state or territorial legislatures limiting abortion. While many States have amended or updated their laws, twenty-one of the laws on the books in 1868 remain in effect today. Indeed, the Texas statute struck down today was, as the majority notes, first enacted in 1857 and "has remained substantially unchanged to the present time." . . .

There apparently was no question concerning the validity of this provision or of any of the other state statutes when the Fourteenth Amendment was adopted. The only conclusion possible from this history is that the drafters did not intend to have the Fourteenth Amendment withdraw from the States the power to legislate with respect to this matter. . . .

∼ Case 6.2 ∼

Justice **POWELL:** "[S]tare decisis, while perhaps never entirely persuasive on a constitutional question, is a doctrine that demands respect in a society governed by the rule of law. We respect it today and reaffirm *Roe.*"

Justice **O'CONNOR:** "The *Roe* framework ... is clearly on a collision course with itself."

Akron v. Akron Center for Reproductive Health
462 U.S. 416, 103 S. Ct. 2481, 76 L. Ed. 2d 687 (1983)

Roe v. Wade did not lay to rest the constitutional questions about a woman's right to have an abortion or a fetus's status as a person. Many other kinds of state legislation remained in force, and state as well as local officials enacted reams of new statutes and ordinances to regulate abortion. In decisions alluded to in this case, the Court struck down just about all of these statutes that were challenged.

The story at the federal level was similar. Senators and representatives introduced dozens of bills to modify the effects of Roe *and proposed a bevy of constitutional amendments to deny a right to abortion. The only bill that became law was the Hyde Amendment, a statutory provision attached to appropriations that, though the specific terms varied from year to year, in general forbade using federal funds for abortions that were not necessary to save the mother's life. Maher v. Roe, 432 U.S. 464 (1977), and Harris v. McRae, 448 U.S. 297 (1980), sustained these restrictions.*

As was mentioned in the introduction of this chapter, Ronald Reagan intended to select judges who would reverse Roe. *When Potter Stewart retired in 1981, Reagan nominated Sandra Day O'Connor to take his place. The first important case involving abortion after her appointment was* Akron.

In 1978 Akron, Ohio, adopted a comprehensive ordinance regulating abortions, which included the following provisions: (1) sec. 1870.03 requiring that all abortions after the first trimester be performed in accredited hospitals; (2) sec. 1870.05 setting up procedures for notifying before an abortion the parents of an unmarried minor; (3) sec. 1870.06 mandating that "the attending physician" before an abortion make certain specified statements, including that "the unborn child is a human life from the moment of conception," and describing the characteristics of the fetus, the dangers of abortion, and the public services available to help women through pregnancy; and (4) sec. 1870.07 ordering, except in an emergency, a twenty-four-hour delay between the time the woman signed a consent form and the abortion was performed.

Three corporations that ran abortion clinics in Akron and a physician who specialized in that work filed suit in a federal district court, asking for an injunction against enforcement of the various regulations. The district court upheld some provisions, but struck down others. Both sides appealed portions of that decision. The court of appeals affirmed in part and reversed in part. Both sides then sought and obtained review.

Justice **POWELL** delivered the opinion of the Court. . . .

These cases come to us a decade after we held in Roe v. Wade (1973) that the right to privacy, grounded in the concept of personal liberty guaranteed by the Constitution, encompasses a woman's right to decide whether to terminate her pregnancy. Legislative responses to the Court's decision have required us on several occasions, and again today, to define the limits of a State's authority to regulate the performance of abortions. And arguments continue to be made, in these cases and elsewhere, that we erred in interpreting the Constitution. Nonetheless, the doctrine of stare decisis, while perhaps never entirely persuasive on a constitutional question, is a doctrine that demands respect in a society governed by the rule of law.° We respect it today and reaffirm *Roe*. . . .

Today, however, the dissenting opinion rejects the basic premise of *Roe* and its progeny. The dissent stops short of arguing flatly that *Roe* should be overruled. Rather, it adopts reasoning that, for all practical purposes, would accomplish precisely that result. . . .

In sum, it appears that the dissent would uphold virtually any abortion regulation under a rational-basis test. It also appears that even where heightened scrutiny is deemed appropriate, the dissent would uphold virtually any abortion-inhibiting regulation because of the State's interest in preserving potential human life. . . . This analysis is wholly incompatible with the fundamental right recognized in *Roe*.

° There are especially compelling reasons for adhering to stare decisis [a policy of law requiring courts to abide by precedents] in applying the principles of *Roe*. That case was considered with special care. It was argued during the 1971 Term, and reargued—with extensive briefing—the following Term. The decision was joined by the Chief Justice and six other Justices. Since *Roe* was decided . . . the Court repeatedly and consistently has accepted and applied the basic principle that a woman has a fundamental right to make the highly personal choice whether or not to terminate her pregnancy. . . . [Footnote by the Court.]

II

In *Roe,* the Court held that the "right of privacy, . . . founded in the Fourteenth Amendment's concept of personal liberty and restrictions upon state action, . . . is broad enough to encompass a woman's decision whether or not to terminate her pregnancy." Although the Constitution does not specifically identify this right, the history of this Court's constitutional adjudication leaves no doubt that "the full scope of the liberty guaranteed by the Due Process Clause cannot be found in or limited by the precise terms of the specific guarantees elsewhere provided in the Constitution." Poe v. Ullman (1961) (Harlan, J., dissenting from dismissal of appeal). Central among these protected liberties is an individual's "freedom of personal choice in matters of marriage and family life." *Roe* (Stewart, J., concurring). See, e.g., Eisenstadt v. Baird (1972); Loving v. Virginia (1967); Griswold v. Connecticut (1965); Pierce v. Society of Sisters (1925); Meyer v. Nebraska (1923). The decision in *Roe* was based firmly on this long-recognized and essential element of personal liberty.

The Court also has recognized, because abortion is a medical procedure, that the full vindication of the woman's fundamental right necessarily requires that her physician be given "the room he needs to make his best medical judgment." Doe v. Bolton (1973). See Whalen v. Roe (1977). The physician's exercise of this medical judgment encompasses both assisting the woman in the decisionmaking process and implementing her decision should she choose abortion. See Colautti v. Franklin (1979).

At the same time, the Court in *Roe* acknowledged that the woman's fundamental right "is not unqualified and must be considered against important state interests in abortion." But restrictive state regulation of the right to choose abortion, as with other fundamental rights subject to searching judicial examination, must be supported by a compelling state interest. We have recognized two such interests that may justify state regulation of abortions.°

First, a State has an "important and legitimate interest in protecting the potentiality of human life." Although the interest exists "throughout the course of the woman's pregnancy," Beal v. Doe (1977), it becomes com-

---

° In addition, the Court repeatedly has recognized that, in view of the unique status of children under the law, the States have a "significant" interest in certain abortion regulations aimed at protecting children "that is not present in the case of an adult." Planned Parenthood v. Danforth (1976). See H. L. v. Matheson (1981). . . . A majority of the Court, however, has indicated that these state and parental interests must give way to the constitutional right of a mature minor or of an immature minor whose best interests are contrary to parental involvement. See, e.g., *Matheson* (Powell, J., concurring) (Marshall, J., dissenting). . . . [Footnote by the Court.]

pelling only at viability, the point at which the fetus "has the capability of meaningful life outside the mother's womb," *Roe*. At viability this interest in protecting the potential life of the unborn child is so important that the State may proscribe abortions altogether, "except when it is necessary to preserve the life or health of the mother." *Roe*.

Second, because a State has a legitimate concern with the health of women who undergo abortions, "a State may properly assert important interests in safeguarding health [and] in maintaining medical standards." We held in *Roe*, however, that this health interest does not become compelling until "approximately the end of the first trimester" of pregnancy. Until that time, a pregnant woman must be permitted, in consultation with her physician, to decide to have an abortion and to effectuate that decision "free of interference by the State."

This does not mean that a State never may enact a regulation touching on the woman's abortion right during the first weeks of pregnancy. Certain regulations that have no significant impact on the woman's exercise of her right may be permissible where justified by important state health objectives. In *Danforth*, we unanimously upheld two Missouri statutory provisions, applicable to the first trimester, requiring the woman to provide her informed written consent to the abortion and the physician to keep certain records, even though comparable requirements were not imposed on most other medical procedures. The decisive factor was that the State met its burden of demonstrating that these regulations furthered important health-related State concerns. But even these minor regulations on the abortion procedure during the first trimester may not interfere with physician-patient consultation or with the woman's choice between abortion and childbirth.

From approximately the end of the first trimester of pregnancy, the State "may regulate the abortion procedure to the extent that the regulation reasonably relates to the preservation and protection of maternal health." *Roe*. The State's discretion to regulate on this basis does not, however, permit it to adopt abortion regulations that depart from accepted medical practice. We have rejected a State's attempt to ban a particular second-trimester abortion procedure, where the ban would have increased the costs and limited the availability of abortions without promoting important health benefits. See *Danforth*....

III

Section 1807.03 of the Akron ordinance requires that any abortion performed "upon a pregnant woman subsequent to the end of the first trimester of her pregnancy" must be "performed in a hospital." A "hospital" is "a general hospital or special hospital devoted to gynecology or obstetrics which is accredited by the Joint Commission on Accreditation of Hospitals or by the American Osteopathic Association." § 1870.1(B). Accreditation by three organizations requires compliance with comprehensive standards governing a wide variety of health and surgical services. The ordinance thus prevents the performance of abortions in outpatient facilities that are not part of an acute-care, full-service hospital. . . .

. . . [W]e now hold that § 1870.03 is unconstitutional.

A . . .

We reaffirm today that a State's interest in health regulation becomes compelling at approximately the end of the first trimester. The existence of a compelling state interest in health, however, is only the beginning of the inquiry. The State's regulation may be upheld only if it is reasonably designed to further that state interest. See *Doe*. . . .

B

There can be no doubt that § 1870.03's second-trimester hospitalization requirement places a significant obstacle in the path of women seeking an abortion. A primary burden created by the requirement is additional cost to the woman. . . . [A] second-trimester abortion costs more than twice as much in a hospital as in a clinic. . . . It therefore is apparent that a second-trimester hospitalization requirement may significantly limit a woman's ability to obtain an abortion.

Akron . . . defends [§ 1870.03] as a reasonable health regulation. This position had strong support at the time of *Roe*, as hospitalization for second-trimester abortions was recommended by the American Public Health Association (APHA) and the American College of Obstetricians and Gynecologists (ACOG). Since then, however, the safety of second-trimester abortions has increased dramatically. The principal reason is that the D[ilation] & E[vacuation] procedure is now widely and successfully used for second-trimester abortions. . . .

. . . [E]xperience indicates that D & E may be performed safely on an outpatient basis in appropriate nonhospital facilities. The evidence is strong enough to have convinced the APHA to abandon its prior recommendation of hospitalization for all second-trimester abortions. . . . Similarly, the ACOG no longer suggests that all second-trimester abortions be performed in a hospital. . . .

These developments, and the professional commentary supporting them, constitute impressive evidence that—at least during the early weeks of the second trimester—D & E abortions may be performed as safely in an outpatient clinic as in a full-service hospital. We conclude, therefore, that "present medical knowledge," *Roe*, convincingly undercuts Akron's justification for requiring that *all* second-trimester abortions be performed in a hospital. . . .

IV

We turn next to § 1870.05(B), the provision prohibiting a physician from performing an abortion on a minor pregnant woman under the age of 15 unless he obtains "the informed written consent of one of her parents or her legal guardian" or unless the minor obtains "an order from a court having jurisdiction over her that the abortion be performed or induced." . . .

The relevant legal standards are not in dispute. The Court has held that "the State may not impose a blanket provision . . . requiring the consent of a parent or person in loco parentis as a condition for abortion of an unmarried minor." *Danforth*. In Bellotti v. Baird (1979) (*Bellotti II*), a majority of the Court indicated that a State's interest in protecting immature minors will sustain a requirement of a consent substitute, either parental or judicial. [Plurality opinion of four Justices.] The *Bellotti II* plurality cautioned, however, that the State must provide an alternative procedure whereby a pregnant minor may demonstrate that she is sufficiently mature to make the abortion decision herself or that, despite her immaturity, an abortion would be in her best interests. Under these decisions, it is clear that Akron may not make a blanket determination that *all* minors under the age of 15 are too immature to make this decision or that an abortion never may be in the minor's best interests without parental approval. . . .

V

The Akron ordinance provides that no abortion shall be performed except "with the informed written consent of the pregnant woman, . . . given freely and without coercion." § 1870.06(A). Furthermore, "in order to insure that the consent for an abortion is truly informed consent," the woman must be "orally informed by her attending physician" of the status of her pregnancy, the development of her fetus, the date of possible viability, the physical and emotional complications that may result from an abortion, and the availability of agencies to provide her with assistance and information with respect to birth control, adoption, and childbirth." § 1870.06(B). In addition, the attending physician must inform her "of the particular risks associated with her own pregnancy and the abortion technique to be employed . . . [and] other information which in his own medical judgment is relevant to her decision as to whether to have an abortion or carry her pregnancy to term." § 1870.06(C). . . .

A

In *Danforth*, we upheld a Missouri law requiring a pregnant woman to "certif[y] in writing her consent to the abortion and that her consent is informed and freely given and is not the result of coercion." . . .

The validity of an informed consent requirement thus rests on the State's interest in protecting the health of the pregnant woman. The decision to have an abortion has "implications far broader than those associated with most other kinds of medical treatment," and thus the State legitimately may seek to ensure that it has been made "in the light of all attendant circumstances—psychological and emotional as well as physical—that might be relevant to the well-being of the patient." This does not mean, however, that a State has unreviewable authority to decide what information a woman must be given before she chooses to have an abortion. It remains primarily the responsibility of the physician to ensure that appropriate information is conveyed to his patient, depending on her particular circumstances. *Danforth's* recognition of the State's interest in ensuring that this information be given will not justify abortion regulations designed to influence the woman's informed choice between abortion or childbirth.

B

... [W]e believe that § 1870.06(B) attempts to extend the State's interest in ensuring "informed consent" beyond permissible limits. First, ... much of the information required is designed not to inform the woman's consent but rather to persuade her to withhold it altogether. Subsection (3) requires the physician to inform his patient that "the unborn child is a human life from the moment of conception," a requirement inconsistent with the Court's holding in *Roe* that a state may not adopt one theory of when life begins to justify its regulation of abortions. Moreover, much of the detailed description of "the anatomical and physiological characteristics of the particular unborn child" required by subsection (3) would involve at best speculation by the physician. And subsection (5), that begins with the dubious statement that "abortion is a major surgical procedure" and proceeds to describe numerous possible physical and psychological complications of abortion, is a "parade of horribles" intended to suggest that abortion is a particularly dangerous procedure.

An additional, and equally decisive, objection to § 1870.06(B) is its intrusion upon the discretion of the pregnant woman's physician. . . . For example, even if the physician believes that some of the risks outlined in subsection (5) are nonexistent for a particular patient, he remains obligated to describe them to her. . . .

C

Section 1870.06(C) presents a different question. Under this provision, the "attending physician" must inform the woman "of the particular risks associated with her own pregnancy and the abortion technique to be employed including providing her with at least a general description of the medical instructions to be followed subsequent to the abortion in order to insure her safe recovery, and shall in addition provide her with such other information which in his own medical judgment is relevant to her decision as to whether to have an abortion or carry her pregnancy to term."

The information required clearly is related to maternal health and to the State's legitimate purpose in requiring informed consent. . . .

We are not convinced, however, that there is as vital a state need for insisting that the physician performing the abortion, or for that matter any physician, personally counsel the patient in the absence of a request. The State's interest is in ensuring that the woman's consent is informed and unpressured; the critical factor is whether she obtains the necessary information and counseling from a qualified person, not the identity of the person from whom she obtains it. . . . [O]n the record before us we cannot say that the woman's consent to the abortion will not be informed if a physician delegates the counseling task to another qualified individual.

In so holding, we do not suggest that the State is powerless to vindicate its interest in making certain the "important" and "stressful" decision to abort "is made with full knowledge of its nature and consequences." *Danforth.* Nor do we imply that a physician may abdicate his essential role as the person ultimately responsible for the medical aspects of the decision to perform the abortion. A State may define the physician's responsibility to include verification that adequate counseling has been provided and that the woman's consent is informed. In addition, the State may establish reasonable minimum qualifications for those people who perform the primary counseling function. . . .

VI

The Akron ordinance prohibits a physician from performing an abortion until 24 hours after the pregnant woman signs a consent form. § 1870.07. . . .

We find that Akron has failed to demonstrate that any legitimate state interest is furthered by an arbitrary and inflexible waiting period. There is no evidence suggesting that the abortion procedure will be performed more safely. Nor are we convinced that the State's legitimate concern that the woman's decision be informed is reasonably served by requiring a 24-hour delay as a matter of course. . . .

Justice **O'CONNOR**, with whom Justice **WHITE** and Justice **REHNQUIST** join, dissenting.

. . . [I]t is apparent from the Court's opinion that neither sound constitutional theory nor our need to decide cases based on the application of neutral principles can accommodate an analytical framework that varies according to the "stages" of pregnancy, where those stages, and their concomitant standards of review, differ according to the level of medical technology available when a particular challenge to state regulation occurs. The Court's analysis of the Akron regulations is inconsistent both with the methods of analysis employed in previous cases dealing with abortion, and with the Court's approach to fundamental rights in other areas.

Our recent cases indicate that a regulation imposed on "a lawful abortion 'is not unconstitutional unless it unduly burdens the right to seek an abortion.' " Maher v. Roe (1977). See also Harris v. McRae (1980). In my view, this "unduly burdensome" standard should be applied to the challenged regulations throughout the entire pregnancy without reference to the particular "stage" of pregnancy involved. If the particular regulation does not "unduly burden[]" the fundamental right, then our evaluation of that regulation is limited to our determination that the regulation rationally relates to a legitimate state purpose. Irrespective of what we may believe is wise or prudent policy in this difficult area, "the Constitution does not constitute us as 'Platonic Guardians' nor does it vest in this Court the authority to strike down laws because they do not meet our standards of desirable social policy, 'wisdom,' or 'common sense.' " Plyler v. Doe (1982) (Burger, C. J., dissenting).

I

The trimester or "three-stage" approach adopted by the Court in *Roe* ... cannot be supported as a legitimate or useful framework for accommodating the woman's right and the State's interests. The decision of the Court today graphically illustrates why the trimester approach is a completely unworkable method. . . .

. . . [T]he State's compelling interest in maternal health changes as medical technology changes, and any health regulation must not "depart from accepted medical practice." In applying this standard, the Court holds that "the safety of second-trimester abortions has increased dramatically" since 1973, when *Roe* was decided. Although a regulation such as one requiring that all second-trimester abortions be performed in hospitals "had strong support" in 1973 "as a reasonable health regulation," this regulation can no longer stand because, according to the Court's diligent research into medical and scientific literature, the dilation and evacuation procedure (D & E), used in 1973 only for first-trimester abortions, "is now widely and successfully used for second trimester abortions." . . .

It is not difficult to see that despite the Court's purported adherence to the trimester approach adopted in *Roe*, the lines drawn in that decision have now been "blurred" because of what the Court accepts as technological advancement in the safety of abortion procedure. . . . [T]he State must continuously and conscientiously study contemporary medical and scientific literature in order to determine whether the effect of a particular regulation is to "depart from accepted medical practice" insofar as particular procedures and particular periods within the trimester are concerned. Assuming that legislative bodies are able to engage in this exacting task, it is difficult to believe that our Constitution *requires* that they do it as a prelude to protecting the health of their citizens. It is even more difficult to believe that this Court, without the resources available to those bodies entrusted with making legislative choices, believes itself competent to make these inquiries and to revise these standards every time the American College of Obstetricians and Gynecologists (ACOG) or similar group revises its views about what is and what is not appropriate medical procedure in this area. . . .

Just as improvements in medical technology inevitably will move *forward* the point at which the State may regulate for reasons of maternal health, different technological improvements will move *backward* the point of viability at which the State may proscribe abortions except when necessary to preserve the life and health of the mother.

In 1973, viability before 28 weeks was considered unusual. . . . However, recent studies have demonstrated increasingly earlier fetal viability. It is certainly reasonable to believe that fetal viability in the first trimester of pregnancy may be possible in the not too distant future. Indeed, the Court has explicitly acknowledged that *Roe* left the point of viability "flexible for anticipated advancements in medical skill." . . .

The *Roe* framework, then, is clearly on a collision course with itself. . . . [I]t is clear that the trimester approach violates the fundamental aspiration of judicial decision making through the application of neutral principles "sufficiently absolute to give them roots throughout the community and continuity over significant periods of time. . . ." A. Cox, *The Role of the Supreme Court in American Government* 114 (1976). The *Roe* framework is inherently tied to the state of medical technology that exists whenever particular litigation ensues. Although legislatures are better suited to make the necessary factual judgments in this area, the Court's framework forces legislatures, as a matter of constitutional law, to speculate about what constitutes "accepted medical practice" at any given time. Without the necessary expertise or ability, courts must then pretend to act as science review boards and examine those legislative judgments.

The Court adheres to the *Roe* framework because the doctrine of stare decisis "demands respect in a society governed by the rule of law." Although respect for stare decisis cannot be challenged, "this Court's considered practice [is] not to apply stare decisis as rigidly in constitutional as in nonconstitutional cases." Glidden Company v. Zdanok (1962). Although we must be mindful of the "desirability of continuity of decision in constitutional questions . . . when convinced of former error, this Court has never felt constrained to follow precedent. In constitutional questions, when correction depends on amendment and not upon legislative action this Court throughout its history has freely exercised its power to reexamine the basis of its constitutional decisions." Smith v. Allwright (1944).

Even assuming that there is a fundamental right to terminate pregnancy in some situations, there is no justification in law or logic for the trimester framework adopted in *Roe*. . . . [T]hat framework is clearly an unworkable means of balancing the fundamental right and the compelling state interests that are indisputably implicated.

II

The Court in *Roe* correctly realized that the State has important interests "in the areas of health and medical standards" and that "[t]he State has a legitimate interest in seeing to it that abortion, like any other medical procedure, is performed under circumstances that insure maximum safety for the patient." The Court also recognized that the State has "*another* important and legitimate interest in protecting the potentiality of human life." (Emphasis in original.) I agree completely that the State has these interests, but in my view, the point at which these interests become compelling does not depend on the trimester of pregnancy. Rather, these interests are present *throughout* pregnancy. . . .

The fallacy inherent in the *Roe* framework is apparent: just because the State has a compelling interest in ensuring maternal safety once an abortion may be more dangerous than childbirth, it simply does not follow that the State has no interest before that point. . . .

The state interest in potential human life is likewise extant throughout pregnancy. In *Roe*, the Court held that although the State had an important and legitimate interest in protecting potential life, that interest could not become compelling until the point at which the fetus was viable. The difficulty with this analysis is clear: *potential* life is no less potential in the first weeks of pregnancy than it is at viability or afterward. At any stage in pregnancy, there is the *potential* for human life. Although the Court refused to "resolve the difficult question of when life begins," the Court chose the point of viability—when the fetus is *capable* of life independent of its mother—to permit the complete proscription of abortion. The choice of viability as the point at which the state interest in *potential* life becomes compelling is no less arbitrary than choosing any point before viability or any point afterward. . . .

III

Although the State possesses compelling interests in the protection of potential human life and in maternal health throughout pregnancy, not every regulation that the State imposes must be measured against the State's compelling interests and examined with strict scrutiny. ". . . *Roe* did not declare an unqualified 'constitutional right to an abortion.' . . . Rather, the right protects the woman from unduly burdensome interference with her freedom to decide whether to terminate her pregnancy." *Maher.* The Court and its individual Justices have repeatedly utilized the "unduly burdensome" standards in abortion cases.

The requirement that state interference "infringe substantially" or "heavily burden" a right before heightened scrutiny is applied is not novel in our fundamental-rights jurisprudence, or restricted to the abortion context. In San Antonio Independent School District v. Rodriguez (1973), we observed that we apply "strict judicial scrutiny" only when legislation may be said to have " 'deprived,' 'infringed,' or 'interfered' with the free exercise of some such fundamental personal right or liberty." . . .

In Carey v. Population Services International (1977), we eschewed the notion that state law had to meet the exacting "compelling state interest" test " 'whenever it implicates sexual freedom.' " Rather, we required that before the "strict scrutiny" standard was employed, it was necssary that the state law "impose[ ]a significant burden" on a protected right or that it "burden an individual's right to prevent conception or terminate pregnancy by *substantially* limiting access to the means of effectuating that decision. . . ." (Emphasis added.) The Court stressed that, "even a burdensome regulation may be validated by a sufficiently compelling state interest." . . .

Indeed, the Court today follows this approach. Although the Court does not use the expression "undue burden," the Court recognizes that even a "significant obstacle" can be justified by a "reasonable" regulation.

The "undue burden" required in the abortion cases represents the required threshold inquiry that must be conducted before this Court can require a State to justify its legislative actions under the exacting "compelling state interest" standard. . . .

The "unduly burdensome" standard is particularly appropriate in the abortion context because of the *nature* and *scope* of the right that is involved. The privacy right involved in the abortion context "cannot be said to be absolute." *Roe.* "*Roe* did not declare an unqualified 'constitutional right to an abortion.' " *Maher.* Rather, the *Roe* right is intended to protect against state action "drastically limiting the availability and safety of the desired service," against the imposition of an "absolute obstacle" on the abortion decision, *Danforth* or against "official interference" and "coercive restraint" imposed on the abortion decision, *Harris* (White, J., concurring). That a state regulation may "inhibit" abortions to some degree does not require that we find that the regulation is invalid. See H. L. v. Matheson (1981). . . .

In determining whether the State imposes an "undue burden," we must keep in mind that when we are concerned with extremely sensitive issues, such as the one involved here, "the appropriate forum for their resolution in a democracy is the legislature. We should not forget that 'legislatures are

ultimate guardians of the liberties and welfare of the people in quite as great a degree as the courts.' Missouri, K. & T. R. Co. v. May (1904) (Holmes, J.)."
Maher. This does not mean that in determining whether a regulation imposes an "undue burden" on the *Roe* right that we defer to the judgments made by state legislatures. "The point is, rather, that when we face a complex problem with many hard questions and few easy answers we do well to pay careful attention to how the other branches of Government have addressed the same problem." Columbia Broadcasting System, Inc. v. Democratic National Committee (1973).

We must always be mindful that "[t]he Constitution does not compel a state to fine-tune its statutes so as to encourage or facilitate abortions. To the contrary, state action 'encouraging childbirth except in the most urgent circumstances' is 'rationally related to the legitimate government objective of protecting potential life.'" *Harris.* . . .

[Justice O'Connor then examined each of the regulations and found all were rationally related to the compelling governmental interest in preserving potential human life and did not impose "an undue burden" on the right to abortion.]

Editors' Note: The vote in Roe *was 7-2; in* Akron, *6-3. In 1986 Thornburgh v. American College of Obst. & Gyn., 90 L. Ed. 2d 779, again questioned the viability of* Roe. *This time the vote to adhere to* Roe *was 5-4, with Chief Justice Burger, in one of his last opinions, joining the three dissenters from* Akron. *(Burger had not been a strong supporter of the initial decision. In fact, at least one of the justices had recorded in his notes of the conference on* Roe *that the Chief Justice had voted to sustain the state regulation.) Burger's replacement as chief justice was William H. Rehnquist, who had been a perennial dissenter in abortion cases; Rehnquist's replacement as associate justice was Antonin Scalia, who was widely believed to favor reversing* Roe.

～ Case 6.3 ～

Justice **WHITE**: "The Court is most vulnerable and comes nearest to illegitimacy when it deals with judge-made constitutional law having little or no cognizable roots in the language or design of the Constitution."

Justice **BLACKMUN**: "[T]his case is about 'the most comprehensive of rights and the right most valued by civilized men,' namely, 'the right to be let alone.' "

Bowers v. Hardwick
__ U.S. __, __ S. Ct. __, 92 L. Ed. 2d 140 (1986)

In 1982 police charged Michael Hardwick with violating sec. 16-6-2 of the Georgia Code by committing sodomy° *in the privacy of his own home with another consenting, male adult. The local district attorney decided not to prosecute. Hardwick then sued in a federal district court, asking for an injunction forbidding Georgia to enforce the statute. Claiming to be a practicing homosexual, he alleged that sec. 16-6-2 threatened him with immediate injury to his constitutional rights to privacy and intimate association. The district court dismissed the suit, but the Court of Appeals for the 11th Circuit reversed. Georgia then sought and obtained review from the U.S. Supreme Court.*

Justice **WHITE** delivered the opinion of the Court. . . .

This case does not require a judgment on whether laws against sodomy between consenting adults in general, or between homosexuals in particular, are wise or desirable. It raises no question about the right or propriety of state legislative decisions to repeal their laws that criminalize homosexual sodomy, or of state court decisions invalidating those laws on state constitutional grounds. The issue presented is whether the Federal Constitution confers a fundamental right upon homosexuals to engage in sodomy and hence invalidates the laws of the many States that still make such conduct illegal and have done so for a very long time. The case also calls for some judgment about the limits of the Court's role in carrying out its constitutional mandate.

We first register our disagreement with the Court of Appeals and with respondent that the Court's prior cases have construed the Constitution to confer a right of privacy that extends to homosexual sodomy and for all

---

° *Sec. 16-6-2 defines sodomy as engagement in "any sexual act involving the sex organs of one person and the mouth or anus of another. . . ."—Eds.*

intents and purposes have decided this case. The reach of this line of cases was sketched in Carey v. Population Services International (1977). Pierce v. Society of Sisters (1925) and Meyer v. Nebraska (1923) were described as dealing with child rearing and education; Prince v. Massachusetts (1944) with family relationships; Skinner v. Oklahoma (1942) with procreation; Loving v. Virginia (1967) with marriage; Griswold v. Connecticut (1965) and Eisenstadt v. Baird (1972) with contraception; and Roe v. Wade (1973) with abortion. The latter three cases were interpreted as construing the Due Process Clause of the Fourteenth Amendment to confer a fundamental individual right to decide whether or not to beget or bear a child.

Accepting the decisions in these cases . . . we think it evident that none of the rights announced in those cases bears any resemblance to the claimed constitutional right of homosexuals to engage in acts of sodomy that is asserted in this case. No connection between family, marriage, or procreation on the one hand and homosexual activity on the other has been demonstrated, either by the Court of Appeals or by respondent. Moreover, any claim that these cases nevertheless stand for the proposition that any kind of private sexual conduct between consenting adults is constitutionally insulated from state proscription is unsupportable. Indeed, the Court's opinion in *Carey* twice asserted that the privacy right, which the *Griswold* line of cases found to be one of the protections provided by the Due Process Clause, did not reach so far.

Precedent aside, however, respondent would have us announce . . . a fundamental right to engage in homosexual sodomy. This we are quite unwilling to do. It is true that despite the language of the Due Process Clauses of the Fifth and Fourteenth Amendments, which appears to focus only on the processes by which life, liberty, or property is taken, the cases are legion in which those Clauses have been interpreted to have substantive content. . . . Among such cases are those recognizing rights that have little or no textual support in the constitutional language. *Myers, Prince,* and *Pierce* fall in this category, as do the privacy cases from *Griswold* to *Carey.*

Striving to assure itself and the public that announcing rights not readily identifiable in the Constitution's text involves much more than the imposition of the Justices' own choice of values on the States and the Federal Government, the Court has sought to identify the nature of the rights qualifying for heightened judicial protection. In Palko v. Connecticut (1937) it was said that this category includes those fundamental liberties that are "implicit in the concept of ordered liberty," such that "neither liberty nor justice would exist if [they] were sacrificed." A different description of fundamental liberties appeared in Moore v. East Cleveland (1977) (opinion of Powell, J.), where they are characterized as those liberties that are "deeply rooted in this Nation's history and tradition."

It is obvious to us that neither of these formulations would extend a fundamental right to homosexuals to engage in acts of consensual sodomy.

Proscriptions against that conduct have ancient roots. . . . Sodomy was a criminal offense at common law and was forbidden by the laws of the original thirteen States when they ratified the Bill of Rights. In 1868, when the Fourteenth Amendment was ratified, all but 5 of the 37 States in the Union had criminal sodomy laws. In fact, until 1961, all 50 States outlawed sodomy, and today, 24 States and the District of Columbia continue to provide criminal penalties for sodomy performed in private and between consenting adults. Against this background, to claim that a right to engage in such conduct is "deeply rooted in this Nation's history and tradition" or "implicit in the concept of ordered liberty" is, at best, facetious.

Nor are we inclined to take a more expansive view of our authority to discover new fundamental rights imbedded in the Due Process Clause. The Court is most vulnerable and comes nearest to illegitimacy when it deals with judge-made constitutional law having little or no cognizable roots in the language or design of the Constitution. That this is so was painfully demonstrated by the face-off between the Executive and the Court in the 1930's, which resulted in the repudiation of much of the substantive gloss that the Court had placed on the Due Process Clause of the Fifth and Fourteenth Amendments. There should be, therefore, great resistance to expand the substantive reach of those Clauses, particularly if it requires redefining the category of rights deemed to be fundamental. Otherwise, the Judiciary necessarily takes to itself further authority to govern the country without express constitutional authority. . . .

Respondent, however, asserts that the result should be different where the homosexual conduct occurs in the privacy of the home. He relies on Stanley v. Georgia (1969), where the Court held that the First Amendment prevents conviction for possessing and reading obscene material in the privacy of his home: "If the First Amendment means anything, it means that a State has no business telling a man, sitting alone in his house, what books he may read or what films he may watch."

Stanley did protect conduct that would not have been protected outside the home, and it partially prevented the enforcement of state obscenity laws; but the decision was firmly grounded in the First Amendment. The right pressed upon us here has no similar support in the text of the Constitution, and it does not qualify for recognition under the prevailing principles for construing the Fourteenth Amendment. Its limits are also difficult to discern. Plainly enough, otherwise illegal conduct is not always immunized whenever it occurs in the home. Victimless crimes, such as the possession and use of illegal drugs do not escape the law where they are committed at home. *Stanley* itself recognized that its holding offered no protection for the possession in the home of drugs, firearms, or stolen goods. And if respondent's submission is limited to the voluntary sexual conduct between consenting adults, it would be difficult, except by fiat, to limit the claimed right to homosexual conduct while leaving exposed to prosecution adultery, incest, and other sexual crimes even though they are committed in the home. We are unwilling to start down that road.

Even if the conduct at issue here is not a fundamental right, respondent asserts that there must be a rational basis for the law and that there is none in this case other than the presumed belief of a majority of the electorate in Georgia that homosexual sodomy is immoral and unacceptable. This is said to be an inadequate rationale to support the law. The law, however, is constantly based on notions of morality, and if all laws representing essentially moral choices are to be invalidated under the Due Process Clause, the courts will be very busy indeed. Even respondent makes no such claim, but insists that majority sentiments about the morality of homosexuality should be declared inadequate. We do not agree, and are unpersuaded that the sodomy laws of some 25 States should be invalidated on this basis.°

Accordingly, the judgment of the Court of Appeals is

Reversed.

Chief Justice **BURGER,** concurring. . . .

Justice **POWELL,** concurring. . . .

I join the opinion of the Court. I agree with the Court that there is no fundamental right—*i.e.,* no substantive right under the Due Process Clause—such as that claimed by respondent. . . . This is not to suggest, however, that respondent may not be protected by the Eighth Amendment of the Constitution. The Georgia statute at issue in this case authorizes a court to imprison a person for up to 20 years for a single private, consensual act of sodomy. In my view, a prison sentence for such conduct— certainly a sentence of long duration—would create a serious Eighth Amendment issue. . . .

In this case, however, respondent has not been tried, much less convicted and sentenced. Moreover, respondent has not raised the Eighth Amendment issue below. For these reasons this constitutional argument is not before us.

Justice **BLACKMUN,** with whom Justice **BRENNAN,** Justice **MARSHALL,** and Justice **STEVENS** join, dissenting.

This case is no more about "a fundamental right to engage in homosexual sodomy," as the Court purports to declare, than Stanley v. Georgia (1969) was about a fundamental right to watch obscene movies, or Katz v. United

---

° Respondent [Hardwick] does not defend the judgment below [the decision of the Court of Appeals for the 11th Circuit] based on the Ninth Amendment, the Equal Protection Clause or the Eighth Amendment. [Footnote by the Court.]

States (1967) was about a fundamental right to place interstate bets from a telephone booth. Rather, this case is about "the most comprehensive of rights and the right most valued by civilized men," namely, "the right to be let alone." Olmstead v. United States (1928) (Brandeis, J., dissenting.)

The statute at issue denies individuals the right to decide for themselves whether to engage in particular forms of private, consensual sexual activity. The Court concludes that § 16-6-2 is valid essentially because "the laws of . . . many States . . . still make such conduct illegal and have done so for a very long time." But the fact that the moral judgments expressed by statutes like § 16-6-2 may be "natural and familiar . . . ought not to conclude our judgment upon the question whether statutes embodying them conflict with the Constitution of the United States." Roe v. Wade (1973), quoting Lochner v. New York (1905) (Holmes, J., dissenting). Like Justice Holmes, I believe that "[i]t is revolting to have no better reason for a rule of law than that so it was laid down in the time of Henry IV. It is still more revolting if the grounds upon which it was laid down have vanished long since, and the rule simply persists from blind imitation of the past." I believe we must analyze respondent's claim in the light of the values that underlie the constitutional right to privacy. If that right means anything, it means that, before Georgia can prosecute its citizens for making choices about the most intimate aspects of their lives, it must do more than assert that the choice they have made is an " 'abominable crime not fit to be named among Christians.' "

I

In its haste . . . the Court relegates the actual statute being challenged to a footnote and ignores the procedural posture of the case before it. A fair reading of the statute and of the complaint clearly reveals that the majority has distorted the question this case presents.

First, the Court's almost obsessive focus on homosexual activity is particularly hard to justify in light of the broad language Georgia has used. Unlike the Court, the Georgia Legislature has not proceeded on the assumption that homosexuals are so different from other citizens that their lives may be controlled in a way that would not be tolerated if it limited the choices of those other citizens. Rather, Georgia has provided that "[a] person commits the offense of sodomy when he performs or submits to any sexual act involving the sex organs of one person and the mouth or anus of another." The sex or status of the persons who engage in the act is irrelevant as a matter of state law. In fact, to the extent I can discern a legislative purpose for Georgia's 1968 enactment of § 16-6-2, that purpose seems to have been to broaden the coverage of the law to reach heterosexual as well as homosexual activity. I therefore see no basis for the Court's decision to treat this case as an "as applied" challenge to § 16-6-2 . . . solely on the grounds that it prohibits homosexual activity. Michael Hardwick's . . .

claim that § 16-6-2 involves an unconstitutional intrusion into his privacy and his right of intimate association does not depend in any way on his sexual orientation.

Second, I disagree with the Court's refusal to consider whether § 16-6-2 runs afoul of the Eighth or Ninth Amendments or the Equal Protection Clause of the Fourteenth Amendment. Respondent's complaint expressly invoked the Ninth Amendment, and he relied heavily before this Court on Griswold v. Connecticut (1965), which identifies that Amendment as one of the specific constitutional provisions giving "life and substance" to our understanding of privacy.... The Court's cramped reading of the issue before it makes for a short opinion, but it does little to make for a persuasive one.

II

"Our cases long have recognized that the Constitution embodies a promise that a certain private sphere of individual liberty will be kept largely beyond the reach of government." Thornburgh v. American Coll. of Obst. & Gyn. (1986). In construing the right to privacy, the Court has proceeded along two somewhat distinct, albeit complementary, lines. First, it has recognized a privacy interest with reference to certain *decisions* that are properly for the individual to make. *E.g.,* Roe v. Wade (1973); Pierce v. Society of Sisters (1925). Second, it has recognized a privacy interest with reference to certain *places* without regard for the particular activities in which the individuals who occupy them are engaged. *E.g.,* United States v. Karo (1984); Payton v. New York (1980); Rios v. United States (1960). The case before us implicates both the decisional and the spatial aspects of the right to privacy.

A

The court concludes today that none of our prior cases dealing with various decisions that individuals are entitled to make free of governmental interference "bears any resemblance to the claimed constitutional right of homosexuals to engage in acts of sodomy that is asserted in this case." While it is true that these cases may be characterized by their connection to protection of the family the Court's conclusion that they extend no further than this boundary ignores the warning in Moore v. East Cleveland (1977) (plurality opinion), against "clos[ing] our eyes to the basic reasons why certain rights associated with the family have been accorded shelter under the Fourteenth Amendment's Due Process Clause." We protect those rights not because they contribute, in some direct and material way, to the general public welfare, but because they form so central a part of an individual's life. "[T]he concept of privacy embodies the 'moral fact that a person belongs to himself and not others nor to society as a whole.'" Thornburgh v. American Coll. of Obst. & Gyn. (Stevens, J., concurring). And so we protect the decision whether to marry precisely because marriage "is an association that promotes a way of life, not causes; a harmony in living, not political faiths; a bilateral loyalty, not commercial or social projects." Griswold v. Connecticut. We protect the decision whether to have a child because parenthood alters so dramatically an individual's self-definition, not because of demographic considerations or the Bible's command to be fruitful and multiply. And we protect the family because it contributes so powerfully to the happiness of individuals, not because of a preference for stereotypical households. The Court recognized in *Roberts* that the "ability independently to define one's identity that is central to any concept of liberty" cannot truly be exercised in a vacuum; we all depend on the "emotional enrichment of close ties with others."

Only the most willful blindness could obscure the fact that sexual intimacy is "a sensitive, key relationship of human existence, central to family life, community welfare, and the development of human personality," Paris Adult Theater I v. Slayton (1973). The fact that individuals define themselves in a significant way through their intimate sexual relationships with others suggests, in a Nation as diverse as ours, that there may be many "right" ways of conducting those relationships, and that much of the richness of a relationship will come from the freedom an individual has to *choose* the form and nature of these intensely personal bonds.

In a variety of circumstances we have recognized that a necessary corollary of giving individuals freedom to choose how to conduct their lives is acceptance of the fact that different individuals will make different choices. . . . The Court claims that its decision today merely refuses to recognize a fundamental right to engage in homosexual sodomy; what the Court really has refused to recognize is the fundamental interest all individuals have in controlling the nature of their intimate associations with others.

B

The behavior for which Hardwick faces prosecution occurred in his own home, a place to which the Fourth Amendment attaches special significance. The Court's treatment of this aspect of the case is symptomatic of its overall refusal to consider the broad principles that have informed our treatment of privacy in specific cases. Just as the right to privacy is more than the mere aggregation of a number of entitlements to engage in specific behavior, so too, protecting the physical integrity of the home is more than merely a means of protecting specific activities that often take place there. Even when our understanding of the contours of the right to privacy depends on "reference to a 'place,'" "the essence of a Fourth Amendment violation is 'not the breaking of [a person's] doors, and the rummaging of his drawers,' but rather is 'the invasion of his indefeasible right of personal security, personal liberty and private property.' " California v. Ciraolo (1986) (Powell, J., dissenting), quoting Boyd v. United States (1886).

The Court's interpretation of the pivotal case of Stanley v. Georgia (1969) is entirely unconvincing. . . . According to the majority here, *Stanley* relied entirely on the First Amendment, and thus, it is claimed, sheds no light on cases not involving printed materials. But that is not what *Stanley* said. Rather, the *Stanley* Court anchored its holding in the Fourth Amendment's special protection for the individual in his home:

> " 'The makers of our Constitution undertook to secure conditions favorable to the pursuit of happiness. They recognized the significance of man's spiritual nature, of his feelings and of his intellect. They knew that only a part of the pain, pleasure and satisfactions of life are to be found in material things. They sought to protect Americans in their beliefs, their thoughts, their emotions and their sensations. . . .
>
> These are the rights that appellant is asserting in the case before us. He is asserting the right to read or observe what he pleases—the right to satisfy his intellectual and emotional needs in the privacy of his own home." Quoting Olmstead v. United States (Brandeis, J., dissenting).

The central place that *Stanley* gives Justice Brandeis' dissent in *Olmstead*, a case raising *no* First Amendment claim, shows that *Stanley* rested as much on the Court's understanding of the Fourth Amendment as it did on the First. Indeed, in *Paris Adult Theatre I* (1973) the Court suggested that reliance on the Fourth Amendment not only supported the Court's outcome in *Stanley* but actually was *necessary* to it: "If obscene material unprotected by the First Amendment in itself carried with it a 'penumbra' of constitutionally protected privacy, this Court would not have found it necessary to decide *Stanley* on the narrow basis of the 'privacy of the home,' which was hardly more than a reaffirmation that 'a man's home is his castle.' " "The right of the people to be secure in their . . . houses," expressly guaranteed by the Fourth Amendment, is perhaps the most "textual" of the various constitutional provisions that inform our understanding of the right to privacy, and thus I cannot agree with the Court's statement that "[t]he right pressed upon us here has no . . . support in the text of the Constitution." Indeed, the right of an individual to conduct intimate relationships in the intimacy of his or her own home seems to me to be the heart of the Constitution's protection of privacy. . . .

III . . .

The core of petitioner's defense of § 16-6-2 . . . is that respondent and others who engage in the conduct prohibited by § 16-6-2 interfere with Georgia's exercise of the " 'right of the Nation and of the States to maintain a decent society,' " *Paris Adult Theater I*, quoting Jacobellis v. Ohio (1964) (Warren, C. J., dissenting). Essentially, petitioner argues, and the Court agrees, that the fact that the acts described in § 16-6-2 "for hundreds of years, if not thousands, have been uniformly condemned as immoral" is a sufficient reason to permit a State to ban them today.

I cannot agree that either the length of time a majority has held its convictions or the passions with which it defends them can withdraw legislation from this Court's scrutiny. As Justice Jackson wrote so eloquently for the Court in West Virginia Board of Education v. Barnette (1943), "we apply the limitations of the Constitution with no fear that freedom to be intellectually and spiritually diverse or even contrary will disintegrate the social organization. . . . [F]reedom to differ is not limited to things that do not matter much. That would be a mere shadow of freedom. The test of its substance is the right to differ as to things that touch the heart of the existing order." It is precisely because the issue raised by this case touches the heart of what makes individuals what they are that we should be especially sensitive to the rights of those whose choices upset the majority.

The assertion that "traditional Judeo-Christian values proscribe" the conduct involved, cannot provide an adequate justification for § 16-6-2. That certain, but by no means all, religious groups condemn the behavior at issue gives the State no license to impose their judgments on the entire citizenry. The legitimacy of secular legislation depends instead on whether the State can advance some justification for its law beyond its conformity to religious doctrine. See, *e.g.*, McGowan v. Maryland (1961); Stone v. Graham (1980). Thus, far from buttressing his case, petitioner's invocation of Leviticus, Romans, St. Thomas Aquinas, and sodomy's heretical status during the Middle Ages undermines his suggestion that § 16-6-2 represents a legitimate use of secular coercive power. A State can no more punish private behavior because of religious intolerance than it can punish such behavior because of racial animus. "The Constitution cannot control such prejudices, but neither can it tolerate them. Private biases may be outside the reach of the law, but the law cannot, directly or indirectly, give them effect." Palmore v. Sidoti (1984). No matter how uncomfortable a certain group may make the majority of this Court, we have held that "[m]ere public intolerance or animosity cannot constitutionally justify the deprivation of a person's physical liberty." O'Connor v. Donaldson (1975).

Nor can § 16-6-2 be justified as a "morally neutral" exercise of Georgia's power to "protect the public environment." Certainly, some private behavior can affect the fabric of society as a whole. Reasonable people may differ about whether particular sexual acts are moral or immoral, but "we have ample evidence for believing that people will not abandon morality, will not think any better of murder, cruelty and dishonesty, merely because some private sexual practice which they abominate is not punished by the law." H. L. A. Hart, *Immorality and Treason*. Petitioner and the Court fail to see the difference between laws that protect public sensibilities and those that enforce private morality. Statutes banning public sexual activity are entirely consistent with protecting the individual's liberty interest in decisions concerning sexual relations: the same recognition that those decisions are intensely private which justifies protecting them from governmental interference can justify protecting individuals from unwilling exposure to the sexual activities of others. But the mere fact that intimate behavior may be punished when it takes place in public cannot dictate how States can regulate intimate behavior that occurs in intimate places. See *Paris Adult Theatre I* ("marital intercourse on a street corner or a theater stage" can be forbidden despite the constitutional protection identified in *Griswold*).

This case involves no real interference with the rights of others, for the mere knowledge that other individuals do not adhere to one's value system cannot be a legally cognizable interest, cf. Diamond v. Charles (1986), let alone an interest that can justify invading the houses, hearts, and minds of citizens who choose to live their lives differently.

IV

It took but three years for the Court to see the error in its analysis in Minersville School District v. Gobitis (1940) and to recognize that the threat to national cohesion posed by a refusal to salute the flag was vastly outweighed by the threat to those same values posed by compelling such a salute. See West Virginia Board of Education v. Barnette (1943). I can only hope that here, too, the Court soon will reconsider its analysis and conclude that depriving individuals of the right to choose for themselves how to conduct their intimate relationships poses a far greater threat to the values most deeply rooted in our Nation's history than tolerance of nonconformity could ever do. Because I think the Court today betrays those values, I dissent.

Justice **STEVENS**, with whom Justice **BRENNAN** and Justice **MARSHALL** join, dissenting. . . .

Because the Georgia statute expresses the traditional view that sodomy is an immoral kind of conduct regardless of the identity of the persons who engage in it, I believe that a proper analysis of its constitutionality requires consideration of two questions: First, may a State totally prohibit the described conduct by means of a neutral law applying without exception to all persons subject to its jurisdiction? If not, may the State save the statute by announcing that it will only enforce the law against homosexuals? The two questions merit separate discussion.

I

Our prior cases make two propositions abundantly clear. First, the fact that the governing majority in a State has traditionally viewed a particular practice as immoral is not a sufficient reason for upholding a law prohibiting the practice; neither history nor tradition could save a law prohibiting miscegenation from constitutional attack. Second, individual decisions by married persons, concerning the intimacies of their physical relationship, even when not intended to produce offspring, are a form of "liberty" protected by the Due Process Clause of the Fourteenth Amendment. Griswold v. Connecticut (1965). Moreover, this protection extends to intimate choices by unmarried as well as married persons. Carey v. Population Services International (1977); Eisenstadt v. Baird (1972).

In consideration of claims of this kind, the Court has emphasized the individual interest in privacy, but its decisions have actually been animated by an even more fundamental concern. As I wrote some years ago:

> "These cases do not deal with the individual's interest in protection from unwarranted public attention, comment, or exploitation. They deal, rather, with the individual's right to make certain unusually important decisions that will affect his own, or his family's, destiny. The Court has referred to such decisions as implicating 'basic values,' as being 'fundamental,' and as being dignified by history and tradition. The character of the Court's language in these cases brings to mind the origins of the American heritage of freedom—the abiding interest in individual liberty that makes certain state intrusions on the citizen's right to decide how he will live his own life intolerable. Guided by history, our tradition of respect for the dignity of individual choice in matters of conscience and the restraints implicit in the federal system, federal judges have accepted the responsibility for recognition and protection of these rights in appropriate cases." Fitzgerald v. Porter Memorial Hospital (CA 7th 1975), cert. den. (1976).

Society has every right to encourage its individual members to follow particular traditions in expressing affection for one another and in gratifying their personal desires. It, of course, may prohibit an individual from imposing his will on another to satisfy his own selfish interests. It also may prevent an individual from interfering with, or violating, a legally sanctioned and protected relationship, such as marriage. And it may explain the relative advantages and disadvantages of different forms of intimate expression. But when individual married couples are isolated from observation by others, the way in which they voluntarily choose to conduct their intimate relations is a matter for them—not the State—to decide. The essential "liberty" that animated the development of the law in cases like *Griswold, Eisenstadt,* and *Carey* surely embraces the right to engage in nonreproductive, sexual conduct that others may consider offensive or immoral.

Paradoxical as it may seem, our prior cases thus establish that a State may not prohibit sodomy within "the sacred precincts of marital bedrooms," *Griswold,* or, indeed, between unmarried heterosexual adults. *Eisenstadt.* In all events, it is perfectly clear that the State of Georgia may not totally prohibit the conduct proscribed by § 16-6-2.

II

If the Georgia statute cannot be enforced as it is written—if the conduct it seeks to prohibit is a protected form of liberty for the vast majority of Georgia's citizens—the State must assume the burden of justifying a selective application of its law. Either the persons to whom Georgia seeks to apply its statute do not have the same interest in "liberty" that others have, or there must be a reason why the State may be permitted to apply a generally applicable law to certain persons that it does not apply to others.

The first possibility is plainly unacceptable. Although the meaning of the principle that "all men are created equal" is not always clear, it surely must mean that every free citizen has the same interest in "liberty" that the members of the majority share. From the standpoint of the individual, the homosexual and the heterosexual have the same interest in deciding how he will live his own life. . . .

The second possibility is similarly unacceptable. A policy of selective application must be supported by a neutral and legitimate interest— something more substantial than a habitual dislike for, or ignorance about, the disfavored group. Neither the State nor the Court has identified any such interest in this case. . . .

Nor, indeed, does the Georgia prosecutor even believe that all homosexuals who violate this statute should be punished. This conclusion is evident from the fact that the respondent in this very case has formally acknowledged in his complaint and in court that he was engaged, and intends to continue to engage, in the prohibited conduct, yet the State has elected not to process criminal charges against him. . . .

7. EQUAL PROTECTION

The Declaration of Independence asserts that "All men are created equal. . . ." The Constitution, as originally adopted and amended by the Bill of Rights, contains no such proclamation, though one might argue that the notion of equality was so obvious to the framers that they never thought to spell it out except indirectly as in forbidding titles of nobility. A more plausible reason for omission was the institution of slavery.

The Thirteenth Amendment opened the way for a constitutional declaration of equality. And the opening section of the Fourteenth Amendment forbids any state to "deny to any person within its jurisdiction the equal protection of the laws." It was reasonable to predict, as the Supreme Court did in its initial interpretation of the amendment,[1] that this clause would protect the civil rights of black people. For sixty years, however, that promise was empty. Reconstruction ended in 1877 and by the early 1890s southern states had enacted laws segregating blacks by race and effectively barring them from voting. The Supreme Court found no constitutional problems with the doctrine of "separate but equal," as Plessy v. Ferguson (1896), the first case in this chapter, illustrates. Moreover, for a time the justices pretended that voting restrictions did not have racial implications.[2]

By the 1930s, however, the justices had grown more sensitive and began trying to bring political practice into line with the Constitution's plain command. In case after case, the Court struck down every challenged state requirement of segregation but without overturning the doctrine of "separate but equal." Finally, in 1954, Brown v. Board of Education held that doctrine had no place in public education, and later decisions completely overruled Plessy. Barely noticed at the time, a companion case to Brown ruled that the due process clause of the Fifth Amendment required the federal government to accord some measure of equal protection;[3] and, once again, later decisions extended that holding to restrict the federal government almost as if there were an equal protection clause in the Bill of Rights.

The school decisions provoked what has been called "a generation of litigation," one liberally sprinkled with violence. The fight for equal

*rights for black people has by no means ended, but passage of the Civil
Rights Act of 1964 put the full force of Congress and the executive
department behind the Constitution's jurisprudence of equality. The
Court, as expected, sustained this legislation. (See Heart of Atlanta
Motel v. United States [1964], Case 7.3.)*

*Race has posed the most dramatic but hardly the only challenge to
equality in America. There is a deep difficulty underlying all questions
of equal treatment. On the one hand, Americans want government to
govern evenhandedly; on the other hand, almost every important piece
of legislation must classify, it must treat people differently. A draft law
that did not exempt physically handicapped people or a tax law that
demanded the same sum of money from the poor as from the rich would
be unjust as well as inefficient.*

*Thus the first great difficulty is to distinguish legitimate from
illegitimate classifications. Over time, the justices created a two-tiered
test for equal protection and later a multitiered test. The two tiers of the
first test are called "rational basis" and "strict scrutiny." The second, or
upper-level, test comes into play where government uses a "suspect
classification" or impinges on a "fundamental right." What classifications
are "suspect" is not yet set. Certainly race and ethnicity are, probably
religion, and, so the Court has said—though the record is less clear—
alienage. The justices have been no more definite about fundamental
rights, as Chapter 6 pointed out.*

*If either a suspect classification or a fundamental right is present
in a case, the Court applies strict scrutiny: It puts the burden of proof on
the government to show (a) that the law serves a "compelling governmental interest" and (b) that the classification or the infringement of
the fundamental right is "necessary" to attain that interest and/or is so
"closely tailored" to achieve that interest as to do the least harm possible.
Needless to say, few statutes survive the strict scrutiny of this upper-
level test.*

*If neither of these two factors is involved, the Court applies the
lower tier of the test, called "rational basis." Here the burden is on the
person attacking the law; all government needs to show is a rational
relationship between the statute and a governmental interest. Few
challenges have succeeded. In 1982, however, the justices gave hints of a
tougher policy. In reviewing a Texas statute denying children of illegal
aliens the right to attend public schools, the Court looked for hard
evidence of a rational connection between the denial and some valid
governmental interest and, finding none, invalidated the law.*[4]

*What about legislative classifications other than race, ethnicity, or
alienage? For classifications by sex, at least, the Court has created a
middle tier of tests. To pass constitutional muster, a statute that
classifies according to sex must serve an "important" governmental*

interest and be "substantially" related to achievement of that objective. (See Mississippi University for Women v. Hogan [1982], Case 7.5.)

Justice Thurgood Marshall has argued that the Court has been— and should be—looking at both classifications and rights as falling along wide spectrums rather than clustering at two or three points, and that the degree of scrutiny judges apply should vary accordingly (see his dissent in San Antonio School District v. Rodriguez [1973], Case 7.4). Justice John Paul Stevens and Chief Justice William H. Rehnquist argue, on the contrary, that because there is only one equal protection clause there should be only one test. But Stevens and Rehnquist are far apart on what that test would look like and how it would operate.

One can charitably describe the doctrines surrounding equal protection as a muddle. But it is crucial to understand that muddle, for the legitimacy of much public policy regarding blacks, Indians, Hispanic-Americans, Asian-Americans, women, and even white males is at stake.

Affirmative action focuses attention on the difficulties here. (See Fullilove v. Klutznick [1980], Case 7.6.) How can government move to undo the damage centuries of slavery before the Civil War and a century of discrimination since have wreaked? Was Justice Harry Blackmun correct in claiming that "to get beyond racism, we must first take account of race"?[5] Or was Antonin Scalia correct when he wrote, before he became a justice, that for government to order affirmative action is to apply the disease of racism as the cure for racism?[6]

This debate offers a glimpse of the importance of the muddle of tiered tests. If race is taboo as a classification, then governmentally mandated affirmative action for blacks is clearly unconstitutional. But if race is a legitimate classification where a compelling *governmental interest exists and the classification is* necessary *or* closely tailored to *achieve that compelling interest, then affirmative action might in some—but not all—circumstances be constitutional.*

---

1. *Slaughter-House Cases*, 16 Wall. 36 (1873).
2. See esp. *Giles v. Harris*, 189 U.S. 475 (1903).
3. *Bolling v. Sharpe*, 347 U.S. 497 (1954).
4. *Plyler v. Doe*, 457 U.S. 202 (1982).
5. Separate opinion in *University of California v. Bakke*, 438 U.S. 265 (1978).
6. *"The Disease as Cure,"* Washington University Law Quarterly (1979), 147.

~ Case 7.1 ~

Justice **BROWN**: "We consider the underlying fallacy of plaintiff's argument to consist in the assumption that the enforced separation of the two races stamps the colored race with a badge of inferiority. If this be so, it is not by reason of anything found in the act, but solely because the colored race chooses to put that construction on it."

Justice **HARLAN**: "Our Constitution is color-blind and neither knows nor tolerates classes among citizens."

Plessy v. Ferguson
163 U.S. 537, 16 S. Ct. 1138, 41 L. Ed. 256 (1896)

In the closing ten to fifteen years of the nineteenth century, the Southern populist movement became a party of political protest and reform. After initial electoral successes, it suffered a series of disastrous defeats. Populists tended to blame their rout on the conservatives' practice of paying poor, illiterate blacks to vote against reform. There was considerable truth to the charge. (In those days, there were few, if any, voter registration laws in the South; voters often expressed their choices orally rather than by secret, written ballot; and where written ballots were used, each party printed its own. Thus there was no way for a voter to support some candidates from one party and others from a second. Moreover, by giving a potential voter a ballot and insuring that he did not take one from the opposing party, a local politico could make certain that bribed voters stayed "honest," just as a boss could, where oral voting was allowed, listen to a voter's choice.)

After 1890 both white reformers and white conservatives realized that both sides could bribe black voters and that lively competition for their ballots might dramatically increase the political power of blacks. Further, southern conservatives believed that blacks were the more natural allies of the reformers, and the reformers—who had campaigned on the same belief—were deeply angered by what they considered a betrayal by blacks. Conservative fear and reformist anger produced during the 1890s a series of laws disenfranchising blacks and segregating them from the larger, more affluent white society.

A Louisiana statute of this kind—Jim Crow laws they were called—forbade whites and blacks to travel together in the same railroad car. Homer Plessy, a black, was arrested and convicted for violating that law. After the supreme court of Louisiana upheld his conviction, he sought review in the U.S. Supreme Court.

Mr. Justice **BROWN** delivered the opinion of the Court. . . .

The object of the [Fourteenth] amendment was undoubtedly to enforce the absolute equality of the two races before the law, but in the nature of things it could not have been intended to abolish distinctions based on color, or to enforce social, as distinguished from political equality, or a commingling of the two races upon terms unsatisfactory to either. Laws permitting, and even requiring, that separation in places where they are liable to be brought into contact do not necessarily imply the inferiority of either race to the other, and have been generally, if not universally, recognized as within the competency of the state legislatures in the exercise of their police power. The most common instance of this is connected with the establishment of separate schools for white and colored children, which has been held to be a valid exercise of the legislative power even by courts of States where the political rights of the colored race have been longest and most earnestly enforced.°

The distinction between laws interfering with the political equality of the negro and those requiring the separation of the two races in schools, theaters, and railway carriages has been frequently drawn by this Court. [The opinion then cites Strauder v. West Virginia as an example of the "political equality" to which blacks were entitled.]

It is claimed by the plaintiff in error that, in any mixed community, the reputation of belonging to the dominant race, in this instance the white race, is property, in the same sense that a right of action, or of inheritance, is property. Conceding this to be so, for the purposes of this case, we are unable to see how this statute deprives him of, or in any way affects his right to, such property. If he be a white man and assigned to a colored coach, he may have his action for damages against the company for being deprived of his so-called property. Upon the other hand, if he be a colored man and be so assigned, he has been deprived of no property, since he is not lawfully entitled to the reputation of being a white man. . . .

So far, then, as a conflict with the Fourteenth Amendment is concerned, the case reduces itself to the question whether the statute of Louisiana is a reasonable regulation, and with respect to this there must necessarily be a large discretion on the part of the legislature. In determining the question of reasonableness it is at liberty to act with reference to the established usages, customs and traditions of the people, and with a view to the promotion of their comfort, and the preservation of the public peace and good order. Gauged by this standard we cannot say that a law which authorizes or even requires the separation of the two races in public conveyances is unreasonable, or more obnoxious to the Fourteenth Amendment than the acts of

---

° *The Court is referring to a state case concerning racial segregation in the schools of Boston but neglects to note that the decision was quickly overturned by an act of the city government and that the judicial decision had predated the Fourteenth Amendment by almost twenty years.—Eds.*

Congress requiring separate schools for colored children in the District of Columbia, the constitutionality of which does not seem to have been questioned, or the corresponding acts of state legislatures.

We consider the underlying fallacy of the plaintiff's argument to consist in the assumption that the enforced separation of the two races stamps the colored race with a badge of inferiority. If this be so, it is not by reason of anything found in the act, but solely because the colored race chooses to put that construction upon it. The argument necessarily assumes that if, as has been more than once the case, and is not unlikely to be so again, the colored race should become the dominant power in the state legislature, and should enact a law in precisely similar terms, it would thereby relegate the white race to an inferior position. We imagine that the white race, at least, would not acquiesce in this assumption. The argument also assumes that social prejudices may be overcome by legislation. . . . Legislation is powerless to eradicate racial instincts or to abolish distinctions based upon physical differences, and the attempt to do so can only result in accentuating the difficulties of the present situation. If the civil and political rights of both races be equal, one cannot be inferior to the other civilly or politically. If one race be inferior to the other socially, the Constitution of the United States cannot put them upon the same plane. . . .

The judgment of the court below is, therefore,

Affirmed.

Mr. Justice **HARLAN** dissenting. . . .

. . . [W]e have before us a state enactment that compels, under penalties, the separation of the two races in railroad passenger coaches, and makes it a crime for a citizen of either race to enter a coach that has been assigned to citizens of the other race. Thus the state regulated the use of a public highway by citizens of the United States solely on the basis of race. However apparent the injustice of such legislation may be, we have only to consider whether it is consistent with the Constitution of the United States. . . .

In respect of civil rights, common to all citizens, the Constitution of the United States does not, I think, permit any public authority to know the race of those entitled to be protected in the enjoyment of such rights. . . . I deny that any legislative body or judicial tribunal may have regard to the race of citizens when the civil rights of those citizens are involved. Indeed such legislation as that here in question is inconsistent, not only with that equality of rights which pertains to citizenship, national and state, but with the personal liberty enjoyed by everyone within the United States. . . .

The white race deems itself to be the dominant race in this country. And so it is, in prestige, in achievements, in education, in wealth, and in power. So, I doubt not, it will continue to be for all time, if it remains true to its great heritage and holds fast to the principles of constitutional liberty. But in view of the Constitution, in the eye of the law, there is in this country no superior, dominant, ruling class of citizens. There is no caste here. Our Constitution is color-blind and neither knows nor tolerates classes among citizens. In respect of civil rights all citizens are equal before the law. The humblest is the peer of the most powerful. The law regards man as man, and takes no account of his surroundings or of his color when his civil rights as guaranteed by the supreme law of the land are involved. It is therefore to be regretted that this high tribunal, the final expositor of the fundamental law of the land, has reached the conclusion that it is competent for a state to regulate the enjoyment by citizens of their civil rights solely on the basis of race.

In my opinion, the judgment of this day rendered will, in time, prove to be quite as pernicious as the decision made by this tribunal in the Dred Scott Case. . . . The present decision, it may well be apprehended, will not [only] stimulate aggressions, more or less brutal and irritating, upon the admitted rights of colored citizens but will encourage the belief that it is possible, by means of state enactments to defeat the beneficent purposes which the people of the United States had in view when they adopted the recent amendments to the Constitution, by one of which the blacks of this country were made citizens of the United States and of the states in which they respectively reside and whose privileges and immunities, as citizens, the states are forbidden to abridge. Sixty millions of whites are in no danger from the presence here of eight millions of blacks. The destinies of the two races in this country are indissolubly linked together, and the interests of both require that the common government of all shall not permit the seeds of race hate to be planted under the sanction of law. What can more certainly arouse race hate, what more certainly create and perpetuate a feeling of distrust between those races, than state enactments which in fact proceed on the ground that colored citizens are so inferior and degraded that they cannot be allowed to sit in public coaches occupied by white citizens? That, as all will admit, is the real meaning of such legislation as was enacted in Louisiana. . . .

The arbitrary separation of citizens, on the basis of race, while they are on a public highway, is a badge of servitude wholly inconsistent with the civil freedom and the equality before the law established by the Constitution. It cannot be justified upon any legal grounds. . . .

. . . We boast of the freedom enjoyed by our people above all other people. But it is difficult to reconcile that boast with a state of the law which, practically, puts the brand of servitude and degradation upon a large class of our fellow-citizens, our equals before the law. The thin disguise of "equal" accommodations for passengers in railroad coaches will not mislead any one, nor atone for the wrong this day done. . . .

~ Case 7.2 ~

Chief Justice **WARREN:** "[I]n the field of public education the doctrine of 'separate but equal' has no place."

Brown v. Board of Education
347 U.S. 483, 74 S. Ct. 686, 98 L. Ed. 873 (1954)

The wrong done by the Court in Plessy *in cloaking "separate but equal" with the mantle of constitutionality begat a new series of wrongs. "Separate" became the rule, "equal" the exception. In case after case, the Court made a mockery of any concept of equal protection. Cumming v. Board, 175 U.S. 528 (1899) upheld a county's providing a high school for whites but none for blacks. Berea College v. Kentucky, 211 U.S. 45 (1908) sustained a state law forbidding private schools to accept both black and white students. The public school systems of the South (and of border states and some nonsouthern states as well) typically spent two or more times more money for each white student than for each black. Indeed, in some instances per capita expenditures for white schools were ten times that for black institutions.*

In time, however, the more flagrant denials of equality came to the Court, and it began to demand higher standards with respect to the opportunities afforded blacks. In 1938 the justices held that Missouri was not providing a black applicant to the state's law school equal rights when the state offered to send him, with his tuition paid, to a law school outside Missouri. Missouri ex rel. Gaines v. Canada, 305 U.S. 337 (1938). Ten years later the Court repeated essentially what it had said in Gaines, this time commanding Oklahoma to admit a black law school applicant if the state provided legal training for whites and refused it for blacks. Sipuel v. Board of Regents, 332 U.S. 631 (1948). Sipuel, it should be noted, illustrated the frustration involved in trying to achieve desegregation through individual lawsuits; until the Court was ready to broaden its rulings, the National Association for the Advancement of Colored People (NAACP), which orchestrated the long campaign of litigation, had a difficult task. Each small victory had to be won again and again. But the NAACP persisted and gradually urged the Supreme Court to require higher standards of equality as a condition of permitting separate facilities. For example, the Court found it unconstitutional to segregate a black student admitted to Oklahoma University's graduate school (he was seated in a special section of a classroom designated "Reserved for Colored") in McLauren v. Oklahoma State Regents, 339 U.S. 637 (1950). In another case the Court held that Texas,

*by providing a law school for blacks near the one provided for whites
and even sharing some faculty and facilities, had still not given blacks
an equal educational opportunity. Sweatt v. Painter, 339 U.S. 629 (1950).
The way was now paved for tackling the NAACP's ultimate objective:
desegregation of the whole public school system.*

*Finally, in the early 1950s the NAACP brought suits against
segregated public schools in Kansas, Delaware, South Carolina, Virginia,
and the District of Columbia. In some instances the physical facilities
were equal; in others local governments were acting to make them so.
But the NAACP was arguing that it was the fact of segregation itself
that was unconstitutional, not merely the relative physical plants or the
amount of money spent per student.*

Mr. Chief Justice **WARREN** delivered the opinion of the Court.

These cases ... are premised on different facts and different local
conditions, but a common legal question justifies their consideration together
in this consolidated opinion.

The plaintiffs contend that segregated public schools are not "equal" and
cannot be made "equal," and that hence they are deprived of the equal
protection of the laws.... Argument was heard in the 1952 Term and
reargument was heard this Term on certain questions propounded by the
Court.

Reargument was largely devoted to the circumstances surrounding the
adoption of the Fourteenth Amendment in 1868.... This discussion and our
own investigation convince us that, although these sources cast some light, it is
not enough to resolve the problem with which we are faced. At best, they are
inconclusive....

An additional reason for the inconclusive nature of the Amendment's
history, with respect to segregated schools, is the status of public education at
that time. In the South, the movement toward free common schools,
supported by general taxation, had not yet taken hold. Education of white
children was largely in the hands of private groups. Education of Negroes was
almost nonexistent, and practically all of the race were illiterate. In fact, any
education of Negroes was forbidden by law in some states.... It is true that
public school education at the time of the Amendment had advanced further
in the North, but the effect of the Amendment on Northern States was
generally ignored in the congressional debates. Even in the North, the
conditions of public education did not approximate those existing today....

In the first cases in this Court construing the Fourteenth Amendment,
decided shortly after its adoption, the Court interpreted it as proscribing all
state-imposed discriminations against the Negro race. The doctrine of
"separate but equal" did not make its appearance in this Court until 1896 in
the case of Plessy v. Ferguson ... involving not education but transportation.

American courts have since labored with the doctrine for over half a century. In this Court, there have been six cases involving the "separate but equal" doctrine in the field of public education. In Cumming v. County Board of Education . . . and Gong Lum v. Rice . . . the validity of the doctrine itself was not challenged. In more recent cases, all on the graduate school level, inequality was found in that specific benefits enjoyed by white students were denied to Negro students of the same educational qualifications. Missouri ex rel. Gaines v. Canada [1938]; Sipuel v. University of Oklahoma [1948]; Sweatt v. Painter [1950]; McLaurin v. Oklahoma State Regents [1950]. In none of these cases was it necessary to reexamine the doctrine to grant relief to the Negro plaintiff. And in Sweatt v. Painter the Court expressly reserved decision on the question whether Plessy v. Ferguson should be held inapplicable to public education.

In the instant cases, that question is directly presented. Here . . . there are findings below that the Negro and white schools involved have been equalized, or are being equalized, with respect to buildings, curricula, qualifications and salaries of teachers, and other "tangible" factors. Our decision, therefore, cannot turn on merely a comparison of these tangible factors in the Negro and white schools involved in each of the cases. We must look instead to the effect of segregation itself on public education.

In approaching this problem, we cannot turn the clock back to 1868 when the Amendment was adopted, or even to 1896 when Plessy v. Ferguson was written. We must consider public education in the light of its full development and its present place in American life throughout the Nation. . . .

Today, education is perhaps the most important function of state and local governments. Compulsory school attendance laws and the great expenditures for education both demonstrate our recognition of the importance of education to our democratic society. It is required in the performance of our most basic public responsibilities, even service in the armed forces. It is the very foundation of good citizenship. Today it is a principal instrument in awakening the child to cultural values, in preparing him for later professional training, and in helping him to adjust normally to his environment. In these days, it is doubtful that any child may reasonably be expected to succeed in life if he is denied the opportunity of an education. Such an opportunity, where the state has undertaken to provide it, is a right which must be made available to all on equal terms.

We come then to the question presented: Does segregation of children in public schools solely on the basis of race, even though the physical facilities and other "tangible" factors may be equal, deprive the children of the minority group of equal educational opportunities? We believe that it does.

In Sweatt v. Painter, in finding that a segregated law school for Negroes could not provide them equal educational opportunities, this Court relied in large part on "those qualities which are incapable of objective measurement but which make for greatness in a law school." In McLaurin v. Oklahoma State Regents the Court, in requiring that a Negro admitted to a white graduate school be treated like all other students, again resorted to intangible considerations: "... his ability to study, to engage in discussions and exchange views with other students, and, in general, to learn his profession." Such considerations apply with added force to children in grade and high schools. To separate them from others of similar age and qualifications solely because of their race generates a feeling of inferiority as to their status in the community that may affect their hearts and minds in a way unlikely ever to be undone. . . .

Whatever may have been the extent of psychological knowledge at the time of Plessy v. Ferguson, this finding is amply supported by modern authority.[*] Any language in Plessy v. Ferguson contrary to this finding is rejected.

We conclude that in the field of public education the doctrine of "separate but equal" has no place. Separate educational facilities are inherently unequal. . . .

Because these are class actions, because of the wide applicability of this decision, and because of the great variety of local conditions, the formulation of decrees in these cases presents problems of considerable complexity. . . . In order that we may have the full assistance of the parties in formulating decrees, the cases will be restored to the docket, and the parties are requested to present further argument [on how to implement this decision]. . . . The Attorney General of the United States is again invited to participate. The Attorneys General of the states requiring or permitting segregation in public education will also be permitted to appear as amici curiae upon request to do so by September 15, 1954, and submission of briefs by October 1, 1954.

It is so ordered.

Editors' Note: Bolling v. Sharpe, decided the same day as Brown, *held that the same principles bound the federal government. Thus segregated public schools were unconstitutional in the District of Columbia.*

---

[*] K. B. Clark, Effect of Prejudice and Discrimination on Personality Development (Midcentury White House Conference on Children and Youth, 1950); Witmer and Kotinsky, Personality in the Making (1952), ch. VI; Deutscher and Chein, The Psychological Effects of Enforced Segregation: A Survey of Social Science Opinion, 26 J Psychol 259 (1948); Chein, What are the Psychological Effects of Segregation Under Conditions of Equal Facilities?, 3 Int J Opinion and Attitude Res 229 (1949); Brameld, Educational Costs, in Discrimination and National Welfare (MacIver, ed. 1949), 44-48; Frazier, The Negro in the United States (1949), 674-681. And see generally Myrdal, An American Dilemma (1944). [This footnote by the Court, number 11 in the original text, provoked attacks on the justices for making a sociological rather than a legal decision.—Eds.]

~ Case 7.3 ~

Justice **CLARK:** "[T]he power of Congress to protect interstate commerce also includes the power to protect local incidents thereof."

Heart of Atlanta Motel v. United States
379 U.S. 241, 85 S. Ct. 348, 13 L. Ed 2d 258 (1964)

The opening section of the Fourteenth Amendment reads:

All persons born or naturalized in the United States and subject to the jurisdiction thereof, are citizens of the United States and of the State wherein they reside. No State shall make or enforce any law which shall abridge the privileges or immunities of citizens of the United States; nor shall any State deprive any person of life, liberty, or property, without due process of law; nor deny to any person within its jurisdiction the equal protection of the laws.

Sec. 5 of the amendment adds:

The Congress shall have power to enforce, by appropriate legislation, the provisions of this article.

Acting under the authority of sec. 5, Congress adopted in 1875 a sweeping civil rights act that forbade private citizens to discriminate, on the basis of race, in operating inns, theaters, or means of transportation. In the Civil Rights Cases (1883) an unsympathetic Supreme Court struck down this statute. In effect, the majority held, despite the wording of sec. 5, Congress did not have power to define and enforce the privileges and immunities of American citizens supposedly recognized by the first two sentences of the amendment. Congress, the Court said, could forbid only state action that violated sec. 1, not private action.

In the mid-1960s, a decade after the Supreme Court had declared unconstitutional segregation in public schools, racial discrimination in state educational institutions was still the norm. Far more rampant was discrimination in most phases of life by private citizens against blacks, Indians, Orientals, and Hispanics. Ignited by the Court's school cases, kept burning by the leadership of Rev. Martin Luther King, Jr., and fanned by President Lyndon B. Johnson, the civil rights movement persuaded Congress that only positive federal action could right the moral and constitutional wrong of racial discrimination.

The Civil Rights Cases, however, remained a barrier. Although in recent years the Court had several times hinted that those old rulings might no longer be valid, Congress treated them as sleeping dogs and in

*the Civil Rights Act of 1964 relied both on the commerce power and sec.
5 to outlaw private discrimination in hotels, restaurants, and large-scale
businesses.*

*As expected, a legal challenge came quickly. The Heart of Atlanta
Motel asked a federal district court in Georgia for a declaratory
judgment—a formal statement by the court defining (declaring) the
litigant's rights—that Title II of the Civil Rights Act of 1964 was
unconstitutional. The U.S. Department of Justice opposed the motel's
request and filed a countersuit, asking the trial court to sustain the
statute and issue an injunction that, in effect, would require the motel
to conform to the terms of Title II. The district court decided for the
federal government, and the owners of the motel appealed to the U.S.
Supreme Court.*

Mr. Justice **CLARK** delivered the opinion of the Court....

... Appellant owns and operates the Heart of Atlanta Motel which has
216 rooms available to transient guests....

... Appellant solicits patronage from outside the State of Georgia
through various advertising media ... and approximately 75% of its regis-
tered guests are from out of State. Prior to the passage of the Act the motel
had followed a practice of refusing to rent rooms to Negroes, and it alleged
that it intended to continue to do so. In an effort to perpetuate that policy this
suit was filed....

The appellant contends that Congress in passing this Act exceeded its
power to regulate commerce ... that the Act violates the Fifth Amendment
because appellant is deprived of the right to choose its customers and operate
its business as it wishes, resulting in a taking of its liberty and property
without due process of law and a taking of its property without just
compensation; and, finally, that by requiring appellant to rent available
rooms to Negroes against its will, Congress is subjecting it to involuntary
servitude in contravention of the Thirteenth Amendment.

The appellees counter that the unavailability to Negroes of adequate
accommodations interferes significantly with interstate travel, and that
Congress, under the Commerce Clause, has power to remove such obstructions and restraints; that the Fifth Amendment does not forbid reasonable
regulation and that consequential damage does not constitute a "taking"
within the meaning of that amendment; that the Thirteenth Amendment
claim fails because it is entirely frivolous to say that an amendment directed
to the abolition of human bondage and the removal of widespread disabilities
associated with slavery places discrimination in public accommodations
beyond the reach of both federal and state law....

The sole question posed is ... the constitutionality of the Civil Rights Act
of 1964 as applied to these facts. The legislative history of the Act indicates

that Congress based the Act on § 5 and the Equal Protection Clause of the Fourteenth Amendment as well as its power to regulate interstate commerce under Art. I, § 8, cl. 3 of the Constitution.

The Senate Commerce Committee made it quite clear that the fundamental object of Title II was to vindicate "the deprivation of personal dignity that surely accompanies denials of equal access to public establishments." At the same time, however, it noted that such an objective has been and could be readily achieved "by congressional action based on the commerce power of the Constitution." . . . Our study of the legislative record, made in the light of prior cases, has brought us to the conclusion that Congress possessed ample power in this regard, and we have therefore not considered the other grounds relied upon. This is not to say that the remaining authority upon which it acted was not adequate, a question upon which we not pass, but merely that since the commerce power is sufficient for our decision here we have considered it alone. . . .

It is said that the operation of the motel here is of a purely local character. But, assuming this to be true, "[i]f it is interstate commerce that feels the pinch, it does not matter how local the operation which applies the squeeze." United States v. Women's Sportswear Mfrs. Ass'n (1949). . . . Thus the power of Congress to promote interstate commerce also includes the power to regulate the local incidents thereof, including local activities in both the States of origin and destination, which might have a substantial and harmful effect upon that commerce. One need only examine the evidence which we have discussed above to see that Congress may—as it has—prohibit racial discrimination by motels serving travelers, however "local" their operations may appear. . . .

We, therefore, conclude that the action of the Congress in the adoption of the Act as applied here to a motel which concededly serves interstate travelers is within the power granted to it by this Court for 140 years. . . .

Affirmed.

Mr. Justice **DOUGLAS**, concurring.

Though I join the Court's opinion, I am somewhat reluctant . . . to rest solely on the Commerce Clause. My reluctance is not due to any conviction that Congress lacks power to regulate commerce in the interests of human rights. It is rather my belief that the right of the people to be free of state action that discriminates against them because of race . . . "occupies a more protected position in our constitutional system than does the movement of cattle, fruit, steel and coal across state lines." . . .

Hence I would prefer to rest on the assertion of legislative power contained in § 5 of the Fourteenth Amendment. . . .

A decision based on the Fourteenth Amendment would have a more settling effect, making unnecessary litigation over whether a particular restaurant or inn is within the commerce definitions of the Act. . . . Under my construction, the Act would apply to all customers in all the enumerated places of public accommodation. And that construction would put an end to all obstructionist strategies and finally close one door on a bitter chapter in American history. . . .

[Justices **BLACK** and **GOLDBERG** also wrote concurring opinions.]

Editors' Note: In a companion case, Katzenbach v. McClung, the Court held that Ollie's Barbecue, a small restaurant in Birmingham, Alabama, was also covered by the act. Although the barbecue was a family-owned business that obtained most of its supplies from within Alabama, the Court noted that a large percentage of that material had originated in other states. Congress, the Court said, had "a rational basis for finding that racial discrimination in restaurants had a direct and adverse effect on the free flow of interstate commerce."

~ Case 7.4 ~

Justice **POWELL:** "[A]t least where wealth is concerned the Equal Protection Clause does not require absolute equality or precisely equal advantages."

Justice **MARSHALL:** "[T]he majority's holding can only be seen as a retreat from our historic commitment to equality of educational opportunity and as unsupportable acquiescence in a system which deprives children in their earliest years of the chance to reach their full potential as citizens."

San Antonio School District v. Rodriguez
411 U.S. 1, 93 S. Ct. 1278, 36 L. Ed. 2d 16 (1973)

Race, the Court established, was a suspect classification. But what about classification by wealth? During the late 1950s and during the 1960s, the justices struck down statutes that rested a citizen's rights to vote, to be represented by counsel, to appeal a conviction, or to obtain a divorce on ability to pay. But what about a state's conditioning the quality of public education (a fundamental right?) on the taxable wealth (a suspect classification?) of its subdivisions? Several state and federal courts ruled that such schemes violated the equal protection clause of the Fourteenth Amendment, and in this case the U.S. Supreme Court squarely faced the issue. The justices also reexamined the nature and complexity of the two-tiered test they had been using in cases involving equal protection. (See the introduction to this chapter for a discussion of that test.)

In Texas the financing of education comes from three sources: state grants, federal grants, and local property taxes. Great disparities in the amount spent per pupil occur because some poor communities do not have enough property of sufficient value to tax for education, whereas more affluent school districts often have ample taxable property. Parents in a school district occupied largely by Mexican-Americans where property values were low brought suit claiming their children were being denied equal education, on the sole basis of the poverty in the area where they lived. This denial, they argued, deprived their children of equal protection of the laws. They won in a federal district court, and Texas then appealed to the U.S. Supreme Court.

Mr. Justice **POWELL** delivered the opinion of the Court. . . .

The wealth discrimination discovered by the District Court in this case and by several other courts that have recently struck down school financing laws in other States is quite unlike any of the forms of wealth discrimination heretofore reviewed by this Court. . . . [T]he courts in these cases have virtually assumed their findings of a suspect classification through a simplistic process of analysis: since, under the traditional systems of financing public schools, some poorer people receive less expensive educations than other more affluent people, these systems discriminate on the basis of wealth. This approach largely ignores the hard threshold questions, including whether it makes a difference for purposes of consideration under the Constitution that the class of disadvantaged "poor" cannot be identified or defined in customary equal protection terms, and whether the relative—rather than absolute—nature of the asserted deprivation is of significant consequence. . . .

The precedents of this Court provide the proper starting point. The individuals or groups of individuals who constituted the class discriminated against in our prior cases shared two distinguishing characteristics: . . . they were completely unable to pay for some desired benefit, and as a consequence, they sustained an absolute deprivation of a meaningful opportunity to enjoy that benefit. In Griffin v. Illinois (1956) and its progeny, the Court invalidated state laws that prevented an indigent criminal defendant from acquiring a transcript, or an adequate substitute for a transcript, for use at several stages of the trial and appeal process. The payment requirements in each case were found to occasion de facto discrimination against those who, because of their indigency, were totally unable to pay for transcripts. . . .

Likewise in Douglas v. California (1963) the Court dealt only with defendants who could not pay for counsel. . . . *Douglas* provides no relief for those on whom the burdens of paying for a criminal defense are, relatively speaking, great but not insurmountable. Nor does it deal with relative differences in the quality of counsel acquired by the less wealthy.

Williams v. Illinois (1970) and Tate v. Short (1971) struck down criminal penalties that subjected indigents to incarceration simply because of their inability to pay a fine. Again, the disadvantaged class was composed only of persons who were totally unable to pay. . . .

Finally, in Bullock v. Carter (1972) the Court invalidated the Texas filing fee requirement for primary elections. . . . The size of the fee, often running into the thousands of dollars . . . effectively barred all potential candidates who were unable to pay. . . . [I]nability to pay occasioned an absolute denial of a position on the primary ballot.

. . . Even cursory examination . . . demonstrates that neither of the two distinguishing characteristics of wealth classifications can be found here. First . . . appellees have made no effort to demonstrate that it operates to the peculiar disadvantage of any class fairly definable as indigent, or as composed of persons whose incomes are beneath any designated poverty level. Indeed, there is reason to believe that the poorest families are not necessarily clustered in the poorest property districts. A recent and exhaustive study of school districts in Connecticut concluded that "[i]t is clearly incorrect . . . to contend that the 'poor' live in 'poor' districts. . . . Thus, the major factual assumption of *Serrano*°—that the educational finance system discriminates against the 'poor'—is simply false in Connecticut." Defining "poor" families as those below the Bureau of the Census "poverty level," the Connecticut study found . . . that the poor were clustered around commercial and industrial areas— those same areas that provide the most attractive sources of property tax income for school districts. Whether a similar pattern would be discovered in Texas is not known, but there is no basis on the record in this case for assuming that the poorest people . . . are concentrated in the poorest districts.

Second, neither appellees nor the District Court addressed the fact that . . . lack of personal resources has not occasioned an absolute deprivation of the desired benefit. The argument here is not that the children in districts having relatively low assessable property values are receiving no public education; rather, it is that they are receiving a poorer quality education than

---

° *Serrano v. Priest (1971), a ruling by the supreme court of California, held that unconstitutional discrimination, based on wealth, results when schools are financed mainly by property taxes. Much the same happened in New Jersey. See Robinson v. Cahill (1972). Note, however, that these decisions relied on state constitutions and not the Fourteenth Amendment.—Eds.*

that available to children in districts having more assessable wealth. . . . [A] sufficient answer . . . is that at least where wealth is involved the Equal Protection Clause does not require absolute equality or precisely equal advantages. Nor, indeed, in view of the infinite variables affecting the educational process, can any system assure equal quality of education except in the most relative sense. Texas asserts that the Minimum Foundation Program provides an "adequate" education for all children in the State. By providing 12 years of free public school education, and by assuring teachers, books, transportation and operating funds, the Texas Legislature has endeavored to "guarantee, for the welfare of the state as a whole, that all people shall have at least an adequate program of education. . . ." No proof was offered at trial persuasively discrediting or refuting the State's assertion. . . .

. . . [A]ppellees and the District Court may have embraced a second or third approach, the second of which might be characterized as a theory of relative or comparative discrimination based on family income. Appellees sought to prove that a direct correlation exists between the wealth of families within each district and the expenditures therein for education. . . .

The principal evidence adduced in support of this comparative discrimination claim is an affidavit submitted by Professor Joele S. Berke of Syracuse University's Educational Finance Policy Institute. The District Court, relying in major part upon this affidavit . . . noted, first, a positive correlation between the wealth of school districts, measured in terms of assessable property per pupil, and their levels of per-pupil expenditures. Second, the court found a similar correlation between district wealth and the personal wealth of its residents, measured in terms of median family income. . . .

Professor Berke's affidavit is based on a survey of approximately 10% of the school districts in Texas. His findings . . . show only that the wealthiest few districts in the sample have the highest median family incomes and spend the most on education, and that the several poorest districts have the lowest family incomes and devote the least amount of money to education. For the remainder of the districts—96 districts comprising almost 90% of the sample—the correlation is inverted, i.e., the districts that spend next to the most money on education are populated by families having next to the lowest median family incomes while the districts spending the least have the highest median family incomes. . . .

However described, it is clear that appellees' suit asks this Court to extend its most exacting scrutiny to review a system that allegedly discriminates against a large, diverse, and amorphous class, unified only by the common factor of residence in districts that happen to have less taxable wealth than other districts. The system of alleged discrimination and the class it defines have none of the traditional indicia of suspectness: the class is not saddled with such disabilities, or subjected to such a history of purposeful unequal treatment, or relegated to such a position of political powerlessness as to command extraordinary protection from the majoritarian political process.

We thus conclude that the Texas system does not operate to the peculiar disadvantage of any suspect class. . . . [Appellees] also assert that the State's system impermissibly interferes with the exercise of a "fundamental" right and that accordingly the prior decisions of this Court require the application of the strict standard of judicial review. . . .

In Brown v. Board of Education (1954), a unanimous Court recognized that "education is perhaps the most important function of state and local governments." . . . What was said there in the context of racial discrimination has lost none of its vitality with the passage of time. . . .

Nothing this Court holds today in any way detracts from our historic dedication to public education. . . . But the importance of a service performed by the State does not determine whether it must be regarded as fundamental for purposes of examination under the Equal Protection Clause. . . .

Lindsey v. Normet (1972) firmly reiterates that social importance is not the critical determinant for subjecting state legislation to strict scrutiny. . . . Mr. Justice White's analysis, in his opinion for the Court, is instructive:

> We do not denigrate the importance of decent, safe, and sanitary housing. But the Constitution does not provide judicial remedies for every social and economic ill. We are unable to perceive in that document any constitutional guarantee of access to dwellings of a particular quality or any recognition of the right of a tenant to occupy the real property of his landlord beyond the term of his lease, without the payment of rent. . . . *Absent constitutional mandate*, the assurance of adequate housing and the definition of landlord-tenant relationships are legislative, not judicial, functions. . . . (Emphasis supplied.)

Similarly, in Dandridge v. Williams (1979), the Court's explicit recognition of the fact that the "administration of public welfare assistance . . . involves the most basic economic needs of impoverished human beings" . . . provided no basis for departing from the settled mode of constitutional analysis of legislative classifications involving questions of economic and social policy. . . .

The lesson of these cases . . . is plain. It is not the province of this Court to create substantive constitutional rights in the name of guaranteeing equal protection of the laws. Thus the key to discovering whether education is "fundamental" is not to be found in comparisons of the relative societal significance of education as opposed to subsistence or housing. Nor is it to be found by weighing whether education is as important as the right to travel. Rather, the answer lies in assessing whether there is a right to education explicitly or implicitly guaranteed by the Constitution. . . .

Education, of course, is not among the rights afforded explicit protection under our Federal Constitution. Nor do we find any basis for saying it is implicitly so protected. . . . It is appellees' contention, however, that education is distinguishable from other services and benefits provided by the State because it bears a peculiarly close relationship to other rights and liberties accorded

225

protection under the Constitution. Specifically, they insist that education . . . is essential to the effective exercise of First Amendment freedoms and to intelligent utilization of the right to vote. . . . The "marketplace of ideas" is an empty forum for those lacking basic communicative tools. Likewise, they argue that the corollary right to receive information becomes little more than a hollow privilege when the recipient has not been taught to read, assimilate, and utilize available knowledge.

A similar line of reasoning is pursued with respect to the right to vote. . . .

We need not dispute any of these propositions. The Court has long afforded zealous protection against unjustifiable governmental interference with the individual's rights to speak and to vote. Yet we have never presumed to possess either the ability or the authority to guarantee to the citizenry the most *effective* speech or the most *informed* electoral choice. . . .

Appellees further urge that the Texas system is unconstitutionally arbitrary because it allows the availability of local taxable resources to turn on "happenstance." . . . But any scheme of local taxation . . . requires the establishment of jurisdictional boundaries that are inevitably arbitrary. It is equally inevitable that some localities are going to be blessed with more taxable assets than others. Nor is local wealth a static quantity. Changes in the level of taxable wealth within any district may result from any number of events, some of which local residents can and do influence. . . .

Moreover, if local taxation for local expenditure is an unconstitutional method of providing for education then it may be an equally impermissible means of providing other necessary services customarily financed largely from local property taxes, including local police and fire protection, public health and hospitals, and public utility facilities of various kinds. We perceive no justification for such a severe denegation of local property taxation and control as would follow from appellees' contentions. . . .

In sum, to the extent that the Texas system of school finance results in unequal expenditures between children who happen to reside in different districts, we cannot say that such disparities are the product of a system that is so irrational as to be invidiously discriminatory. Texas has acknowledged its shortcomings and has persistently endeavored—not without some success—to ameliorate the differences in levels of expenditures without sacrificing the benefits of local participation. The Texas plan is not the result of hurried, ill-conceived legislation. It certainly is not the product of purposeful discrimination against any group or class. On the contrary, it is rooted in decades of experience in Texas and elsewhere, and in major part is the product of responsible studies by qualified people. . . . One also must remember that the system here challenged is not peculiar to Texas. . . . In its essential characteristics the Texas plan . . . reflects what many educators for a half century have thought was an enlightened approach to a problem for which there is no perfect solution. We are unwilling to assume for ourselves a level of wisdom superior to that of legislators, scholars, and educational authorities in 49 States, especially where the alternatives proposed are only recently conceived and nowhere yet tested. The constitutional standard under the Equal Protection Clause is whether the challenged state action rationally furthers a legitimate state purpose or interest. McGinnis v. Royster (1973). We hold that the Texas plan abundantly satisfies this standard. . . .

Reversed.

Mr. Justice **STEWART** concurring. . . .

Mr. Justice **BRENNAN** dissenting. . . .

Mr. Justice **WHITE,** with whom Mr. Justice **DOUGLAS** and Mr. Justice **BRENNAN** join, dissenting. . . .

Mr. Justice **MARSHALL,** with whom Mr. Justice **DOUGLAS** concurs, dissenting.

The Court today decides, in effect, that a State may constitutionally vary the quality of education which it offers its children in accordance with the amount of taxable wealth located in the school districts within which they reside. . . . More unfortunately, though, the majority's holding can only be seen as a retreat from our historic commitment to equality of educational opportunity and as unsupportable acquiescence in a system which deprives children in their earliest years of the chance to reach their full potential as citizens. . . .

In my judgment, the right of every American to an equal start in life, so far as the provision of a state service as important as education is concerned, is far too vital to permit state discrimination on grounds as tenuous as those presented by this record. Nor can I accept the notion that it is sufficient to remit these appellees to the vagaries of the political process which . . . has proven singularly unsuited to the task of providing a remedy for this discrimination. . . .

The consequences, in terms of objective educational inputs, of the variations in district funding . . . are apparent from the data introduced before the District Court. For example, in 1968-1969, 100% of the teachers in the property rich Alamo Heights School District had college degrees. By contrast, during the same school year only 80.02% of the teachers had college degrees in the property poor Edgewood Independent School District. Also, in 1968-1969, approximately 47% of the teachers in the Edgewood District were on emergency teaching permits, whereas only 11% of the teachers in Alamo Heights were on such permits. This is undoubtedly a reflection of the fact that Edgewood's teacher salary scale was approximately 80% of Alamo

227

Heights'. And, not surprisingly, the teacher-student ratio varies significantly between the two districts. . . .

At the very least . . . the burden of proving that these disparities do not in fact affect the quality of children's education must fall upon the appellants. . . . Yet appellants made no effort in the District Court to demonstrate that educational quality is not affected by variations in funding and in resulting inputs. And, in this Court, they have argued no more than that the relationship is ambiguous. This is hardly sufficient to overcome appellees' prima facie showing of state created discrimination. . . .

. . . [A]ppellants and the majority may believe that the Equal Protection Clause cannot be offended by substantially unequal state treatment of persons who are similarly situated so long as the State provides everyone with some unspecified amount of education which evidently is "enough." The basis for such a novel view is far from clear. It is, of course, true that the Constitution does not require precise equality in the treatment of all persons. . . . But this Court has never suggested that because some "adequate" level of benefits is provided to all, discrimination in the provision of services is therefore constitutionally excusable. The Equal Protection Clause is not addressed to the minimal sufficiency but rather to the unjustifiable inequalities of state action. It mandates nothing less than that "all persons similarly circumstanced shall be treated alike." F. S. Royster Guano Co. v. Virginia (1920).

Even if the Equal Protection Clause encompassed some theory of constitutional adequacy, discrimination in the provision of educational opportunity would certainly seem to be a poor candidate for its application. . . .

The Court has repeatedly held that state discrimination which adversely affects a "fundamental interest" . . . or is based on a distinction of a suspect character . . . must be carefully scrutinized to ensure that the scheme is necessary to promote a substantial, legitimate state interest. . . . The majority today concludes, however, that the Texas scheme is not subject to such a strict standard of review. . . . Instead, in its view, the Texas scheme must be tested by nothing more than that lenient standard of rationality . . . traditionally applied to discriminatory state action in the context of economic and commercial matters. . . . I cannot accept such an emasculation of the Equal Protection Clause. . . .

. . . The Court apparently seeks to establish today that equal protection cases fall into one of two neat categories which dictate the appropriate standard of review—strict scrutiny or mere rationality. But this Court's decisions in the field of equal protection defy such easy categorization. A principled reading of what this Court has done reveals that it has applied a spectrum of standards in reviewing discrimination. . . . This spectrum clearly comprehends variations in the degree of care with which the Court will scrutinize particular classifications, depending, I believe, on the constitutional and societal importance of the interest adversely affected and the recognized invidiousness of the basis upon which the particular classification is drawn....

I therefore cannot accept the majority's labored efforts to demonstrate that fundamental interests, which call for strict scrutiny of the challenged classification, encompass only established rights which we are somehow bound to recognize from the text of the Constitution itself. To be sure, some interests which the Court has deemed to be fundamental for purposes of equal protection analysis are themselves constitutionally protected rights. Thus, discrimination against the guaranteed right of freedom of speech has called for strict judicial scrutiny.... But it will not do to suggest that the "answer" to whether an interest is fundamental for purposes of equal protection analysis is *always* determined by whether that interest "is a right ... explicitly or implicitly guaranteed by the Constitution."...

I would like to know where the Constitution guarantees the right to procreate, Skinner v. Oklahoma (1942) or the right to vote in state elections, Reynolds v. Sims (1964) or the right to an appeal from a criminal conviction, e.g., Griffin v. Illinois (1956). These are instances in which, due to the importance of the interests at stake, the Court has displayed a strong concern with the existence of discriminatory state treatment....

The majority is, of course, correct when it suggests that the process of determining which interests are fundamental is a difficult one. But I do not think the problem is insurmountable. And I certainly do not accept the view that the process need necessarily degenerate into an unprincipled, subjective "picking-and-choosing." ... The task in every case should be to determine the extent to which constitutionally guaranteed rights are dependent on interests not mentioned in the Constitution. As the nexus between the specific constitutional guarantee and the nonconstitutional interest draws closer, the nonconstitutional interest becomes more fundamental and the degree of judicial scrutiny applied when the interest is infringed on a discriminatory basis must be adjusted accordingly.... Only if we closely protect the related interests from state discrimination do we ultimately ensure the integrity of the constitutional guarantee itself....

... It is true that this Court has never deemed the provision of free public education to be required by the Constitution.... Nevertheless, the fundamental importance of education is amply indicated by the prior decisions of this Court, by the unique status accorded public education by our society, and by the close relationship between education and some of our most basic constitutional values.

The special concern of this Court with the educational process of our country is a matter of common knowledge. Undoubtedly, this Court's most famous statement on the subject is that contained in Brown v. Board of Education....

Only last Term the Court recognized that "[p]roviding public schools ranks at the very apex of the function of a State." Wisconsin v. Yoder (1972).

This is clearly borne out by the fact that in 48 of our 50 States the provision of public education is mandated by the state constitution. No other state function is so uniformly recognized as an essential element of our society's well-being. In large measure, the explanation for the special importance attached to education must rest ... on the facts that "some degree of education is necessary to prepare citizens to participate effectively and intelligently in our open political system ... " and that "education prepares individuals to be self-reliant and self-sufficient participants in society." ...

Education directly affects the ability of a child to exercise his First Amendment interests both as a source and as a receiver of information and ideas, whatever interests he may pursue in life. ...

Of particular importance is the relationship between education and the political process. ... Education serves the essential function of instilling in our young an understanding of and appreciation for the principles and operation of our governmental processes. Education may instill the interest and provide the tools necessary for political discourse and debate. Indeed, it has frequently been suggested that education is the dominant factor affecting political consciousness and participation. ... But of most immediate and direct concern must be the demonstrated effect of education on the exercise of the franchise by the electorate. The right to vote in federal elections ... has been afforded special protection because it is "preservative of other basic civil and political rights," Reynolds v. Sims. Data from the Presidential Election of 1968 clearly demonstrate a direct relationship between participation in the electoral process and level of educational attainment; and, as this Court recognized in Gaston County v. United States (1969), the quality of education offered may influence a child's decision to "enter or remain in school." It is this very sort of intimate relationship between a particular personal interest and specific constitutional guarantees that has heretofore caused the Court to attach special significance, for purposes of equal protection analysis, to individual interests such as procreation and the exercise of the state franchise.

While ultimately disputing little of this, the majority seeks refuge in the fact that the Court has "never presumed to possess either the ability or the authority to guarantee to the citizenry the most *effective* speech or the most *informed* electoral choice." ... This serves only to blur what is in fact at stake. With due respect, the issue is neither provision of the most *effective* speech nor of the most *informed* vote. Appellees do not now seek the best education Texas might provide. They do seek, however, an end to state discrimination resulting from the unequal distribution of taxable district property wealth that directly impairs the ability of some districts to provide the same educational opportunity that other districts can provide with the same or even substantially less tax effort. ...

∼ Case 7.5 ∼

Justice **O'CONNOR:** "[T]he party seeking to uphold a statute that classifies individuals on the basis of their gender must carry the burden of showing an 'exceedingly persuasive justification' for the classification."

Justice **POWELL:** "By applying heightened equal protection analysis to this case, the Court frustrates the liberating spirit of the Equal Protection Clause."

Mississippi University for Women v. Hogan
458 U.S. 718, 102 S. Ct. 3331, 73 L Ed. 2d 1090 (1982)

Rodriguez *settled at least for a time that wealth is not a suspect classification and education is not a fundamental right. Justice Marshall's dissent, however, shook belief that the Court had been—or even should have been—applying a two-tiered test. He claimed that the Court's approach had been much more nuanced, using in fact a multitiered test.*

The issue of classification by sex brought to the fore again the issue of proper tests for constitutionality. Four of the justices wanted to rule sex "suspect" and so invoke the upper-level test, but five of their colleagues refused to go so far. Still, the Court managed to invalidate several sexist regulations. Then in 1976 Craig v. Boren, *429 U.S. 119, brought the matter to a head. The legal drinking age in Oklahoma was twenty-one, but the state had allowed females over eighteen to purchase 3.2 beer. In striking down this statute as a denial of equal protection, the justices added "a middle tier" to their testing apparatus: "To withstand constitutional challenge . . . classifications by gender must serve* important *governmental objectives and must be* substantially *related to those objectives." [Emphasis added.] Commentators quickly noted the differences between "important" and "compelling" governmental objectives and between "directly and necessarily" and "substantially" related. Justice Powell, the author of the opinion in* Rodriguez, *filed a separate. opinion agreeing that in cases involving classification by sex the Court applied "a more critical examination" than usual.*

In 1981 two opinions written by Justice Rehnquist raised doubts about this compromise. The first, Michael M. v. Superior Court, *450 U.S. 464, found no sexual discrimination in a conviction of a seventeen-and-a-half-year-old male for statutory rape of a sixteen-and-a-half-year-old female. For four of the five justices in the majority, Rehnquist wrote:*

We do not apply so-called "strict scrutiny" to [gender-based] classifications. Our cases have held, however, that the traditional minimal rationality test takes on a somewhat "sharper focus" when gender-based classifications are challenged. See Craig v. Boren (1976) (Powell, J., concurring).

Conceding that the purpose of punishing males for intercourse with females under eighteen but not females for intercourse with males under eighteen was "somewhat less than clear," Rehnquist accepted the state's argument that it was to prevent pregnancies among teen-agers and that this was a "strong interest."

In the second case, Rostker v. Goldberg, 433 U.S. 57, Rehnquist wrote for the Court, upholding by a 6-3 vote the Military Selective Service Act, which requires only males to register for the draft. The majority found Congress's restricting of compulsory service to males to be reasonable. The opinion, full of deference toward congressional power to raise armies and wage war, finessed the question of requiring any standard stricter than a rational basis. Some observers, however, discounted Rostker's signifying change because it involved congressional powers that the Court had traditionally been reluctant to question. Michael M. was more difficult to discount, though Rehnquist had made a slight bow toward a form of heightened scrutiny.

Mississippi University for Women, a state institution in Columbus, provided a new test of the compromise's vitality. From its founding, MUW had limited enrollment to women. Joe Hogan, a male nurse resident in Columbus, applied for admission to the School of Nursing to obtain a bachelor's degree in his field. Solely on the basis of his sex, MUW denied him admission to a degree-granting program, though he was allowed to audit classes. He sued for an injunction in a federal district court, lost, and won on appeal. Mississippi then sought and obtained review.

Justice **O'CONNOR** delivered the opinion of the Court.

This case presents the narrow issue of whether a state statute that excludes males from enrolling in a state-supported professional nursing school violates the Equal Protection Clause of the Fourteenth Amendment. . . .

II

We begin our analysis aided by several firmly-established principles. Because the challenged policy expressly discriminates among applicants on the basis of gender, it is subject to scrutiny under the Equal Protection Clause of the Fourteenth Amendment. Reed v. Reed (1971). That this statute discriminates against males rather than against females does not exempt it from scrutiny or reduce the standard of review. Caban v. Mohammed (1979);

Orr v. Orr (1979). Our decisions also establish that the party seeking to uphold a statute that classifies individuals on the basis of their gender must carry the burden of showing an "exceedingly persuasive justification" for the classification. Kirchberg v. Feenstra (1981); Personnel Administrator of Massachusetts v. Feeney (1979). The burden is met only by showing at least that the classification serves "important governmental objectives and that the discriminatory means employed" are "substantially related to the achievement of those objectives." Wengler v. Druggists Mutual Insurance Co. (1980).

Although the test for determining the validity of a gender-based classification is straightforward, it must be applied free of fixed notions concerning the roles and abilities of males and females. Care must be taken in ascertaining whether the statutory objective itself reflects archaic and stereotypic notions. Thus, if the statutory objective is to exclude or "protect" members of one gender because they are presumed to suffer from an inherent handicap or to be innately inferior, the objective itself is illegitimate. See Frontiero v. Richardson (1973) (plurality opinion).

If the State's objective is legitimate and important, we next determine whether the requisite direct, substantial relationship between objective and means is present. The purpose of requiring that close relationship is to assure that the validity of a classification is determined through reasoned analysis rather than through the mechanical application of traditional, often inaccurate, assumptions about the proper roles of men and women....

III

A

The State's primary justification for maintaining the single-sex admissions policy of MUW's School of Nursing is that it compensates for discrimination against women and, therefore, constitutes educational affirmative action. As applied to the School of Nursing, we find the State's argument unpersuasive.

In limited circumstances, a gender-based classification favoring one sex can be justified if it intentionally and directly assists members of the sex that is disproportionately burdened. See Schlesinger v. Ballard (1975). However, we consistently have emphasized that "the mere recitation of a benign, compensatory purpose is not an automatic shield which protects against any inquiry into the actual purposes underlying a statutory scheme." Weinberger v. Wiesenfeld (1975). The same searching analysis must be made, regardless of whether the State's objective is to eliminate family controversy, *Reed*, to achieve administrative efficiency, *Frontiero*, or to balance the burdens borne by males and females.

It is readily apparent that a State can evoke a compensatory purpose to justify an otherwise discriminatory classification only if members of the

233

gender benefited by the classification actually suffer a disadvantage related to the classification. We considered such a situation in Califano v. Webster (1977), which involved a challenge to a statutory classification that allowed women to eliminate more low-earning years than men for purposes of computing Social Security retirement benefits. Although the effect of the classification was to allow women higher monthly benefits than were available to men with the same earning history, we upheld the statutory scheme, noting that it took into account that women "as such have been unfairly hindered from earning as much as men" and "work[ed] directly to remedy" the resulting economic disparity.

A similar pattern of discrimination against women influenced our decision in *Schlesinger*. There, we considered a federal statute that granted female Naval officers a 13-year tenure of commissioned service before mandatory discharge, but accorded male officers only a nine-year tenure. We recognized that, because women were barred from combat duty, they had had fewer opportunities for promotion than had their male counterparts. By allowing women an additional four years to reach a particular rank before subjecting them to mandatory discharge, the statute directly compensated for other statutory barriers to advancement.

In sharp contrast, Mississippi has made no showing that women lacked opportunities to obtain training in the field of nursing or to attain positions of leadership in that field when the MUW School of Nursing opened its door or that women currently are deprived of such opportunities. In fact, in 1970, the year before the School of Nursing's first class enrolled, women earned 94 percent of the nursing baccalaureate degrees conferred in Mississippi and 98.6 percent of the degrees earned nationwide. That year was not an aberration; one decade earlier, women had earned all the nursing degrees conferred in Mississippi and 98.9 percent of the degrees conferred nation-wide. As one would expect, the labor force reflects the same predominance of women in nursing. . . .

Rather than compensate for discriminatory barriers faced by women, MUW's policy of excluding males from admission to the School of Nursing tends to perpetuate the stereotyped view of nursing as an exclusively woman's job. . . . Thus, we conclude that, although the State recited a "benign, compensatory purpose," it failed to establish that the alleged objective is the actual purpose underlying the discriminatory classification.

The policy is invalid also because it fails the second part of the equal protection test, for the State has made no showing that the gender-based classification is substantially and directly related to its proposed compensatory objective. To the contrary, MUW's policy of permitting men to attend classes as auditors fatally undermines its claim that women, at least those in the School of Nursing, are adversely affected by the presence of men. . . .

[Affirmed.]

Chief Justice **BURGER,** dissenting.

I agree generally with Justice Powell's dissenting opinion. I write separately, however, to emphasize that the Court's holding today is limited to the context of a professional nursing school. Since the Court's opinion relies heavily on its finding that women have traditionally dominated the nursing profession, it suggests that a State might well be justified in maintaining, for example, the option of an all-women's business school or liberal arts program.

Justice **BLACKMUN,** dissenting. . . .

I have come to suspect that it is easy to go too far with rigid rules in this area of claimed sex discrimination, and to lose—indeed destroy—values that mean much to some people by forbidding the State from offering them a choice while not depriving others of an alternate choice. Justice Powell in his separate opinion advances this theme well.

While the Court purports to write narrowly, declaring that it does not decide the same issue with respect to "separate but equal" undergraduate institutions for females and males, or with respect to units of MUW other than its School of Nursing, there is inevitable spillover from the Court's ruling today. That ruling, it seems to me, places in constitutional jeopardy any state-supported educational institution that confines its student body in any area to members of one sex, even though the State elsewhere provides an equivalent program to the complaining applicant. The Court's reasoning does not stop with the School of Nursing of the Mississippi University for Women.

I hope that we do not lose all values that some think are worthwhile (and are not based on differences of race or religion) and relegate ourselves to needless conformity. The ringing words of the Equal Protection Clause of the Fourteenth Amendment—what Justice Powell aptly describes as its "liberating spirit,"—do not demand that price.

Justice **POWELL,** with whom Justice **REHNQUIST** joins, dissenting.

The Court's opinion bows deeply to conformity. Left without honor—indeed, held unconstitutional—is an element of diversity that has characterized much of American education and enriched much of American life. The Court in effect holds today that no State now may provide even a single institution of higher learning open only to women students. It gives no heed to the efforts of the State of Mississippi to provide abundant opportunities for young men and young women to attend coeducational institutions, and none to the preferences of the more than 40,000 young women who over the years have evidenced their approval of an all-women's college by choosing Mississippi University for Women (MUW) over seven coeducational universities within the State. The Court decides today that the Equal Protection Clause makes it unlawful for the State to provide women with a traditionally popular and respected choice of educational environment. It does so in a case instituted by one man, who represents no class, and whose primary concern is personal convenience.

It is undisputed that women enjoy complete equality of opportunity in Mississippi's public system of higher education. Of the State's eight universities and 16 junior colleges, all except MUW are coeducational. At least two other Mississippi universities would have provided respondent with the nursing curriculum that he wishes to pursue. . . .

I

Coeducation, historically, is a novel educational theory. From grade school through high school, college, and graduate and professional training, much of the nation's population during much of our history has been educated in sexually segregated classrooms. At the college level, for instance, until recently some of the most prestigious colleges and universities—including most of the Ivy League—had long histories of single-sex education. As Harvard, Yale, and Princeton remained all-male colleges well into the second half of this century, the "Seven Sister" institutions established a parallel standard of excellence for women's colleges. . . .

The sexual segregation of students has been a reflection of, rather than an imposition upon, the preference of those subject to the policy. It cannot be disputed, for example, that the highly qualified women attending the leading women's colleges could have earned admission to virtually any college of their choice. Women attending such colleges have chosen to be there, usually expressing a preference for the special benefits of single-sex institutions. Similar decisions were made by the colleges that elected to remain open to women only.

The arguable benefits of single-sex colleges also continue to be recognized by students of higher education. . . .

II

The issue in this case is whether a State transgresses the Constitution when—within the context of a public system that offers a diverse range of campuses, curricula, and educational alternatives—it seeks to accommodate the legitimate personal preferences of those desiring the advantages of an all-women's college. In my view, the Court errs seriously by assuming—without argument or discussion—that the equal protection standard generally applicable to sex discrimination is appropriate here. That standard was designed to free women from "archaic and overbroad generalizations. . . ." *Schlesinger.* In no previous case have we applied it to invalidate state efforts to *expand* women's choices. Nor are there prior sex discrimination decisions by this Court in which a male plaintiff, as in this case, had the choice of an equal benefit.

The cases cited by the Court therefore do not control the issue now before us. In most of them women were given no opportunity for the same benefit as men. Cases involving male plaintiffs are equally inapplicable. . . .

By applying heightened equal protection analysis to this case, the Court frustrates the liberating spirit of the Equal Protection Clause. It forbids the States from providing women with an opportunity to choose the type of university they prefer. And yet it is these women whom the Court regards as the *victims* of an illegal, stereotyped perception of the role of women in our society. The Court reasons this way in a case in which no woman has complained, and the only complainant is a man who advances no claims on behalf of anyone else. His claim, it should be recalled, is not that he is being denied a substantive educational opportunity, or even the right to attend an all-male or a coeducational college. It is *only* that the colleges open to him are located at inconvenient distances.

III . . .

In sum, the practice of voluntarily chosen single-sex education is an honored tradition in our country. . . . Mississippi's accommodation of such student choices is legitimate because it is completely consensual and is important because it permits students to decide for themselves the type of college education they think will benefit them most. Finally, Mississippi's policy is substantially related to its long-respected objective.

IV

A distinctive feature of America's tradition has been respect for diversity. This has been characteristic of the peoples from numerous lands who have built our country. It is the essence of our democratic system. At stake in this case as I see it is the preservation of a small aspect of this diversity. But that aspect is by no means insignificant, given our heritage of available choice between single-sex and coeducational institutions of higher learning. The Court answers that there is discrimination—not just that which may be tolerable, as for example between those candidates for admission able to contribute most to an educational institution and those able to contribute less—but discrimination of constitutional dimension. But, having found "discrimination," the Court finds it difficult to identify the victims. It hardly can claim that women are discriminated against. A constitutional case is held to exist solely because one man found it inconvenient to travel to any of the other institutions made available to him by the State of Mississippi. In essence he insists that he has a right to attend a college in his home community. This simply is not a sex discrimination case. The Equal Protection Clause was never intended to be applied to this kind of case.

~ Case 7.6 ~

Chief Justice **BURGER:** "[W]e reject the contention that in the remedial context the Congress must act in a wholly 'color-blind' fashion."

Justice **STEWART:** "Under our Constitution, any official action that treats a person differently on account of his race or ethnic origin is inherently suspect and presumptively invalid."

Fullilove v. Klutznick
448 U.S. 448, 100 S. Ct. 2758, 65 L. Ed. 2d 902 (1980)

The end of governmentally mandated discrimination represents, of course, a remarkable advance toward the ideals of the American Constitution. But how much good does it do to tell a group whose ancestors were first enslaved and then, for at least a century after emancipation, discriminated against, that they—who probably also felt some of the painful effects of governmental discrimination—will now be treated the same as the rest of society? How much does it help black people whom the state denied an education equal to that of whites that they now can compete on equal legal terms with whites? Giving some sort of preference in opportunities to acquire higher education and get jobs is one obvious remedy.

On the other hand, if the Constitution is colorblind, can government link preferential treatment to race? If government is remedying an abuse against a particular individual whom its past policy has injured, the answer is easy. But what if those most injured are now long dead and it is impossible to identify those who have suffered or are now suffering indirect injury from past discrimination? Can government give preference to a whole class of people, where that class is identified solely by-race?

It is with these questions that individual citizens, many states, and the federal government have wrestled in trying to right the grievous wrongs-of racist policies of the past. Congress has both required some and allowed more "affirmative action" as a remedy, but the extent of that requirement and authorization is not clear since Congress has also, consonant with the equal protection clause, forbidden discrimination (preference?) by race.

The Court first fully addressed these questions in California v. Bakke, 438 U.S. 265 (1978), a challenge to a "benign quota" by which the University of California at Davis reserved a minimum of one-sixth of the places in its medical school for blacks, Mexican-Americans, American Indians, and Asians. As a result of that policy, some members of these minorities were admitted with much lower grade-point averages and scores on standardized aptitude tests than those of rejected white applicants. The Court divided 4-1-4. Four justices said that both Congress and the Fourteenth Amendment allowed such quotas; four said it was unnecessary to address the constitutional issue because Congress had outlawed such schemes of racial preference. The ninth justice, Lewis F. Powell, Jr., said that the question whether Congress had outlawed such programs was not before the Court and that, although there was no constitutional ban against affirmative action programs in general, this particular one violated the equal protection clause.

Fullilove and a slew of other cases, some of which are discussed in a note after this reading, brought the issue back to Court. In sec. 103(f)(2) of the Public Works Employment Act of 1977, Congress provided that:

> Except to the extent that the Secretary [of Commerce] determines otherwise, no grant shall be made under this Act for any local public works project unless the applicant gives satisfactory assurance to the Secretary that at least ten per centum of the amount of each grant shall be expended for minority business enterprises. For the purposes of this paragraph, the term "minority business enterprise" (MBE) means a business at least 50 per centum of which is owned by minority group members or, in the case of a publicly owned business, at least 51 per centum of the stock of which is owned by minority group members. For the purposes of the preceding sentence, minority group members are citizens of the United States who are Negroes, Spanish-speaking, Orientals, Eskimos, and Aleuts.

Later that year several contracting and subcontracting firms filed suit in a federal district court, asking for an injunction against the secretary of commerce as well as city and state officials in New York who accepted grants under sec. 103(f)(2). The contractors claimed that the section, on its face, violated the equal protection clause and the "equal protection component" of the Fifth Amendment. Both the district court and the court of appeals upheld the constitutionality of sec. 103(f)(2). The contractors obtained review from the Supreme Court.

Mr. Chief Justice **BURGER** announced the judgment of the Court and delivered an opinion in which Mr. Justice **WHITE** and Mr. Justice **POWELL** joined. . . .

III

When we are required to pass on the constitutionality of an Act of

Congress, we assume "the gravest and most delicate duty that this Court is called on to perform." Blodgett v. Holden (1927) (opinion of Holmes, J.). A program that employs racial or ethnic criteria, even in a remedial context, calls for close examination; yet we are bound to approach our task with appropriate deference to the Congress, a coequal branch charged by the Constitution with the power to "provide for the . . . general Welfare of the United States" and "to enforce by appropriate legislation" the equal protection guarantees of the Fourteenth Amendment. In Columbia Broadcasting System, Inc. v. Democratic National Committee (1973), we accorded "great weight to the decisions of Congress" even though the legislation implicated fundamental constitutional rights guaranteed by the First Amendment. The rule is not different when a congressional program raises equal protection concerns.

Here we pass, not on a choice made by a single judge or a school board but on a considered decision of the Congress and the President. However, in no sense does that render it immune from judicial scrutiny and it "is not to say we 'defer' to the judgment of the Congress . . . on a constitutional question," or that we would hesitate to invoke the Constitution should we determine that Congress has overstepped the bounds of its constitutional power. *Columbia Broadcasting*. . . .

Our analysis proceeds in two steps. At the outset, we must inquire whether the *objectives* of this legislation are within the power of Congress. If so, we must go on to decide whether the limited use of racial and ethnic criteria, in the context presented, is a constitutionally permissible *means* for achieving the congressional objectives and does not violate the equal protection component of the Due Process Clause of the Fifth Amendment.

A

1   In enacting the MBE provision, it is clear that Congress employed an amalgam of its specifically delegated powers. The Act, by its very nature, is primarily an exercise of the Spending Power. . . . This Court has recognized that the power to "provide for the . . . general Welfare" is an independent grant of legislative authority, distinct from other broad congressional powers. Buckley v. Valeo (1976); United States v. Butler (1936). Congress has frequently employed the Spending Power to further broad policy objectives by conditioning receipt of federal monies upon compliance by the recipient with federal statutory and administrative directives. This Court has repeatedly upheld against constitutional challenge the use of this technique to induce governments and private parties to cooperate voluntarily with federal policy. . . .

The MBE program is structured within this familiar legislative pattern. . . .

. . . The reach of the Spending Power, within its sphere, is at least as broad as the regulatory powers of Congress. If, pursuant to its regulatory powers, Congress could have achieved the objectives of the MBE program, then it may do so under the Spending Power. And we have no difficulty perceiving a basis for accomplishing the objectives of the MBE program through the Commerce Power ... and through the power to enforce the equal protection guarantees of the Fourteenth Amendment....

2 We turn first to the Commerce Power.... Had Congress chosen to do so, it could have drawn on the Commerce Clause to regulate the practices of prime contractors on federally funded public works projects. Katzenbach v. McClung (1964); Heart of Atlanta Motel v. United States (1964). The legislative history of the MBE provision shows that there was a rational basis for Congress to conclude that the subcontracting practices of prime contractors could perpetuate the prevailing impaired access by minority businesses to public contracting opportunities, and that this inequity has an effect on interstate commerce. Thus Congress could take necessary and proper action to remedy the situation....

... Insofar as the MBE program pertains to the actions of private prime contractors, the Congress could [also] have achieved its objectives under the Commerce Clause. We conclude that in this respect the objectives of the MBE provision are within the scope of the Spending Power.

3 In certain contexts, there are limitations on the reach of the Commerce Power to regulate the actions of state and local governments. National League of Cities v. Usery (1976).° To avoid such complications, we look to § 5 of the Fourteenth Amendment for the power to regulate the procurement practices of state and local grantees of federal funds. A review of our cases persuades us that the objectives of the MBE program are within the power of Congress under § 5 "to enforce by appropriate legislation" the equal protection guarantees of the Fourteenth Amendment.

In Katzenbach v. Morgan (1966), we equated the scope of this authority with the broad powers expressed in the Necessary and Proper Clause. "Correctly viewed, § 5 is a positive grant of legislative power authorizing Congress to exercise its discretion in determining whether and what legislation is needed to secure the guarantees of the Fourteenth Amendment."...

... Congress reasonably determined that the prospective elimination of [discriminatory] barriers to minority firm access to public contracting opportunities generated by the 1977 Act was appropriate to ensure that those businesses were not denied equal opportunity to participate in federal grants to state and local governments, which is one aspect of the equal protection of the laws. Insofar as the MBE program pertains to the actions of state and local grantees, Congress could have achieved its objectives by use of its power

---

° *Garcia v. San Antonio MTA (1985; see Case 3.4) overruled* Usery, *but the general point is still valid.—Eds.*

under § 5 of the Fourteenth Amendment. We conclude that in this respect the objectives of the MBE provision are within the scope of the Spending Power. . . .

B

We now turn to the question whether, as a means to accomplish these plainly constitutional objectives, Congress may use racial and ethnic criteria, in this limited way, as a condition attached to a federal grant. We are mindful that "[i]n no matter should we pay more deference to the opinion of Congress than in its choice of instrumentalities to perform a function that is within its power," National Mutual Insurance Co. v. Tidewater Transfer Co. (1949) (opinion of Jackson, J.). However, . . . [w]e recognize [that the equal protection component of the Due Process Clause of the Fifth Amendment requires] careful judicial evaluation to assure that any congressional program that employs racial or ethnic criteria to accomplish the objective of remedying the present effects of past discrimination is narrowly tailored to the achievement of that goal. . . .

1   As a threshold matter, we reject the contention that in the remedial context the Congress must act in a wholly "color-blind" fashion. . . . [I]n Board of Education v. Swann (1971), we . . . held that "[j]ust as the race of students must be considered in determining whether a constitutional violation has occurred, so also must race be considered in formulating a remedy." . . .

When we have discussed the remedial powers of a federal court, we have been alert to the limitation that "[t]he power of the federal courts to restructure the operation of local and state governmental entities 'is not plenary. . . .' [A] federal court is required to tailor 'the scope of the remedy' to fit the nature and extent of the . . . violation." Dayton Board of Education v. Brinkman [I] (1977). Here we deal, . . . not with the limited remedial powers of a federal court, . . . but with the broad remedial powers of Congress. It is fundamental that in no organ of government, state or federal, does there repose a more comprehensive remedial power than in the Congress, expressly charged by the Constitution with competence and authority to enforce equal protection guarantees. Congress not only may induce voluntary action to assure compliance with existing federal statutory or constitutional antidiscrimination provisions, but also, where Congress has authority to declare certain conduct unlawful, it may, as here, authorize and induce state action to avoid such conduct.

2   A more specific challenge to the MBE program is the charge that it impermissibly deprives nonminority businesses of access to at least some portion of the government contracting opportunities generated by the Act. . . .

. . . [A]lthough we may assume that the complaining parties are innocent of any discriminatory conduct, it was within congressional power to act on the assumption that in the past some nonminority businesses may have reaped competitive benefit over the years from the virtual exclusion of minority firms from these contracting opportunities.

3   Another challenge to the validity of the MBE program is the assertion that it is underinclusive—that it limits its benefit to specified minority groups rather than extending its remedial objective to all businesses whose access to government contracting is impaired by the effects of disadvantage or discrimination. Such an extension would, of course, be appropriate for Congress to provide; it is not a function for the courts.

Even in this context, the well-established concept that a legislature may take one step at a time to remedy only part of a broader problem is not without relevance. See Dandridge v. Williams (1970); Williamson v. Lee Optical (1955). . . .

The Congress has not sought to give select minority groups a preferred standing in the construction industry, but has embarked on a remedial program to place them on a more equitable footing with respect to public contracting opportunities. There has been no showing in this case that Congress has inadvertently effected an invidious discrimination by excluding from coverage an identifiable minority group that has been the victim of a degree of disadvantage and discrimination equal to or greater than that suffered by the groups encompassed by the MBE program. . . .

4   It is also contended that the MBE program is overinclusive—that it bestows a benefit on businesses identified by racial or ethnic criteria which cannot be justified on the basis of competitive criteria or as a remedy for the present effects of identified prior discrimination. It is conceivable that a particular application of the program may have this effect; however, the peculiarities of specific applications are not before us in this case. . . .

IV

Congress, after due consideration, perceived a pressing need to move forward with new approaches in the continuing effort to achieve the goal of equality of economic opportunity. In this effort, Congress has necessary latitude to try new techniques such as the limited use of racial and ethnic criteria to accomplish remedial objectives. . . . That the program may press the outer limits of congressional authority affords no basis for striking it down. . . .

In a different context . . . Mr. Justice Brandeis had this to say:

> To stay experimentation in things social and economic is a grave responsibility. Denial of the right to experiment may be fraught with serious consequences to the Nation. New State Ice Co. v. Liebmann (1932) (dissenting opinion).

Any preference based on racial or ethnic criteria must necessarily receive a most searching examination to make sure that it does not conflict with constitutional guarantees. This case is one which requires; and which has received, that kind of examination. This opinion does not adopt, either expressly or implicitly, the formulas of analysis articulated in such cases as University of California Regents v. Bakke (1978). However, our analysis demonstrates that the MBE provision would survive judicial review under either "test" articulated in the several *Bakke* opinions. The MBE provision . . . does not violate the Constitution.

Affirmed.

Mr. Justice **POWELL**, concurring.

Although I would place greater emphasis than The Chief Justice on the need to articulate judicial standards of review in conventional terms, . . . I join [his] opinion and write separately to apply the analysis set forth by my opinion in *Bakke*.

. . . Section 103(f) (2) employs a racial classification that is constitutionally prohibited unless it is a necessary means of advancing a compelling governmental interest. . . .

. . . In my view, the effect of the set-aside° is limited and so widely dispersed that its use is consistent with fundamental fairness.

. . . [T]he set-aside is a reasonably necessary means of furthering the compelling governmental interest in redressing the discrimination that affects minority contractors. Any marginal unfairness to innocent nonminority contractors is not sufficiently significant—or sufficiently identifiable—to outweigh the governmental interest served by § 103(f) (2). When Congress acts to remedy identified discrimination, it may exercise discretion in choosing a remedy that is reasonably necessary to accomplish its purpose. Whatever the exact breadth of that discretion, I believe that it encompasses the selection of the set-aside in this case. . . .

Distinguishing the rights of all citizens to be free from racial classifications from the rights of some citizens to be made whole is a perplexing, but necessary, judicial task. When we first confronted such an issue in *Bakke,* I concluded that the Regents of the University of California were not competent to make, and had not made, findings sufficient to uphold the use of the race-conscious remedy they adopted. . . . [U]se of racial classifications, which are fundamentally at odds with the ideals of a democratic society implicit in the Due Process and Equal Protection Clauses, cannot be imposed simply to serve transient social or political goals, however worthy they may be. But the issue here turns on the scope of congressional power, and Congress has been given a unique constitutional role in the enforcement of the post-

---

° *The term* set-aside *refers to Congress's requiring that 10 percent of federal grants for local public works projects be set aside to pay businesses owned by members of the specified minorities.—Eds.*

Civil War Amendments. In this case, where Congress determined that minority contractors were victims of purposeful discrimination and where Congress chose a reasonably necessary means to effectuate its purpose, I find no constitutional reason to invalidate § 103(f) (2).

Mr. Justice **MARSHALL,** with whom Mr. Justice **BRENNAN,** and Mr. Justice **BLACKMUN** join, concurring in judgment.

My resolution of the constitutional issue in this case is governed by the separate opinion I coauthored in *Bakke*. In my view, the 10% minority set-aside provision . . . passes constitutional muster under the standard announced in that opinion. . . .

Mr. Justice **STEWART,** with whom Mr. Justice **REHNQUIST** joins, dissenting. . . .

"Our Constitution is color-blind, and neither knows nor tolerates classes among citizens. . . . The law regards man as man, and takes no account of his surroundings or of his color. . . ." Those words were written by a Member of this Court 84 years ago. Plessy v. Ferguson [1896] (Harlan, J., dissenting). [Mr. Justice Harlan's] colleagues disagreed with him, and held that a statute that required the separation of people on the basis of their race was constitutionally valid because it was a "reasonable" exercise of legislative power and had been "enacted in good faith for the promotion [of] the public good. . . ." Today, the Court upholds a statute that accords a preference to citizens who are "Negroes, Spanish-speaking, Orientals, Indians, Eskimos, and Aleuts," for much the same reasons. I think today's decision is wrong for the same reason that *Plessy* was wrong. . . .

The equal protection standard of the Constitution has one clear and central meaning—it absolutely prohibits invidious discrimination by government. . . . Under our Constitution, any official action that treats a person differently on account of his race or ethnic origin is inherently suspect and presumptively invalid. Bolling v. Sharpe [1954]; Korematsu v. United States [1944]. . . .

. . . In short, racial discrimination is by definition invidious discrimination.

The rule cannot be any different when the persons injured by a racially biased law are not members of a racial minority. The guarantee of equal protection is "universal in [its] application, to all persons . . . without regard to any differences of race, of color, or of nationality." Yick Wo v. Hopkins [1886]. . . . From the perspective of a person detrimentally affected by a racially discriminatory law, the arbitrariness and unfairness is entirely the same, whatever his skin color and whatever the law's purpose, be it purportedly "for the promotion of the public good" or otherwise. . . .

... [The Court's] self-evident truisms [about Congress's powers to spend, to regulate commerce, and to enforce § 5 of the Fourteenth Amendment] do not begin to answer the question before us in this case. For in the exercise of its powers, Congress must obey the Constitution just as the legislatures of all the States must.... If a law is unconstitutional, it is no less unconstitutional just because it is a product of the Congress of the United States....

Mr. Justice **STEVENS,** dissenting....

Our historic aversion to titles of nobility is only one aspect of our commitment to the proposition that the sovereign has a fundamental duty to govern impartially. When government accords different treatment to different persons, there must be a reason for the difference. Because racial characteristics so seldom provide a relevant basis for disparate treatment, and because classifications based on race are potentially so harmful to the entire body politic, it is especially important that the reasons for any such classification be clearly identified and unquestionably legitimate....

... I assume that the wrong committed against the Negro class is both so serious and so pervasive that it would constitutionally justify an appropriate classwide recovery.... But that serious classwide wrong cannot in itself justify the particular classification Congress has made in this Act. Racial classifications are simply too pernicious to permit any but the most exact connection between justification and classification. Quite obviously, the history of discrimination against black citizens in America cannot justify a grant of privileges to Eskimos or Indians.

Even if we assume that each of the six racial subclasses has suffered its own special injury at some time in our history, surely it does not necessarily follow that each of those subclasses suffered harm of identical magnitude.... There is no reason to assume, and nothing in the legislative history suggests, much less demonstrates, that each of these subclasses is equally entitled to reparations from the United States Government.

At best, the statutory preference is a somewhat perverse form of reparation for the members of the injured classes. For those who are the most disadvantaged within each class are the least likely to receive any benefit from the special privilege even though they are the persons most likely still to be suffering the consequences of the past wrong. A random distribution to a favored few is a poor form of compensation for an injury shared by many.

... [If the history of discrimination against Negroes] can justify such a random distribution of benefits on racial lines, ... it will serve not merely as a basis for remedial legislation, but rather as a permanent source of justification for grants of special privileges. For if there is no duty to attempt either to measure the recovery by the wrong or to distribute that recovery within the injured class in an evenhanded way, our history will adequately support a legislative preference for almost any ethnic, religious, or racial group with the political strength to negotiate "a piece of the action" for its members.

Although I do not dispute the validity of the assumption that each of the subclasses identified in the Act has suffered a severe wrong at some time in the past, I cannot accept this slapdash statute as a legitimate method of providing classwide relief. . . .

III

The legislative history of the Act discloses that there is a group of legislators in Congress identified as the "Black Caucus" and that members of that group argued that if the Federal Government was going to provide $4,000,000,000 of new public contract business, their constituents were entitled to "a piece of the action." . . .

The legislators' interest in providing their constituents with favored access to benefits distributed by the Federal Government is, in my opinion, a plainly impermissible justification for this racial classification.

IV

The interest in facilitating and encouraging the participation by minority business enterprises in the economy is unquestionably legitimate. Any barrier to such entry and growth . . . should be vigorously and thoroughly removed. . . . This statute, however, is not designed to remove any barriers to entry. Nor does its sparse legislative history detail any insuperable or even significant obstacles to entry into the competitive market. . . .

This Act has a character that is fundamentally different from a carefully drafted remedial measure like the Voting Rights Act of 1965. . . . Whereas the enactment of the Voting Rights Act was preceded by exhaustive hearings and debates concerning discriminatory denial of access to the electoral process, and became effective in specific States only after specific findings were made, this statute authorizes an automatic nationwide preference for all members of a diverse racial class regardless of their possible interest in the particular geographic areas where the public contracts are to be performed. . . .

A comparable approach in the electoral context would support a rule requiring that at least 10% of the candidates elected to the legislature be members of specified racial minorities. Surely that would be an effective way of ensuring black citizens the representation that has long been their due. Quite obviously, however, such a measure would merely create the kind of inequality that an impartial sovereign cannot tolerate. Yet that is precisely the kind of "remedy" that this Act authorizes. In both political and economic contexts, we have a legitimate interest in seeing that those who were disadvantaged in the past may succeed in the future. But neither an election nor a market can be equally accessible to all if race provides a basis for placing a special value on votes or dollars. . . .

V

A judge's opinion that a statute reflects a profoundly unwise policy determination is an insufficient reason for concluding that it is unconstitutional. Congress has broad power to spend money to provide for the "general Welfare of the United States," to "regulate Commerce among the several States," to enforce the Civil War Amendments, and to discriminate between aliens and citizens. But the exercise of these broad powers is subject to the constraints imposed by the Due Process Clause of the Fifth Amendment. That Clause has both substantive and procedural components; it performs the office of both the Due Process and Equal Protection Clauses of the Fourteenth Amendment in requiring that the federal sovereign act impartially.

Unlike Mr. Justice Stewart and Mr. Justice Rehnquist, however, I am not convinced that the [Due Process] Clause contains an absolute prohibition against any statutory classification based on race. I am nonetheless persuaded that it does impose a special obligation to scrutinize any governmental decisionmaking process that draws nationwide distinctions between citizens on the basis of their race and incidentally also discriminates against noncitizens in the preferred racial classes. For just as procedural safeguards are necessary to guarantee impartial decisionmaking in the judicial process, so can they play a vital part in preserving the impartial character of the legislative process. . . .

Although it is traditional for judges to accord the same presumption of regularity to the legislative process no matter how obvious it may be that a busy Congress has acted precipitately, I see no reason why the character of their procedures may not be considered relevant to the decision whether the legislative product has caused a deprivation of liberty or property without due process of law. Whenever Congress creates a classification that would be subject to strict scrutiny under the Equal Protection Clause of the Fourteenth Amendment if it had been fashioned by a state legislature, it seems to me that judicial review should include a consideration of the procedural character of the decisionmaking process. A holding that the classification was not adequately preceded by a consideration of less drastic alternatives or adequately explained by a statement of legislative purpose would be far less intrusive than a final determination that the substance of the decision is not "narrowly tailored to the achievement of that goal." . . .

In all events, rather than take the substantive position expressed in Mr. Justice Stewart's dissenting opinion, I would hold this statute unconstitutional on a narrower ground. It cannot fairly be characterized as a "narrowly tailored" racial classification because it simply raises too many serious questions that Congress failed to answer or even to address in a responsible way. The risk that habitual attitudes toward classes of persons, rather than analysis of the relevant characteristics of the class, will serve as a basis for a legislative classification is present when benefits are distributed as well as when burdens are imposed. In the past, traditional attitudes too often provided the only explanation for discrimination against women, aliens, illegitimates, and black citizens. Today there is a danger that awareness of past injustice will lead to automatic acceptance of new classifications that are not in fact justified by attributes characteristic of the class as a whole.

When Congress creates a special preference, or a special disability, for a class of persons, it should identify the characteristic that justifies the special treatment. When the classification is defined in racial terms, I believe that such particular identification is imperative.

In this case, only two conceivable bases for differentiating the preferred classes from society as a whole have occurred to me: (1) that they were the victims of unfair treatment in the past and (2) that they are less able to compete in the future. Although the first of these factors would justify an appropriate remedy for past wrongs, ... this statute is not such a remedial measure. The second factor is simply not true. Nothing in the record of this case, the legislative history of the Act, or experience that we may notice judicially provides any support for such a proposition. It is up to Congress to demonstrate that its unique statutory preference is justified by a relevant characteristic that is shared by the members of the preferred class. In my opinion, because it has failed to make that demonstration, it has also failed to discharge its duty to govern impartially embodied in the Fifth Amendment. ...

Editors' Note: Here, as in Bakke, *there was no opinion for the Court. Thus, while the justices sustained the program, there was no institutional explanation why they did so, only somewhat different explanations offered by individual justices. Even had there been an opinion of the Court, one would not expect so large a problem as affirmative action to go away merely because the Court had spoken clearly. The issue has returned and undoubtedly will return again. Consider the examples of the following paragraphs.*

In Firefighters Union v. Stotts, *467 U.S. 561 (1984), the Court examined a policy of Memphis, Tennessee, which as an economy measure reduced the number of public servants, on the basis of last hired, first fired. While not racist in intent, the plan had a disproportionate impact on blacks because only recently—and as the result of a lawsuit—had they been hired in large numbers as municipal employees. Despite this disproportionate effect, five justices upheld the plan.*

Wygant v. Jackson Board of Education, 90 L. Ed. 2d 260 (1986), struck down as a denial of equal protection a city's lay-off plan for public school teachers that generally operated by seniority but also provided that blacks and whites would be laid off in proportionate numbers, with the result that some whites with long seniority were laid off while some blacks with much less seniority retained their jobs. As in Bakke *and* Fullilove, *there was no opinion for the Court.*

On the other hand, Sheet Metal Workers v. EEOC, *92 L. Ed. 2d 344 (1986), sustained—over arguments by the Reagan administration—a lower court decree requiring a union not only to cease discriminatory admissions practices against blacks and Hispanics but to work toward a goal of nonwhite membership of 29 percent. Again there was no opinion of the Court, but five members of the majority thought it important that the union had had a long history of discrimination and had disobeyed orders from administrative agencies as well as courts to stop those practices.*

8. RIGHTS OF THE ACCUSED

Crime and criminal justice pose once again the basic questions that James Madison put to the framing generation: How can a nation construct a government that is strong enough to govern yet not so strong as to oppress? The Preamble of the Constitution speaks of one of the nation's purposes as ensuring "domestic Tranquility." Nevertheless, compared to most nations in the developed world, the United States is ridden not merely with lawless behavior but with violent lawless behavior that threatens the rights of all decent citizens—and even those of many criminals. Whether it is organized as a big business Mafia-style or random as in individual assaults by drug addicts or retarded juvenile delinquents, crime is widespread. The FBI estimates that each year about twelve million crimes against property and more than a million against people are committed in the United States.

Creating "law and order" is hardly easy, for the two are separate concepts and may even conflict. If order were the primary value, giving police unlimited authority to seek and punish criminals might seem rational. If, however, law is to be uppermost, then police, like the rest of society, have to be restrained. In the recent past, we have had the examples of Nazi Germany and fascist Italy to remind us how, in the name of order, police can terrorize their own people, memories that the governments of the Soviet Union, People's Republic of China, South Africa, and Chile, for example, keep alive. The real question is how to preserve order with law, that is, order with adherence to rules that allow the guilty to be arrested and punished and the innocent to go free.

The U.S. constitutional system's primary mission is protecting the innocent—from foreign enemies, from domestic criminals, and from the U.S. federal and state governments. Obviously the political system has done a better job with the first and third objectives than with the second. To accomplish the last objective, the Fourth, Fifth, Sixth, and Eighth amendments detail procedural safeguards. (And the Ninth reserves unlisted rights.) The Supreme Court has "incorporated" most of these provisions of the Bill of Rights into the due process clause of the Fourteenth Amendment, making them equally applicable against state governments as against the federal. Thus the Constitution, as histori-

cally interpreted, prefers liberty over police efficiency.

Under the amendments as originally ratified and their "incorporation" into the Fourteenth Amendment, an accused has rights to an attorney, to silence, to be protected against unreasonable searches and seizures and "cruel and unusual punishments," and, in general, to go free on bail between arrest and trial. But what do these rights mean to poor people who cannot afford their own attorneys or cannot post bail or are not sufficiently educated to understand their right to silence and their protection from illegal searches? Must arresting officers inform suspects of their rights? Must the government appoint attorneys to defend the poor? *Miranda v. Arizona (1966; see Case 8.1)* marked the culmination of a long series of decisions that had coped piecemeal with these questions.

In a nation that spends much of its leisure watching television shows about police, Miranda has become a household word. There is now even a verb to Mirandize, meaning to explain to a person his or her rights. But widespread use is not quite the same as full acceptance. Miranda is among the most controversial rulings of this century and remains the object of a long campaign for reversal.

Further aggravating opponents of Miranda has been the "exclusionary rule": Evidence obtained in violation of a suspect's statutory or constitutional rights cannot be used in court against that person. The justices first applied this rule against the federal government and later, as they incorporated more and more of the Bill of Rights into the Fourteenth Amendment, against the states as well.

The exclusionary rule is judge-made. The words of the constitutional document do not command it, require it, or even directly imply it. The judicial explanation for creating the rule is that without it, most of the Bill of Rights would be no more than a set of pious admonitions: Police could search anyone's person and property at will until they found incriminating evidence, or they could extract confessions by fraud, trickery, or perhaps even torture. The obvious means of enforcing the Constitution simply do not work in such situations. District attorneys are not likely to prosecute police who give them the evidence to become famous, and, in civil suits, jurors are not apt to make police pay damages to convicts. With the rule, police and prosecutors cannot use the evidence they have illegally obtained and, under the doctrine of the "fruit of the poisoned tree," neither can they use any evidence obtained through leads provided by the illegally obtained evidence.

Still, it is apparent that the exclusionary rule allows many guilty persons to go free. Weighing the values here is a delicate and subtle business, one that causes bitter disagreements not only among judges, police, and legislators but also among judges themselves. United States v. Leon (1984; see Case 8.2) provides acrid evidence of the closeness and significance of the issues as well as the emotional heat surrounding them.

~ Case 8.1 ~

Chief Justice **WARREN**: "[A]n interrogation environment is created for no purpose other than to subjugate the individual [suspect] to the will of his examiner. . . . To be sure, this is not physical intimidation, but it is equally destructive of human dignity."

Justice **HARLAN**: "[T]he thrust of the new rules is to negate all pressures, to reinforce the nervous or ignorant suspect, and ultimately to discourage any confession at all. The aim in short is . . . voluntariness with a vengeance."

Miranda v. Arizona
384 U.S. 436, 86 S. Ct. 1602, 16 L. Ed. 2d 694 (1966)

One of the most troublesome problems in a constitutional democracy centers on the treatment that police accord to persons suspected of committing crimes. The Bill of Rights, especially the Fourth, Fifth, Sixth, and Eighth amendments, restricts the authority of federal officials. State officials are limited by the far more general terms of the due process and equal protection clauses of the Fourteenth Amendment. Gradually, however, the Supreme Court has come to hold that the due process clause of the Fourteenth Amendment incorporates most of the Bill of Rights, and thus, in criminal matters, state and federal officials must conform to the same constitutional standards in dealing with suspects.

Because criminals often try to free themselves by claiming that earlier admissions of guilt were coerced from them and because police have a history of employing various forms of trickery, psychological coercion, and even physical violence to extract admissions of guilt, the use of confessions as evidence at trials has posed its own special difficulties. As Justice Harlan's dissent in this case indicates, the Court has not followed a straight, logical road in its decision making. For many years before this case, however, the justices had consistently held that, as a minimum, a confession could not be used in a state or federal court unless it had been "voluntary." Voluntary, alas, is a word that has many shades of meaning.

These four cases, one each from state courts in Arizona, California, and New York and another from a federal court in California, involved prosecutors' use of admissions of guilt by defendants. In none of the instances was there serious evidence of police brutality or gross psycho-

logical pressure against defendants. On the other hand, in none of these cases had police informed the accused, before he confessed, that he had a constitutional right to remain silent and to be represented by a lawyer. (Before these cases the Court had never ruled that a suspect had the right to have an attorney present at interrogation if the suspect could not afford to pay the lawyer's fee.) Here, by its own choice, the Court directly confronted the question of whether a confession could be "voluntary" if the suspect did not understand his right to silence.

Mr. Chief Justice **WARREN** delivered the opinion of the Court.

The cases before us raise questions which go to the roots of our concepts of American criminal jurisprudence.... More specifically, we deal with the admissibility of statements obtained from an individual who is subjected to custodial police interrogation and the necessity for procedures which assure that the individual is accorded his privilege under the Fifth Amendment to the Constitution not to be compelled to incriminate himself....

We start ... with the premise that our holding is not an innovation in our jurisprudence, but is an application of principles long recognized ... an explication of basic rights that are enshrined in our Constitution—that "No person ... shall be compelled in any criminal case to be a witness against himself," and that "the accused shall ... have the Assistance of Counsel...." These precious rights were fixed in our Constitution only after centuries of persecution and struggle. And in the words of Chief Justice Marshall, they were secured "for ages to come, and ... designed to approach immortality as nearly as human institutions can approach it," Cohens v. Virginia [1821]....

I ...

... From extensive factual studies undertaken in the early 1930's ... it is clear that police violence and the "third degree" flourished at that time. In a series of cases decided by this Court long after these studies, the police resorted to physical brutality—beating, hanging, whipping—and to sustained and protracted questioning incommunicado in order to extort confessions. The Commission on Civil Rights in 1961 found much evidence to indicate that "some policemen still resort to physical force to obtain confessions.".... The use of physical brutality and violence is not, unfortunately, relegated to the past or to any part of the country....

The examples given ... are undoubtedly the exception now, but they are sufficiently widespread to be the object of concern. Unless a proper limitation upon custodial interrogation is achieved ... there can be no assurance that practices of this nature will be eradicated in the foreseeable future....

... [T]he modern practice of in-custody interrogation is psychologically rather than physically oriented.... "[T]his Court has recognized that coercion can be mental as well as physical, and that the blood of the accused is not the only hallmark of an unconstitutional inquisition." . . . Interrogation still takes place in privacy. Privacy results in secrecy and this in turn results in a gap in our knowledge as to what in fact goes on. . . . A valuable source of information about present police practices, however, may be found in various police manuals and texts . . . used by law enforcement agencies themselves as guides. . . .

The officers are told by the manuals that the "principal psychological factor contributing to a successful interrogation is *privacy*—being alone with the person under interrogation."

> ". . . [T]he interrogation should take place in the investigator's office or at least in a room of his own choice. The subject should be deprived of every psychological advantage. In his own home he may be confident, indignant, or recalcitrant. He is more keenly aware of his rights. . . . Moreover his family and other friends are nearby, their presence lending moral support. In his own office, the investigator possesses all the advantages. The atmosphere suggests the invincibility of the forces of the law."

To highlight the isolation and unfamiliar surroundings, the manuals instruct the police to display an air of confidence in the suspect's guilt and . . . to maintain only an [apparent] interest in confirming certain details. . . . The interrogator should direct his comments toward the reasons why the subject committed the act, rather than court failure by asking the subject whether he did it. . . .

. . . The officers are instructed to minimize the moral seriousness of the offense, to cast blame on the victim or on society. These tactics are designed to put the subject in a psychological state where his story is but an elaboration of what the police purport to know already—that he is guilty. . . .

The texts thus stress that the major qualities an interrogator should possess are patience and perseverance: . . .

> ". . . Where emotional appeals and tricks are employed to no avail, [the investigator] must rely on an oppressive atmosphere of dogged persistence. He must interrogate steadily and without relent, leaving the subject no prospect of surcease. He must dominate his subject and overwhelm him with his inexorable will to obtain the truth. He should interrogate for a spell of several hours pausing only for the subject's necessities . . . to avoid a charge of duress. . . . In a serious case, the interrogation may continue for days, with the required intervals for food and sleep, but with no respite from the atmosphere of domination. It is possible in this way to induce the subject to talk without resorting to duress or coercion. The method should be used only when the guilt of the subject appears highly probable."

The manuals suggest that the suspect be offered legal excuses for his actions in order to obtain an initial admission of guilt. . . . Having then obtained the admission . . . the interrogator is advised to refer to circumstantial evidence which negates the self-defense explanation. This should enable him to secure the entire story. . . .

When the techniques described above prove unavailing, the texts recommend they be alternated with a show of some hostility. One ploy often used has been termed the "friendly-unfriendly" or the "Mutt and Jeff" act:

> ". . . [T]wo agents are employed. Mutt, the relentless investigator, who knows the subject is guilty. . . . [H]e's going to send the subject away for the full term. Jeff, on the other hand, is obviously a kindhearted man. . . . He has a brother who was involved in a little scrape like this. He disapproves of Mutt and his tactics and will arrange to get him off the case if the subject will cooperate. He can't hold Mutt off for very long. . . . The technique is applied by having both investigators present while Mutt acts out his role. Jeff may stand by quietly and demur at some of Mutt's tactics. When Jeff makes his plea for cooperation, Mutt is not in the room."

The interrogators sometimes are instructed to induce a confession out of trickery. The technique here is quite effective in crimes which require identification. . . . [T]he interrogator may . . . place the subject among a group of men in a line-up. "The witness or complainant (previously coached, if necessary) studies the line-up and confidently points out the subject as the guilty party." Then the questioning resumes "as though there were now no doubt about the guilt of the subject." . . .

The manuals also contain instructions for police on how to handle the individual who refuses to discuss the matter entirely, or who asks for an attorney or relatives. The examiner is to concede him the right to remain silent. . . . [H]owever, the officer is told to point out the incriminating significance of the suspect's refusal to talk:

> "Joe, you have a right to remain silent. That's your privilege and I'm the last person in the world who'll try to take it away from you. . . . But let me ask you this. Suppose you were in my shoes . . . and you called me in to ask me about this and I told you, 'I don't want to answer any of your questions.' You'd think I had something to hide. . . . That's exactly what I'll have to think about you. . . . So let's sit here and talk this whole thing over." . . .

In the event that the subject wishes to speak to a relative or an attorney: . . .

> "[T]he interrogator should respond by suggesting that the subject first tell the truth to the interrogator himself rather than get anyone else involved. . . . If the request is for an attorney, the interrogator may suggest that the subject save himself or his family the expense of any such professional service, particularly if he is innocent of the offense under investigation. The interrogator may also add, "Joe, I'm only looking for the truth, and if you're telling the truth, that's it. You can handle this by yourself.""

... [T]he setting prescribed by the manuals and observed in practice becomes clear: ... To be alone with the subject is essential to prevent distraction and to deprive him of any outside support. The aura of confidence in his guilt undermines his will to resist. He merely confirms the preconceived story the police seek to have him describe. ...

... [T]he very fact of custodial interrogation exacts a heavy toll on individual liberty and trades on the weakness of individuals.

In these cases, we might not find the defendants' statements to have been involuntary in traditional terms. Our concern for adequate safeguards to protect precious Fifth Amendment rights is, of course, not lessened in the slightest. In each of the cases, the defendant was thrust into an unfamiliar atmosphere and run through menacing police interrogation procedures. The potentiality for compulsion is forcefully apparent. ...

It is obvious that such an interrogation environment is created for no purpose other than to subjugate the individual to the will of his examiner. This atmosphere carries its own badge of intimidation. To be sure, this is not physical intimidation, but it is equally destructive of human dignity. ... [It] is at odds with one of our Nation's most cherished principles—that the individual may not be compelled to incriminate himself. Unless adequate protective devices are employed to dispel the compulsion inherent in custodial surroundings, no statement obtained from the defendant can truly be the product of his free choice. ...

III ...

... In order to combat these pressures and to permit a full opportunity to exercise the privilege against self-incrimination, the accused must be adequately and effectively apprised of his rights and the exercise of those rights must be fully honored.

It is impossible for us to foresee the potential alternatives for protecting the privilege which might be devised by Congress or the States. ... Therefore we cannot say that the Constitution necessarily requires adherence to any particular solution. ... Our decision in no way creates a constitutional straitjacket which will handicap sound efforts at reform. ... We encourage Congress and the States to continue their laudable search for increasingly effective ways of protecting the rights of the individual while promoting efficient enforcement of our criminal laws. However, unless we are shown other procedures which are at least as effective in apprising accused persons of their right of silence and in assuring a continuous opportunity to exercise it, the following safeguards must be observed.

At the outset, if a person in custody is to be subjected to interrogation, he must first be informed in clear and unequivocal terms that he has the right to remain silent. ...

The warning ... must be accompanied by the explanation that anything said can and will be used against the individual in court. This warning is needed in order to make him aware not only of the privilege, but also of the consequences of forgoing it. . . .

The circumstances surrounding in-custody interrogation can operate very quickly to overbear the will of one merely made aware of his privilege by his interrogators. Therefore, the right to have counsel present at the interrogation is indispensable to the protection of the Fifth Amendment privilege. . . . Our aim is to assure that the individual's right to choose between silence and speech remains unfettered throughout the interrogation process. . . . Thus, the need for counsel to protect the Fifth Amendment privilege comprehends not merely a right to consult with counsel prior to questioning, but also to have counsel present during any questioning if the defendant so desires.

An individual need not make a pre-interrogation request for a lawyer. . . . No effective waiver of the right to counsel during interrogation can be recognized unless specifically made after the warnings we here delineate have been given. The accused who does not know his rights and therefore does not make a request may be the person who most needs counsel.

Accordingly we hold that an individual held for interrogation must be clearly informed that he has the right to consult with a lawyer and to have the lawyer with him during interrogation. . . . As with the warnings of the right to remain silent and that anything stated can be used in evidence against him, this warning is an absolute prerequisite to interrogation. . . .

. . . The financial ability of the individual has no relationship to the scope of the rights involved here. . . . The need for counsel in order to protect the privilege exists for the indigent as well as the affluent. . . .

In order fully to apprise a person interrogated of the extent of his rights . . . it is necessary to warn him not only that he has the right to consult with an attorney, but also that if he is indigent a lawyer will be appointed to represent him. . . .

Once warnings have been given, the subsequent procedure is clear. If the individual indicates in any manner, at any time prior to or during questioning, that he wishes to remain silent, the interrogation must cease. . . . If the individual states that he wants an attorney, the interrogation must cease until an attorney is present. At that time, the individual must have an opportunity to confer with the attorney and to have him present during any subsequent questioning. If the individual cannot obtain an attorney and he indicates that he wants one before speaking to police, they must respect his decision to remain silent.

This does not mean . . . that each police station must have a "station house lawyer" present at all times to advise prisoners. It does mean, however, that if police propose to interrogate a person they must make known to him that he is entitled to a lawyer and that if he cannot afford one, a lawyer will be provided for him prior to any interrogation. If authorities conclude that they will not provide counsel during a reasonable period of time in which investigation in the field is carried out, they may refrain from doing so without violating the person's Fifth Amendment privilege so long as they do not question him during that time.

If the interrogation continues without the presence of an attorney and a statement is taken, a heavy burden rests on the government to demonstrate that the defendant knowingly and intelligently waived his privilege against self-incrimination and his right to retained or appointed counsel. . . .

An express statement that the individual is willing to make a statement and does not want an attorney followed closely by a statement could constitute a waiver. But a valid waiver will not be presumed simply from the silence of the accused after warnings are given or simply from the fact that a confession was in fact eventually obtained. . . .

Whatever the testimony of the authorities as to waiver of rights by an accused, the fact of lengthy interrogation or incommunicado incarceration before a statement is made is strong evidence that the accused did not validly waive his rights. . . . Moreover, any evidence that the accused was threatened, tricked, or cajoled into a waiver will, of course, show that the defendant did not voluntarily waive his privilege. . . .

Our decision is not intended to hamper the traditional function of police officers in investigating crime. . . . When an individual is in custody on probable cause, the police may, of course, seek out evidence in the field to be used at trial against him. Such investigation may include inquiry of persons not under restraint. General on-the-scene questioning as to facts surrounding a crime or other general questioning of citizens in the fact-finding process is not affected by our holding. It is an act of responsible citizenship for individuals to give whatever information they may have to aid in law enforcement. . . .

. . . Confessions remain a proper element in law enforcement. Any statement given freely and voluntarily without any compelling influences is, of course, admissible in evidence. . . . There is no requirement that police stop a person who enters a police station and states that he wishes to confess to a crime. . . .

IV . . .

. . . The whole thrust of our foregoing discussion demonstrates that the Constitution has prescribed the rights of the individual when confronted with the power of government when it provided in the Fifth Amendment that an individual cannot be compelled to be a witness against himself. That right cannot be abridged. As Mr. Justice Brandeis once observed:

"... Our Government is the potent, the omnipresent teacher. For good or for ill, it teaches the whole people by its example. Crime is contagious. If the Government becomes a lawbreaker, it breeds contempt for law; it invites every man to become a law unto himself; it invites anarchy...." Olmstead v. United States (1928) (dissenting opinion).

...[W]e are not unmindful of the burdens which law enforcement officials must bear.... This Court, while protecting individual rights, has always given ample latitude to law enforcement agencies in the legitimate exercise of their duties. The limits we have placed on the interrogation process should not constitute an undue interference with a proper system of law enforcement....

Over the years the Federal Bureau of Investigation has compiled an exemplary record of effective law enforcement while advising any suspect or arrested person, at the outset of an interview, that he is not required to make a statement, that any statement may be used against him in court, that the individual may obtain the services of an attorney of his own choice and, more recently, that he has a right to free counsel if he is unable to pay. A letter received from the Solicitor General in response to a question from the Bench makes it clear that the present pattern of warnings and respect for the rights of the individual followed as a practice by the FBI is consistent with the procedure which we delineate today....

Therefore ... the judgments of the Supreme Court of Arizona ... of the New York Court of Appeals ... and of the Court of Appeals for the Ninth Circuit ... are reversed. The judgment of the Supreme Court of California ... is affirmed.

It is so ordered.

Mr. Justice **CLARK** [dissenting in part and concurring in part]. ...

Mr. Justice **HARLAN,** whom Mr. Justice **STEWART** and Mr. Justice **WHITE** join, dissenting.

I believe the decision of the Court represents poor constitutional law and entails harmful consequences for the country at large. How serious these consequences may prove to be only time can tell. But the basic flaws in the Court's justification seem to me readily apparent....

I. Introduction ...

... The new rules are not designed to guard against police brutality.... Those who use third-degree tactics and deny them in court are equally able and destined to lie as skillfully about warnings and waivers. Rather, the thrust of the new rules is to negate all pressures, to reinforce the nervous or ignorant suspect, and ultimately to discourage any confession at all. The aim in short is ... voluntariness with a vengeance.

To incorporate this notion into the Constitution requires a strained reading of history and precedent and a disregard of the very pragmatic concerns that alone may on occasion justify such strains. . . .

II. Constitutional Premises

It is most fitting to begin . . . by surveying the limits on confessions the Court has evolved under the Due Process Clause of the Fourteenth Amendment. . . . [T]hese cases show that there exists a workable and effective means of dealing with confessions in a judicial manner. . . .

The earliest confession cases in this Court emerged from federal prosecutions and were settled on a nonconstitutional basis, the Court adopting the common-law rule that the absence of inducements, promises, and threats made a confession voluntary and admissible. . . .

This new line of decisions, testing admissibility by the Due Process Clause, began in 1936 with Brown v. Mississippi. . . . While the voluntariness rubric was repeated in many instances . . . the Court never pinned it down to a single meaning but . . . infused it with a number of different values. . . . [T]here was initial emphasis on reliability . . . supplemented by concern over the legality and fairness of the police practices . . . and eventually by close attention to the individual's state of mind and capacity for effective choice. . . . The outcome was a continuing re-evaluation on the facts of each case of *how much* pressure on the suspect was permissible.

Among the criteria often taken into account were threats or imminent danger . . . physical deprivations such as lack of sleep or food . . . repeated or extended interrogation . . . limits on access to counsel or friends . . . length and legality of detention under state law . . . and individual weaknesses or incapacities. . . . Apart from direct physical coercion, however, no single default or fixed combination of defaults guaranteed exclusion. . . .

. . . The Court's opinion . . . fails to show that the Court's new rules are well supported, let alone compelled, by Fifth Amendment precedents. Instead, the new rules actually derive from quotation and analogy drawn from precedents under the Sixth Amendment, which should properly have no bearing on police interrogation.

The Court's opening contention, that the Fifth Amendment governs police station confessions . . . has little to commend itself in the present circumstances. Historically, the privilege against self-incrimination did not bear at all on the use of extra-legal confessions, for which distinct standards evolved. . . .

Having decided that the Fifth Amendment privilege does apply in the police station, the Court reveals that the privilege imposes more exacting restrictions than does the Fourteenth Amendment's voluntariness test. It then emerges . . . that the Fifth Amendment requires for an admissible confession that it be given by one distinctly aware of his right not to speak and shielded from "the compelling atmosphere" of interrogation.... From these key premises, the Court finally develops the safeguards of warning, counsel, and so forth. I do not believe these premises are sustained by precedents under the Fifth Amendment.

The important premise is that pressure on the suspect must be eliminated though it be only the subtle influence of the atmosphere and surroundings. The Fifth Amendment, however, has never been thought to forbid *all* pressure to incriminate one's self in the situations covered by it. On the contrary, it has been held that failure to incriminate one's self can result in denial of removal of one's case from state to federal court ... in refusal of a military commission ... and in numerous other adverse consequences.... This is not to say that short of jail or torture any sanction is permissible in any case; policy and history alike may impose sharp limits.... To support its requirement of a knowing and intelligent waiver, the Court cites [several cases].... All these cases imparting glosses to the Sixth Amendment concerned counsel at trial or an appeal. While the Court finds no pertinent difference between judicial proceedings and police interrogation, I believe the differences are so vast as to disqualify wholly the Sixth Amendment precedents as suitable analogies....

The only attempt in this Court to carry the right to counsel into the station house occurred in [Escobedo v. Illinois (1963)], the Court repeating several times that that stage was no less "critical" than trial itself.... This is hardly persuasive when we consider that a grand jury inquiry, the filing of a certiorari petition, and certainly the purchase of narcotics by an undercover agent from a prospective defendant may all be equally "critical" yet provision of counsel and advice of that score have never been thought compelled by the Constitution in such cases. The sound reason why this right is so freely extended for a criminal trial is the severe injustice risked by confronting an untrained defendant with a range of technical points of law, evidence, and tactics familiar to the prosecutor but not to himself. This danger shrinks markedly in the police station where indeed the lawyer in fulfilling his professional responsibilities of necessity may become an obstacle to truthfinding.... The Court's summary citation of the Sixth Amendment cases here seems to me best described as "the domino method of constitutional adjudication ... wherein every explanatory statement in a previous opinion is made the basis for extension to a wholly different situation."...

III. Policy Considerations

... [A]s an expression of public policy, the Court's new regime proves so dubious that there can be no due compensation for its weakness in constitutional law. The foregoing discussion has shown, I think, how mistaken is the Court in implying that the Constitution has struck the balance in favor of the approach the Court takes.... Legal history has been stretched before to satisfy deep needs of society. In this instance, however, the Court has not and cannot make the powerful showing that its new rules are plainly desirable in the context of our society, something which is surely demanded before those rules are engrafted onto the Constitution and imposed on every State and county in the land. . . .

. . . Until today, the role of the Constitution has been only to sift out *undue* pressure, not to assure spontaneous confessions.

The Court's new rules aim to offset these minor pressures and disadvantages intrinsic to any kind of police interrogation. The rules do not serve due process interests in preventing blatant coercion since . . . they do nothing to contain the policeman who is prepared to lie from the start. . . .

. . . There can be little doubt that the Court's new role would markedly decrease the number of confessions. To warn the suspect that he may remain silent and remind him that his confession may be used in court are minor obstructions. To require also an express waiver by the suspect and an end to questioning whenever he demurs must heavily handicap questioning. And to suggest or provide counsel for the suspect simply invites the end of the interrogation. . . .

How much harm this decision will inflict on law enforcement cannot fairly be predicted with accuracy. Evidence on the role of confessions is notoriously incomplete. . . . [T]he Court is taking a real risk with society's welfare in imposing its new regime on the country. The social costs of crime are too great to call the new rules anything but a hazardous experimentation.

While passing over the costs and risks of its experiment, the Court portrays the evils of normal police questioning in terms which I think are exaggerated. . . . Society has always paid a stiff price for law and order, and peaceful interrogation is not one of the dark moments of the law. . . .

Mr. Justice **WHITE**, with whom Mr. Justice **HARLAN** and Mr. Justice **STEWART** join, dissenting. . . .

Editors' Notes: Miranda elicited an angry reaction from hardliners on crime, and in the Crime Control Act of 1968 Congress responded by saying that a confession obtained in the absence of the warnings listed in Miranda need not be inadmissible evidence in a federal trial. The Senate Judiciary Committee conceded that the Court, as then constituted, would probably invalidate that section of the statute; but, noting that the decision had been 5-4, the committee expressed the hope that by the time a case under the 1968 act was decided, some of the five justices in the majority would have left the bench and a new majority might sustain the section.

Despite campaign rhetoric, the Nixon administration did not enforce the act so as to provoke a judicial test of its constitutionality. On the other hand, Nixon did have the opportunity to nominate four new justices, three of whom replaced members of the majority in Miranda. *With some of the four dissenters in* Miranda, *these new justices have prevented the expansion of* Miranda's *libertarian doctrine and have somewhat curtailed its impact.*

Nevertheless, police now routinely give the warnings required by Miranda. *Justice Harlan's dissent expressed deep concern that such obedience would drastically curtail the number of confessions police obtained. Although the evidence on this point is not wholly conclusive, it seems that the warnings have not caused a dramatic decrease in confessions, partially because most nonprofessional criminals whom the police detain for questioning either do not understand the warnings or fear that a state-appointed attorney will cooperate with the police.*

In February 1976 Ernesto Miranda, who gave his name to this case, was murdered in a barroom in Tucson, Arizona. Police quickly arrested his alleged killer and, standing near Miranda's body, read to the suspect from what has come to be called a Miranda card the warnings specified by the Supreme Court.

~ Case 8.2 ~

Justice **WHITE:** "The substantial social costs exacted by the exclusionary rule for the vindication of Fourth Amendment rights have long been a source of concern."

Justice **STEVENS:** "It is of course true that the exclusionary rule exerts a high price.... But that price ... is ... one the Fourth Amendment requires us to pay."

United States v. Leon
468 U.S. 897, 104 S. Ct. 3405, 82 L. Ed. 2d 677 (1984)

Weeks v. United States, 232 U.S. 383 (1914), exluded from use in federal trials evidence obtained by unlawful searches and seizures. Mapp v. Ohio, 307 U.S. 643 (1961), extended this exclusionary rule to state trials and provoked bitter and long-lasting opposition by police, prosecutors, and many other public officials, including state and federal judges. In this case, police had obtained a facially valid search warrant

Alberto Leon to large-scale drug dealing. Partially on the basis of this evidence, a federal grand jury indicted him for conspiracy to possess and distribute cocaine. At a pretrial hearing, however, the district judge found that, although the police had acted in good faith, the affidavit on which the warrant was based had been insufficient to establish "probable cause," as required by the Fourth Amendment. Thus the district judge ruled that the seized evidence must be excluded from the trial. The Department of Justice appealed to the Court of Appeals for the Ninth Circuit and, after that tribunal affirmed, sought and obtained review from the United States Supreme Court.

Justice **WHITE** delivered the opinion of the Court. . . .

Language in opinions of this Court and of individual Justices has sometimes implied that the exclusionary rule is a necessary corollary of the Fourth Amendment, Mapp v. Ohio (1961); Olmstead v. United States (1928), or that the rule is required by the conjunction of the Fourth and Fifth Amendments. These implications need not detain us long. The Fifth Amendment theory has not withstood critical analysis or the test of time, see Anderson v. Maryland (1976), and the Fourth Amendment "has never been interpreted to proscribe the introduction of illegally seized evidence in all proceedings or against all persons." Stone v. Powell (1976).

The Fourth Amendment contains no provision expressly precluding the use of evidence obtained in violation of its commands, and an examination of its origin and purposes makes clear that the use of fruits of a past unlawful search or seizure "work[s] no new Fourth Amendment wrong." United States v. Calandra (1974). The wrong condemned by the Amendment is "fully accomplished" by the unlawful search or seizure itself, and the exclusionary rule is neither intended nor able to "cure the invasion of the defendant's rights which he has already suffered." *Stone* (White, J., dissenting). The rule thus operates as "a judicially created remedy designed to safeguard Fourth Amendment rights generally through its deterrent effect, rather than a personal constitutional right of the person aggrieved." *Calandra.*

Whether the exclusionary sanction is appropriately imposed in a particular case, our decisions make clear, is "an issue separate from the question whether the Fourth Amendment rights of the party seeking to invoke the rule were violated by police conduct." Illinois v. Gates (1983). Only the former question is currently before us, and it must be resolved by weighing the costs and benefits of preventing the use in the prosecution's case-in-chief of inherently trustworthy tangible evidence obtained in reliance on a search warrant issued by a detached and neutral magistrate that ultimately is found to be defective.

The substantial social costs exacted by the exclusionary rule for the vindication of Fourth Amendment rights have long been a source of concern.

"Our cases have consistently recognized that unbending application of the exclusionary sanction to enforce ideals of governmental rectitude would impede unacceptably the truth-finding functions of judge and jury." United States v. Payner (1980). An objectionable collateral consequence of this interference with the criminal justice system's truth-finding function is that some guilty defendants may go free to receive reduced sentences as a result of favorable plea bargains. Particularly when law enforcement officers have acted in objective good faith or their transgressions have been minor, the magnitude of the benefit conferred on such guilty defendants offends basic concepts of the criminal justice system. *Stone.* Indiscriminate application of the exclusionary rule, therefore, may well "generat[e] disrespect for the law and the administration of justice." Accordingly, "[a]s with any remedial device, the application of the rule has been restricted to those areas where its remedial objectives are thought most efficaciously served." *Calandra.* . . .

Close attention to those remedial objectives has characterized our recent decisions concerning the scope of the Fourth Amendment exclusionary rule. The Court has, to be sure, not seriously questioned, "in the absence of a more efficacious sanction, the continued application of the rule to suppress evidence from the [prosecution's] case where a Fourth Amendment violation has been substantial and deliberate. . . ." Franks v. Delaware (1978); *Stone.* Nevertheless, the balancing approach that has evolved in various contexts— including criminal trials—"forcefully suggest[s] that the exclusionary rule be more generally modified to permit the introduction of evidence obtained in the reasonable good-faith belief that a search or seizure was in accord with the Fourth Amendment." *Gates* (White, J., concurring in the judgment).

Justice **BRENNAN,** with whom Justice **MARSHALL** joins, dissenting.

Ten years ago in *Calandra* (1974), I expressed the fear that the Court's decision "may signal that a majority of my colleagues have positioned themselves to reopen the door [to evidence secured by official lawlessness] still further and abandon altogether the exclusionary rule in search-and-seizure cases." Since then, in case after case, I have witnessed the Court's gradual but determined strangulation of the rule. It now appears that the Court's victory over the Fourth Amendment is complete. That today's decision represents the *piece de resistance* of the Court's past efforts cannot be doubted, for today the court sanctions the use in the prosecution's case-in-chief of illegally obtained evidence against the individual whose rights have been violated—a result that had previously been thought to be foreclosed.

The Court seeks to justify this result on the ground that the "costs" of adhering to the exclusionary rule in cases like those before us exceed the "benefits." But the language of deterrence and of cost/benefit analysis, if used indiscriminately, can have a narcotic effect. It creates an illusion of technical precision and ineluctability. It suggests that not only constitutional principle but also empirical data supports the majority's result. When the Court's analysis is examined carefully, however, it is clear that we have not been treated to an honest assessment of the merits of the exclusionary rule, but have instead been drawn into a curious world where the "costs" of excluding illegally obtained evidence loom to exaggerated heights and where the "benefits" of such exclusion are made to disappear with a mere wave of the hand.

The majority ignores the fundamental constitutional importance of what is at stake here. While the machinery of law enforcement and indeed the nature of crime itself have changed dramatically since the Fourth Amendment became part of the Nation's fundamental law in 1791, what the Framers understood then remains true today—that the task of combatting crime and convicting the guilty will in every era seem of such critical and pressing concern that we may be lured by the temptations of expediency into forsaking our commitment to protecting individual liberty and privacy. It was for that very reason that the Framers of the Bill of Rights insisted that law enforcement efforts be permanently and unambiguously restricted in order to preserve personal freedoms. In the constitutional scheme they ordained, the sometimes unpopular task of ensuring that the government's enforcement efforts remain within the strict boundaries fixed by the Fourth Amendment was entrusted to the courts. . . .

Justice **STEVENS** [concurring in *Leon* and dissenting in a similar case decided the same day] . . . .

It is appropriate to begin with the plain language of the Fourth Amendment:

"The right of the people to be secure in their persons, houses, papers, and effects, against unreasonable searches and seizures, shall not be violated; and no Warrants shall issue but upon probable cause, supported by Oath or affirmation, and particularly describing the place to be searched, and the persons or things to be seized."

The Court assumes that the searches in these cases violated the Fourth Amendment, yet refuses to apply the exclusionary rule because the Court concludes that it was "reasonable" for the police to conduct them. In my opinion an official search and seizure cannot be both "unreasonable" and "reasonable" at the same time. The doctrinal vice in the Court's holding is its failure to consider the separate purposes of the two prohibitory clauses in the Fourth Amendment.

The first clause prohibits unreasonable searches and seizures and the second prohibits the issuance of warrants that are not supported by probable cause or that do not particularly describe the place to be searched and the persons or things to be seized. We have, of course, repeatedly held that warrantless searches are presumptively unreasonable, and that there are only a few carefully delineated exceptions to that basic presumption. But when such an exception has been recognized, analytically we have necessarily concluded that the warrantless activity was not "unreasonable" within the meaning of the first clause. Thus, any Fourth Amendment case may present two separate questions: whether the search was conducted pursuant to a warrant issued in accordance with the second clause, and, if not, whether it was nevertheless "reasonable" within the meaning of the first. On these questions, the constitutional text requires that we speak with one voice. We cannot intelligibly assume arguendo that a search was constitutionally unreasonable but that the seized evidence is admissible because the same search was reasonable.

I . . .

In *Leon*, there is also a substantial question whether the warrant complied with the Fourth Amendment. There was a strong dissent on the probable cause issue when *Leon* was before the Court of Appeals, and that dissent has been given added force by this Court's intervening decision in *Gates* (1983), which constituted a significant development in the law. It is probable, though admittedly not certain, that the Court of Appeals would now conclude that the warrant in *Leon* satisfied the Fourth Amendment if it were given the opportunity to reconsider the issue in the light of *Gates*. Adherence to our normal practice following the announcement of a new rule would therefore postpone, and probably obviate, the need for the promulgation of the broad new rule the Court announces today. . . .

Judges, more than most, should understand the value of adherence to settled procedures. By adopting a set of fair procedures, and then adhering to them, courts of law ensure that justice is administered with an even hand. "These are subtle matters, for they concern the ingredients of what constitutes justice. Therefore, justice must satisfy the appearance of justice." Offutt v. United States (1954). Of course, this Court has a duty to face questions of constitutional law when necessary to the disposition of an actual case or controversy. Marbury v. Madison (1803). But when the Court goes beyond what is necessary to decide the case before it, it can only encourage the perception that it is pursuing its own notions of wise social policy, rather than adhering to its judicial role. I do not believe the Court should reach out to decide what is undoubtedly a profound question concerning the administration of criminal justice before assuring itself that this question is actually and of necessity presented by the concrete facts before the Court. Although it may appear that the Court's broad holding will serve the public interest in enforcing obedience to the rule of law, for my part, I remain firmly convinced that "the preservation of order in our communities will be best insured by adherence to established and respected procedures." Groppi v. Leslie° (en banc) (Stevens, J., dissenting), rev'd (1972). . . .

° *A decision of the U.S. Court of Appeals, Seventh Circuit.—Eds.*

IV . . .

The exclusionary rule is designed to prevent violations of the Fourth Amendment. "Its purpose is to deter—to compel respect for the constitutional guaranty in the only effectively available way, by removing the incentive to disregard it." Elkins v. United States (1960). If the police cannot use evidence obtained through warrants issued on less than probable cause, they have less incentive to seek those warrants, and magistrates have less incentive to issue them.

Today's decisions do grave damage to that deterrent function. Under the majority's new rule, even when the police know their warrant application is probably insufficient, they retain an incentive to submit it to a magistrate, on the chance that he may take the bait. No longer must they hesitate and seek additional evidence in doubtful cases. . . .

The Court is of course correct that the exclusionary rule cannot deter when the authorities have no reason to know that their conduct is unconstitutional. But when probable cause is lacking, then by definition a reasonable person under the circumstances would not believe there is a fair likelihood that a search will produce evidence of a crime. Under such circumstances well-trained professionals must know that they are violating the Constitution. The Court's approach—which, in effect, encourages the police to seek a warrant even if they know the existence of probable cause is doubtful—can only lead to an increased number of constitutional violations.

Thus, the Court's creation of a double standard of reasonableness inevitably must erode the deterrence rationale that still supports the exclusionary rule. But we should not ignore the way it tarnishes the role of the judiciary in enforcing the Constitution. For the original rationale for the exclusionary rule retains its force as well as its relevance:

> "The tendency of those who execute the criminal laws of the country to obtain conviction by means of unlawful seizures . . . should find no sanction in the judgments of the courts which are charged at all times with the support of the Constitution and to which people of all conditions have a right to appeal for the maintenance of such fundamental rights." Weeks v. United States (1914).

Thus, "Courts which sit under our Constitution cannot and will not be made party to lawless invasions of the constitutional rights of citizens by permitting unhindered governmental use of the fruits of such invasions. . . ." Terry v. Ohio (1968). . . . Today, for the first time, this Court holds that although the Constitution has been violated, no court should do anything about it at any time and in any proceeding. In my judgment, the Constitution requires more. Courts simply cannot escape their responsibility for redressing constitutional violations if they admit evidence obtained through unreasonable searches and seizures, since the entire point of police conduct that violates the Fourth Amendment is to obtain evidence for use at trial. If such evidence is admitted, then the courts become not merely the final and necessary link in an unconstitutional chain of events, but its actual motivating force. "If the existing code does not permit district attorneys to have a hand in such dirty business it does not permit the judge to allow such iniquities to succeed." *Olmstead* (1928) (Holmes, J., dissenting). Nor should we so easily concede the existence of a constitutional violation for which there is no remedy. To do so is to convert a Bill of Rights into an unenforced honor code that the police may follow in their discretion. The Constitution requires more; it requires a *remedy*. If the Court's new rule is to be followed, the Bill of Rights should be renamed.

It is of course true that the exclusionary rule exerts a high price—the loss of probative evidence of guilt. But that price is one courts have often been required to pay to serve important social goals. That price is also one the Fourth Amendment requires us to pay, assuming as we must that the Framers intended that its strictures "shall not be violated." For in all such cases, as Justice Stewart has observed, "the same extremely relevant evidence would not have been obtained had the police officer complied with the commands of the fourth amendment in the first place."

> "[T]he forefathers thought this was not too great a price to pay for that decent privacy of home, papers and effects which is indispensable to individual dignity and self-respect. They may have overvalued privacy, but I am not disposed to set their command at naught." Harris v. United States (1947) (Jackson, J., dissenting).

We could, of course, facilitate the process of administering justice to those who violate the criminal laws by ignoring the commands of the Fourth Amendment—indeed, by ignoring the entire Bill of Rights—but it is the very purpose of a Bill of Rights to identify values that may not be sacrificed to expediency. In a just society those who govern, as well as those who are governed, must obey the law. . . .

APPENDIX: THE CONSTITUTION
OF THE UNITED STATES

We the People of the United States, in Order to form a more perfect Union, establish Justice, insure domestic Tranquility, provide for the common defence, promote the general Welfare, and secure the Blessings of Liberty to ourselves and our Posterity, do ordain and establish this Constitution for the United States of America.

Article I

Section 1

All legislative Powers herein granted shall be vested in a Congress of the United States, which shall consist of a Senate and House of Representatives.

Section 2

The House of Representatives shall be composed of Members chosen every second Year by the People of the several States, and the Electors in each State shall have the Qualifications requisite for Electors of the most numerous Branch of the State Legislature.

No Person shall be a Representative who shall not have attained to the age of twenty five Years, and been seven Years a Citizen of the United States, and who shall not, when elected, be an Inhabitant of that State in which he shall be chosen.

[Representatives and direct Taxes shall be apportioned among the several States which may be included within this Union, according to their respective Numbers, which shall be determined by adding to the whole Number of free Persons, including those bound to Service for a Term of Years, and excluding Indians not taxed, three fifths of all other Persons.] [1] The actual Enumeration shall be made within three Years after the first Meeting of the Congress of the United States, and within every subsequent Term of ten Years, in such Manner as they shall by Law direct. The Number of Representatives shall not exceed one for every thirty Thousand, but each State shall have at Least one Representative; and until such enumeration shall be made, the State of New

Hampshire shall be entitled to chuse three, Massachusetts eight, Rhode-Island and Providence Plantations one, Connecticut five, New-York six, New Jersey four, Pennsylvania eight, Delaware one, Maryland six, Virginia ten, North Carolina five, South Carolina five, and Georgia three.

When vacancies happen in the Representation from any State, the Executive Authority thereof shall issue Writs of Election to fill such Vacancies.

The House of Representatives shall chuse their Speaker and other Officers; and shall have the sole Power of Impeachment.

Section 3

The Senate of the United States shall be composed of two Senators from each State, [chosen by the Legislature thereof,] [2] for six Years; and each Senator shall have one Vote.

Immediately after they shall be assembled in Consequence of the first Election, they shall be divided as equally as may be into three Classes. The Seats of the Senators of the first Class shall be vacated at the Expiration of the second Year, of the second Class at the Expiration of the fourth Year, and of the third Class at the Expiration of the sixth Year, so that one third may be chosen every second Year; [and if Vacancies happen by Resignation, or otherwise, during the Recess of the Legislature of any State, the Executive thereof may make temporary Appointments until the next Meeting of the Legislature, which shall then fill such Vacancies.] [3]

No Person shall be a Senator who shall not have attained to the Age of thirty Years, and been nine Years a Citizen of the United States, and who shall not, when elected, be an Inhabitant of that State for which he shall be chosen.

The Vice President of the United States shall be President of the Senate, but shall have no Vote, unless they be equally divided.

The Senate shall chuse their other Officers, and also a President pro tempore, in the Absence of the Vice President, or when he shall exercise the Office of President of the United States.

The Senate shall have the sole Power to try all Impeachments. When sitting for that Purpose, they shall be on Oath or Affirmation. When the President of the United States is tried the Chief Justice shall preside: And no Person shall be convicted without the Concurrence of two thirds of the Members present.

Judgment in Cases of Impeachment shall not extend further than to removal from Office, and disqualification to hold and enjoy any Office of honor, Trust or Profit under the United States: but the Party convicted shall nevertheless be liable and subject to Indictment, Trial, Judgment and Punishment, according to Law.

Section 4

The Times, Places and Manner of holding Elections for Senators and Representatives, shall be prescribed in each State by the Legislature thereof; but the Congress may at any time by Law make or alter such Regulations, except as to the Places of chusing Senators.

The Congress shall assemble at least once in every Year, and such Meeting shall [be on the first Monday in December],⁴ unless they shall by Law appoint a different Day.

Section 5

Each House shall be the Judge of the Elections, Returns and Qualifications of its own Members, and a Majority of each shall constitute a Quorum to do Business; but a smaller Number may adjourn from day to day, and may be authorized to compel the Attendance of absent Members, in such Manner, and under such Penalties as each House may provide.

Each House may determine the Rules of its Proceedings, punish its Members for disorderly Behaviour, and, with the Concurrence of two thirds, expel a Member.

Each House shall keep a Journal of its Proceedings, and from time to time publish the same, excepting such Parts as may in their Judgment require Secrecy; and the Yeas and Nays of the Members of either House on any question shall, at the Desire of one fifth of those Present, be entered on the Journal.

Neither House, during the Session of Congress, shall, without the Consent of the other, adjourn for more than three days, nor to any other Place than that in which the two Houses shall be sitting.

Section 6

The Senators and Representatives shall receive a Compensation for their Services, to be ascertained by Law, and paid out of the Treasury of the United States. They shall in all Cases, except Treason, Felony and Breach of the Peace, be privileged from Arrest during their Attendance at the Session of their respective Houses, and in going to and returning from the same; and for any Speech or Debate in either House, they shall not be questioned in any other Place.

No Senator or Representative shall, during the Time for which he was elected, be appointed to any civil Office under the Authority of the United States, which shall have been created, or the Emoluments whereof shall have been encreased during such time; and no Person holding any Office under the United States, shall be a Member of either House during his Continuance in Office.

Section 7

All Bills for raising Revenue shall originate in the House of Representatives; but the Senate may propose or concur with amendments as on other Bills.

Every Bill which shall have passed the House of Representatives and the Senate, shall, before it become a Law, be presented to the President of the United States; If he approve he shall sign it, but if not he shall return it, with his Objections to that House in which it shall have originated, who shall enter the Objections at large on their Journal, and proceed to reconsider it. If after such Reconsideration two thirds of that House shall agree to pass the Bill, it shall be sent, together with the Objections, to the other House, by which it shall likewise be reconsidered, and if approved by two thirds of that House, it shall become a Law. But in all such Cases the Votes of both Houses shall be determined by yeas and Nays, and the Names of the Persons voting for and against the Bill shall be entered on the Journal of each House respectively. If any Bill shall not be returned by the President within ten Days (Sunday excepted) after it shall have been presented to him, the Same shall be a Law, in like Manner as if he had signed it, unless the Congress by their Adjournment prevent its Return, in which Case it shall not be a Law.

Every Order, Resolution, or Vote to which the Concurrence of the Senate and House of Representatives may be necessary (except on a question of Adjournment) shall be presented to the President of the United States; and before the Same shall take Effect, shall be approved by him, or being disapproved by him, shall be repassed by two thirds of the Senate and House of Representatives, according to the Rules and Limitations prescribed in the Case of a Bill.

Section 8

The Congress shall have Power To lay and collect Taxes, Duties, Imposts and Excises, to pay the Debts and provide for the common Defence and general Welfare of the United States; but all Duties, Imposts and Excises shall be uniform throughout the United States;

To borrow Money on the credit of the United States;

To regulate Commerce with foreign Nations, and among the several States, and with the Indian Tribes;

To establish an uniform Rule of Naturalization, and uniform Laws on the subject of Bankruptcies throughout the United States;

To coin Money, regulate the Value thereof, and of foreign Coin, and fix the Standard of Weights and Measures;

To provide for the Punishment of counterfeiting the Securities and current Coin of the United States;

To establish Post Offices and post Roads;

To promote the Progress of Science and useful Arts, by securing for limited Times to Authors and Inventors the exclusive Right to their respective Writings and Discoveries;

To constitute Tribunals inferior to the supreme Court;

To define and punish Piracies and Felonies commited on the high Seas, and Offences against the Law of Nations;

To declare War, grant Letters of Marque and Reprisal,and make Rules concerning Captures on Land and Water;

To raise and support Armies, but no Appropriation of Money to that Use shall be for a longer Term than two Years;

To provide and maintain a Navy;

To make Rules for the Government and Regulation of the land and naval Forces;

To provide for calling forth the Militia to execute the Laws of the Union, suppress Insurrections and repel Invasions;

To provide for organizing, arming, and disciplining, the Militia, and for governing such Part of them as may be employed in the Service of the United States, reserving to the States respectively, the Appointment of the Officers, and the Authority of training the Militia according to the discipline prescribed by Congress;

To exercise exclusive Legislation in all Cases whatsoever, over such District (not exceeding ten Miles square) as may, by Cession of Particular States, and the Acceptance of Congress, become the Seat of the Government of the United States, and to exercise like Authority over all Places purchased by the Consent of the Legislature of the State in which the Same shall be, for the Erection of Forts, Magazines, Arsenals, dock-Yards, and other needful Buildings; — And

To make all Laws which shall be necessary and proper for carrying into Execution the foregoing Powers, and all other Powers vested by this Constitution in the Government of the United States, or in any Department or Officer thereof.

Section 9

The Migration or Importation of such Persons as any of the States now existing shall think proper to admit, shall not be prohibited by the Congress prior to the Year one thousand eight hundred and eight, but a Tax or duty may be imposed on such Importation, not exceeding ten dollars for each Person.

The Privilege of the Writ of Habeas Corpus shall not be suspended, unless when in Cases of Rebellion or Invasion the public Safety may require it.

No Bill of Attainder or ex post facto Law shall be passed.

No capitation, or other direct, Tax shall be laid, unless in Proportion to the Census of Enumeration herein before directed to be taken.[5]

No Tax or Duty shall be laid on Articles exported from any State.

No Preference shall be given by any Regulation of Commerce or Revenue to the Ports of one State over those of another; nor shall Vessels bound to, or from, one State, be obliged to enter, clear or pay Duties in another.

No Money shall be drawn from the Treasury, but in Consequence of Appropriations made by Law; and a regular Statement and Account of the Receipts and Expenditures of all public Money shall be published from time to time.

No Title of Nobility shall be granted by the United States: And no Person holding any Office of Profit or Trust under them, shall, without the Consent of the Congress, accept of any present, Emolument, Office, or Title, of any kind whatever, from any King, Prince or foreign State.

Section 10

No State shall enter into any Treaty, Alliance, or Confederation; grant Letters of Marque and Reprisal; coin Money; emit Bills of Credit; make any Thing but gold and silver Coin a Tender in Payment of Debts; pass any Bill of Attainder, ex post facto Law, or Law impairing the Obligation of Contracts, or grant any Title of Nobility.

No State shall, without the Consent of the Congress, lay any Imposts or Duties on Imports or Exports, except what may be absolutely necessary for executing its inspection Laws: and the net Produce of all Duties and Imposts, laid by any State on Imports or Exports, shall be for the Use of the Treasury of the United States; and all such Laws shall be subject to the Revision and Controul of the Congress.

No State shall, without the Consent of Congress, lay any Duty of Tonnage, keep Troops, or Ships of War in time of Peace, enter into any Agreement or Compact with another State, or with a foreign Power, or engage in War, unless actually invaded, or in such imminent Danger as will not admit of delay.

Article II

Section 1

The executive Power shall be vested in a President of the United States of America. He shall hold his Office during the Term of four Years, and, together with the Vice President, chosen for the same Term, be elected, as follows.

Each State shall appoint, in such Manner as the Legislature thereof may direct, a Number of Electors, equal to the whole Number of Senators and

Representatives to which the State may be entitled in the Congress: but no Senator or Representative, or Person holding an Office of Trust or Profit under the United States, shall be appointed an Elector.

[The Electors shall meet in their respective States, and vote by Ballot for two Persons, of whom one at least shall not be an Inhabitant of the same State with themselves. And they shall make a List of all the Persons voted for, and of the Number of Votes for each; which List they shall sign and certify, and transmit sealed to the Seat of the Government of the United States, directed to the President of the Senate. The President of the Senate shall, in the Presence of the Senate and House of Representatives, open all the Certificates, and the Votes shall then be counted. The Person having the greatest Number of Votes shall be the President, if such Number be a Majority of the whole Number of Electors appointed; and if there be more than one who have such Majority, and have an equal Number of Votes, then the House of Representatives shall immediately chuse by Ballot one of them for President; and if no Person have a Majority, then from the five highest on the list the said House shall in like Manner chuse the President. But in chusing the President, the Votes shall be taken by States, the Representation from each State having one Vote; a quorum for this Purpose shall consist of a Member or Members from two thirds of the States, and a Majority of all the States shall be necessary to a Choice. In every Case, after the Choice of the President, the Person having the greatest Number of Votes of the Electors shall be the Vice President. But if there should remain two or more who have equal Votes, the Senate shall chuse from them by Ballot the Vice President.] [6]

The Congress may determine the Time of chusing the Electors, and the Day on which they shall give their Votes; which Day shall be the same throughout the United States.

No Person except a natural born Citizen, or a Citizen of the United States, at the time of the Adoption of this Constitution, shall be eligible to the Office of President; neither shall any Person be eligible to that Office who shall not have attained to the Age of thirty five Years, and been fourteen Years a Resident within the United States.

In Case of the Removal of the President from Office, or of his Death, Resignation, or Inability to discharge the Powers and Duties of the said Office,[7] the Same shall devolve on the Vice President, and the Congress may by Law provide for the Case of Removal, Death, Resignation or Inability, both of the President and Vice President, declaring what Officer shall then act as President, and such Officer shall act accordingly, until the Disability be removed, or a President shall be elected.

The President shall, at stated Times, receive for his Services, a Compensation, which shall neither be increased nor diminished during the Period for which he shall have been elected, and he shall not receive within that Period any other Emolument from the United States, or any of them.

Before he enter on the Execution of his Office, he shall take the following Oath or Affirmation: — "I do solemnly swear (or affirm) that I will faithfully execute the Office of President of the United States, and will to the best of my Ability, preserve, protect and defend the Constitution of the United States."

Section 2

The President shall be Commander in Chief of the Army and Navy of the United States, and of the Militia of the several States, when called into the actual Service of the United States; he may require the Opinion, in writing, of the principal Officer in each of the executive Departments, upon any Subject relating to the Duties of their respective Offices, and he shall have Power to grant Reprieves and Pardons for Offenses against the United States, except in Cases of Impeachment.

He shall have Power, by and with the Advice and Consent of the Senate, to make Treaties, provided two thirds of the Senators present concur; and he shall nominate, and by and with the Advice and Consent of the Senate, shall appoint Ambassadors, other public Ministers and Consuls, Judges of the supreme Court, and all other Officers of the United States, whose Appointments are not herein otherwise provided for, and which shall be established by Law: but the Congress may by Law vest the Appointment of such inferior Officers, as they think proper, in the President alone, in the Courts of Law, or in the Heads of Departments.

The President shall have Power to fill up all Vacancies that may happen during the Recess of the Senate, by granting Commissions which shall expire at the End of their next Session.

Section 3

He shall from time to time give to the Congress Information of the State of the Union, and recommend to their Consideration such Measures as he shall judge necessary and expedient; he may, on extraordinary Occasions, convene both Houses, or either of them, and in Case of Disagreement between them, with Respect to the Time of Adjournment, he may adjourn them to such Time as he shall think proper; he shall receive Ambassadors and other public Ministers; he shall take Care that the Laws be faithfully executed, and shall Commission all the Officers of the United States.

Section 4

The President, Vice President and all Civil Officers of the United States, shall be removed from office on Impeachment for, and Conviction of, Treason, Bribery, or other high Crimes and Misdemeanors.

Article III

Section 1

The judicial Power of the United States, shall be vested in one supreme Court, and in such inferior Courts as the Congress may from time to time ordain and establish. The Judges, both of the supreme and inferior Courts, shall hold their Offices during good Behaviour, and shall, at stated Times, receive for their Services, a Compensation, which shall not be diminished during their Continuance in Office.

Section 2

The judicial Power shall extend to all Cases, in Law and Equity, arising under this Constitution, the Laws of the United States, and Treaties made, or which shall be made, under their Authority; — to all Cases affecting Ambassadors, other public Ministers and Consuls; — to all Cases of admiralty and maritime Jurisdiction; — to Controversies to which the United States shall be a Party; — to Controversies between two or more States; — between a State and Citizens of another State; [8] — between Citizens of different States; — between Citizens of the same State claiming Lands under Grants of different States, and between a State, or the Citizens thereof, and foreign States, Citizens or Subjects.[8]

In all Cases affecting Ambassadors, other public Ministers and Consuls, and those in which a State shall be Party, the supreme Court shall have original Jurisdiction. In all the other Cases before mentioned, the supreme Court shall have appellate Jurisdiction, both as to Law and Fact, with such Exceptions, and under such Regulations as the Congress shall make.

The Trial of all Crimes, except in cases of Impeachment, shall be by Jury; and such Trial shall be held in the State where the said Crimes shall have been committed; but when not committed within any State, the Trial shall be at such Place or Places as the Congress may by Law have directed.

Section 3

Treason against the United States, shall consist only in levying War against them, or in adhering to their Enemies, giving them Aid and Comfort. No Person shall be convicted of Treason unless on the Testimony of two Witnesses to the same overt Act, or on Confession in open Court.

The Congress shall have Power to declare the Punishment of Treason, but no Attainder of Treason shall work Corruption of Blood, or Forfeiture except during the Life of the Person attainted.

279

Article IV

Section 1

Full Faith and Credit shall be given in each State to the public Acts, Records, and judicial Proceedings of every other State. And the Congress may by general Laws prescribe the Manner in which such Acts, Records and Proceedings shall be proved, and the Effect thereof.

Section 2

The Citizens of each State shall be entitled to all Privileges and Immunities of Citizens in the several States.

A Person charged in any State with Treason, Felony, or other Crime, who shall flee from Justice, and be found in another State, shall on Demand of the executive Authority of the State from which he fled, be delivered up, to be removed to the State having Jurisdiction of the Crime.

[No Person held to Service or Labour in one State, under the Laws thereof, escaping into another, shall, in Consequence of any Law or Regulation therein, be discharged from such Service or Labour, but shall be delivered up on Claim of the Party to whom such Service or Labour may be due.] [9]

Section 3

New States may be admitted by the Congress into this Union; but no new State shall be formed or erected within the Jurisdiction of any other State; nor any State be formed by the Junction of two or more States, or Parts of States, without the Consent of the Legislatures of the States concerned as well as of the Congress.

The Congress shall have Power to dispose of and make all needful Rules and Regulations respecting the Territory or other Property belonging to the United States; and nothing in this Constitution shall be so construed as to Prejudice any Claims of the United States, or of any particular State.

Section 4

The United States shall guarantee to every State in this Union a Republican Form of Government, and shall protect each of them against Invasion; and on Application of the Legislature, or of the Executive (when the Legislature cannot be convened) against domestic Violence.

Article V

The Congress, whenever two thirds of both Houses shall deem it necessary, shall propose Amendments to this Constitution, or, on the Application of the Legislatures of two thirds of the several States, shall call a Convention for proposing Amendments, which, in either Case, shall be valid to all Intents and Purposes, as Part of this Constitution, when ratified by the Legislatures of three fourths of the several States, or by Conventions in three fourths thereof, as the one or the other Mode of Ratification may be proposed by the Congress; Provided [that no Amendment which may be made prior to the Year One thousand eight hundred and eight shall in any Manner affect the first and fourth Clauses in the Ninth Section of the first Article; and] [10] that no State, without its Consent, shall be deprived of its equal Suffrage in the Senate.

Article VI

All Debts contracted and Engagements entered into, before the Adoption of this Constitution, shall be as valid against the United States under this Constitution, as under the Confederation.

This Constitution, and the Laws of the United States which shall be made in Pursuance thereof; and all Treaties made, or which shall be made, under the Authority of the United States, shall be the supreme Law of the Land; and the Judges in every State shall be bound thereby, any Thing in the Constitution or Laws of any State to the Contrary notwithstanding.

The Senators and Representatives before mentioned, and the Members of the several State Legislatures, and all executive and judicial Officers, both of the United States and of the several States, shall be bound by Oath or Affirmation, to support this Constitution; but no religious Test shall ever be required as a Qualification to any Office or public Trust under the United States.

Article VII

The Ratification of the Conventions of nine States, shall be sufficient for the Establishment of this Constitution between the States so ratifying the Same. Done in Convention by the Unanimous Consent of the States present the Seventeenth Day of September in the Year of our Lord one thousand seven hundred and Eighty seven and of the Independence of the United States of America the Twelfth In witness whereof We have hereunto subscribed our Names, George Washington, President and deputy from Virginia.

New Hampshire: John Langdon,
Nicholas Gilman.

Massachusetts: Nathaniel Gorham,
Rufus King.

Connecticut:	William Samuel Johnson, Roger Sherman.
New York:	Alexander Hamilton
New Jersey:	William Livingston, David Brearley, William Paterson, Jonathan Dayton.
Pennsylvania:	Benjamin Franklin, Thomas Mifflin, Robert Morris, George Clymer, Thomas FitzSimons, Jared Ingersoll, James Wilson, Gouverneur Morris.
Delaware:	George Read, Gunning Bedford Jr., John Dickinson, Richard Bassett, Jacob Broom.
Maryland:	James McHenry, Daniel of St. Thomas Jenifer, Daniel Carroll.
Virginia:	John Blair, James Madison Jr.
North Carolina:	William Blount, Richard Dobbs Spaight, Hugh Williamson.
South Carolina:	John Rutledge, Charles Cotesworth Pinckney, Charles Pinckney, Pierce Butler.
Georgia:	William Few, Abraham Baldwin.

[The language of the original Constitution, not including the Amendments, was adopted by a convention of the states on Sept. 17, 1787, and was subsequently ratified by the states on the following dates: Delaware, Dec. 7, 1787; Pennsylvania, Dec. 12, 1787; New Jersey, Dec. 18, 1787; Georgia, Jan. 2, 1788; Connecticut, Jan. 9, 1788; Massachusetts, Feb. 6, 1788; Maryland, April 28, 1788; South Carolina, May 23, 1788; New Hampshire, June 21, 1788.

Ratification was completed on June 21, 1788.

The Constitution subsequently was ratified by Virginia, June 25, 1788; New York, July 26, 1788; North Carolina, Nov. 21, 1789; Rhode Island, May 29, 1790; and Vermont, Jan. 10, 1791.]

Amendment I

(First ten amendments ratified Dec. 15, 1791)

Congress shall make no law respecting an establishment of religion, or prohibiting the free exercise thereof; or abridging the freedom of speech, or of the press; or the right of the people peaceably to assemble, and to petition the Government for a redress of grievances.

Amendment II

A well regulated Militia, being necessary to the security of a free State, the right of the people to keep and bear Arms, shall not be infringed.

Amendment III

No Soldier shall, in time of peace be quartered in any house, without the consent of the Owner, nor in time of war, but in a manner to be prescribed by law.

Amendment IV

The right of the people to be secure in their persons, houses, papers, and effects, against unreasonable searches and seizures, shall not be violated, and no Warrants shall issue, but upon probable cause, supported by Oath or affirmation, and particularly describing the place to be searched, and the persons or things to be seized.

Amendment V

No person shall be held to answer for a capital, or otherwise infamous crime, unless on a presentment or indictment of a Grand Jury, except in cases arising in the land or naval forces, or in the Militia, when in actual service in time of War or public danger; nor shall any person be subject for the same offence to be twice put in jeopardy of life or limb; nor shall be compelled in any criminal case to be a witness against himself, nor be deprived of life, liberty, or property, without due process of law; nor shall private property be taken for public use, without just compensation.

Amendment VI

In all criminal prosecutions, the accused shall enjoy the right to a speedy and public trial, by an impartial jury of the State and district wherein the crime shall have been committed, which district shall have been previously ascertained by law, and to be informed of the nature and cause of the accusation; to be confronted with the witnesses against him; to have compulsory process for obtaining witnesses in his favor, and to have the Assistance of Counsel for his defence.

Amendment VII

In Suits at common law, where the value in controversy shall exceed twenty dollars, the right of trial by jury shall be preserved, and no fact tried by a jury, shall be otherwise re-examined in any Court of the United States, than according to the rules of the common law.

Amendment VIII

Excessive bail shall not be required, nor excessive fines imposed, nor cruel and unusual punishments inflicted.

Amendment IX

The enumeration in the Constitution, of certain rights, shall not be construed to deny or disparage others retained by the people.

Amendment X

The powers not delegated to the United States by the Constitution, nor prohibited by it to the States, are reserved to the States respectively, or to the people.

Amendment XI (Ratified Feb. 7, 1795)

The Judicial power of the United States shall not be construed to extend to any suit in law or equity, commenced or prosecuted against one of the United States by Citizens of another State, or by Citizens or Subjects of any Foreign State.

Amendment XII (Ratified June 15, 1804)

The Electors shall meet in their respective states and vote by ballot for President and Vice-President, one of whom, at least, shall not be an inhabitant of the same state with themselves; they shall name in their ballots the person voted for as President, and in distinct ballots the person voted for as Vice-President, and they shall make distinct lists of all persons voted for as President, and of all persons voted for as Vice-President, and of the number of votes for each, which lists they shall sign and certify, and transmit sealed to the seat of the government of the United States, directed to the President of the Senate; — The President of the Senate shall, in the presence of the Senate and House of Representatives, open all the certificates and the votes shall then be counted; — The person having the greatest number of votes for President, shall be the President, if such number be a majority of the whole number of Electors appointed; and if no person have such majority, then from the persons having the highest numbers not exceeding three on the list of those voted for as President, the House of Representatives shall choose immediately, by ballot, the President. But in choosing the President, the votes shall be taken by states, the representation from each state having one vote; a quorum for this purpose shall consist of a member or members from two-thirds of the states, and a majority of all the states shall be necessary to a choice. [And if the House of Representatives shall not choose a President whenever the right of choice shall devolve upon them, before the fourth day of March next following, then the Vice-President shall act as President, as in the case of the death or other constitutional disability of the President —] [11] The person having the greatest number of votes as Vice-President, shall be the Vice-President, if such number be a majority of the whole number of Electors appointed, and if no person have a majority, then from the two highest numbers on the list, the Senate shall choose the Vice-President; a quorum for the purpose shall consist of two-thirds of the whole number of Senators, and a majority of the whole number shall be necessary to a choice. But no person constitutionally ineligible to the office of President shall be eligible to that of Vice-President of the United States.

Amendment XIII (Ratified Dec. 6, 1865)

Section 1

Neither slavery nor involuntary servitude, except as a punishment for crime whereof the party shall have been duly convicted, shall exist within the United States, or any place subject to their jurisdiction.

Section 2

Congress shall have power to enforce this article by appropriate legislation.

Amendment XIV (Ratified July 9, 1868)

Section 1

All persons born or naturalized in the United States and subject to the jurisdiction thereof, are citizens of the United States and of the State wherein they reside. No State shall make or enforce any law which shall abridge the privileges or immunities of citizens of the United States; nor shall any State deprive any person of life, liberty, or property, without due process of law; nor deny to any person within its jurisdiction the equal protection of the laws.

Section 2

Representatives shall be apportioned among the several States according to their respective numbers, counting the whole number of persons in each State, excluding Indians not taxed. But when the right to vote at any election for the choice of electors for President and Vice President of the United States, Representatives in Congress, the Executive and Judicial officers of a State, or the members of the Legislature thereof, is denied to any of the male inhabitants of such State, being twenty-one years of age,[12] and citizens of the United States, or in any way abridged, except for participation in rebellion, or other crime, the basis of representation therein shall be reduced in the proportion which the number of such male citizens shall bear to the whole number of male citizens twenty-one years of age in such State.

Section 3

No person shall be a Senator or Representative in Congress, or elector of President and Vice President, or hold any office, civil or military, under the United States, or under any State, who, having previously taken an oath, as a member of Congress, or as an officer of the United States, or as a member of any State legislature, or as an executive or judicial officer of any State, to support the Constitution of the United States, shall have engaged in insurrection or rebellion against the same, or given aid or comfort to the enemies thereof. But Congress may by a vote of two-thirds of each House, remove such disability.

Section 4

The validity of the public debt of the United States, authorized by law, including debts incurred for payment of pensions and bounties for services in suppressing insurrection or rebellion, shall not be questioned. But neither the United States nor any State shall assume or pay any debt or obligation incurred in aid of insurrection or rebellion against the United States, or any claim for the loss or emancipation of any slave; but all such debts, obligations and claims shall be held illegal and void.

Section 5

The Congress shall have power to enforce, by appropriate legislation, the provisions of this article.

Amendment XV (Ratified Feb. 3, 1870)

Section 1

The right of citizens of the United States to vote shall not be denied or abridged by the United States or by any State on account of race, color, or previous condition of servitude.

Section 2

The Congress shall have power to enforce this article by appropriate legislation.

Amendment XVI (Ratified Feb. 3, 1913)

The Congress shall have power to lay and collect taxes on incomes, from whatever source derived, without apportionment among the several States, and without regard to any census or enumeration.

Amendment XVII (Ratified Apr. 8, 1913)

The Senate of the United States shall be composed of two Senators from each State, elected by the people thereof, for six years; and each Senator shall have one vote. The electors in each State shall have the qualifications requisite for electors of the most numerous branch of the State legislatures.

When vacancies happen in the representation of any State in the Senate, the executive authority of such State shall issue writs of election to fill such vacancies: *Provided,* That the legislature of any State may empower the executive thereof to make temporary appointments until the people fill the vacancies by election as the legislature may direct.

This amendment shall not be so construed as to affect the election or term of any Senator chosen before it becomes valid as part of the Constitution.

Amendment XVIII (Ratified Jan. 16, 1919) [13]

Section 1

After one year from the ratification of this article the manufacture, sale, or transportation of intoxicating liquors within, the importation thereof into, or the exportation thereof from the United States and all territory subject to the jurisdiction thereof for beverage purposes is hereby prohibited.

Section 2

The Congress and the several States shall have concurrent power to enforce this article by appropriate legislation.

Section 3

This article shall be inoperative unless it shall have been ratified as an amendment to the Constitution by the legislatures of the several States, as provided in the Constitution, within seven years from the date of the submission hereof to the States by the Congress.

Amendment XIX (Ratified Aug. 18, 1920)

The right of citizens of the United States to vote shall not be denied or abridged by the United States or by any State on account of sex.

Congress shall have power to enforce this article by appropriate legislation.

Amendment XX (Ratified Jan. 23, 1933)

Section 1

The terms of the President and Vice President shall end at noon on the 20th day of January, and the terms of Senators and Representatives at noon on the 3d day of January, of the years in which such terms would have ended if this article had not been ratified; and the terms of their successors shall then begin.

Section 2

The Congress shall assemble at least once in every year, and such meeting shall begin at noon on the 3d day of January, unless they shall by law appoint a different day.

Section 3[14]

If, at the time fixed for the beginning of the term of the President, the President elect shall have died, the Vice President elect shall become President. If a President shall not have been chosen before the time fixed for the beginning of his term, or if the President elect shall have failed to qualify, then the Vice President elect shall act as President until a President shall have qualified; and the Congress may by law provide for the case wherein neither a President elect nor a Vice President elect shall have qualified, declaring who shall then act as President, or the manner in which one who is to act shall be selected, and such person shall act accordingly until a President or Vice President shall have qualified.

Section 4

The Congress may by law provide for the case of the death of any of the persons from whom the House of Representatives may choose a President whenever the right of choice shall have devolved upon them, and for the case of the death of any of the persons from whom the Senate may choose a Vice President whenever the right of choice shall have devolved upon them.

Section 5

Sections 1 and 2 shall take effect on the 15th day of October following the ratification of this article.

Section 6

This article shall be inoperative unless it shall have been ratified as an amendment to the Constitution by the legislatures of three-fourths of the several States within seven years from the date of its submission.

Amendment XXI (Ratified Dec. 5, 1933)

Section 1

The eighteenth article of amendment to the Constitution of the United States is hereby repealed.

Section 2

The transportation or importation into any State, Territory or possession of the United States for delivery or use therein of intoxicating liquors, in violation of the laws thereof, is hereby prohibited.

Section 3

This article shall be inoperative unless it shall have been ratified as an amendment to the Constitution by conventions in the several States, as provided in the Constitution, within seven years from the date of the submission hereof to the States by the Congress.

Appendix

Amendment XXII (Ratified Feb. 27, 1951)

Section 1

No person shall be elected to the office of the President more than twice, and no person who has held the office of President, or acted as President, for more than two years of a term to which some other person was elected President shall be elected to the office of the President more than once. But this Article shall not apply to any person holding the office of President when this Article was proposed by the Congress, and shall not prevent any person who may be holding the office of President, or acting as President, during the term within which this Article become operative from holding the office of President or acting as President during the remainder of such term.

Section 2

This Article shall be inoperative unless it shall have been ratified as an amendment to the Constitution by the legislatures of three-fourths of the several States within seven years from the date of its submission to the States by the Congress.

Amendment XXIII (Ratified March 29, 1961)

Section 1

The District constituting the seat of Government of the United States shall appoint in such manner as the Congress may direct:

A number of electors of President and Vice President equal to the whole number of Senators and Representatives in Congress to which the District would be entitled if it were a State, but in no event more than the least populous State; they shall be in addition to those appointed by the States, but they shall be considered, for the purposes of the election of President and Vice President, to be electors appointed by a State; and they shall meet in the District and perform such duties as provided by the twelfth article of amendment.

Section 2

The Congress shall have power to enforce this article by appropriate legislation.

Amendment XXIV (Ratified Jan. 23, 1964)

Section 1

The right of citizens of the United States to vote in any primary or other election for President or Vice President, for electors for President or Vice President, or for Senator or Representative in Congress, shall not be denied or abridged by the United States or any State by reason of failure to pay any poll tax or other tax.

Section 2

The Congress shall have power to enforce this article by appropriate legislation.

Amendment XXV (Ratified Feb. 10, 1967)

Section 1

In case of the removal of the President from office or of his death or resignation, the Vice President shall become President.

Section 2

Whenever there is a vacancy in the office of the Vice President, the President shall nominate a Vice President who shall take office upon confirmation by a majority vote of both Houses of Congress.

Section 3

Whenever the President transmits to the President pro tempore of the Senate and the Speaker of the House of Representatives his written declaration that he is unable to discharge the powers and duties of his office, and until he transmits to them a written declaration to the contrary, such powers and duties shall be discharged by the Vice President as Acting President.

Section 4

Whenever the Vice President and a majority of either the principal officers of the executive departments or of such other body as Congress may by law provide, transmit to the President pro tempore of the Senate and the Speaker of the House of Representatives their written declaration that the President is unable to discharge the powers and duties of his office, the Vice

President shall immediately assume the powers and duties of the office as Acting President.

Thereafter, when the President transmits to the President pro tempore of the Senate and the Speaker of the House of Representatives his written declaration that no inability exists, he shall resume the powers and duties of his office unless the Vice President and a majority of either the principal officers of the executive department or of such other body as Congress may by law provide, transmit within four days to the President pro tempore of the Senate and the Speaker of the House of Representatives their written declaration that the President is unable to discharge the powers and duties of his office. Thereupon Congress shall decide the issue, assembling within forty-eight hours for that purpose if not in session. If the Congress, within twenty-one days after receipt of the latter written declaration, or, if Congress is not in session, within twenty-one days after Congress is required to assemble, determines by two-thirds vote of both houses that the President is unable to discharge the powers and duties of his office, the Vice President shall continue to discharge the same as Acting President; otherwise, the President shall resume the powers and duties of his office.

Amendment XXVI (Ratified July 1, 1971)

Section 1

The right of citizens of the United States, who are eighteen years of age or older, to vote shall not be denied or abridged by the United States or by any State on account of age.

Section 2

The Congress shall have power to enforce this article by appropriate legislation.

---

1. The part in brackets was changed by section 2 of the Fourteenth Amendment.
2. The part in brackets was changed by section 1 of the Seventeenth Amendment.
3. The part in brackets was changed by the second paragraph of the Seventeenth Amendment.
4. The part in brackets was changed by section 2 of the Twentieth Amendment.
5. The Sixteenth Amendment gave Congress the power to tax incomes.
6. The material in brackets has been superseded by the Twelfth Amendment.
7. This provision has been affected by the Twenty-fifth Amendment.
8. These clauses were affected by the Eleventh Amendment.
9. This paragraph has been superseded by the Thirteenth Amendment.

10. Obsolete.
11. The part in brackets has been superseded by section 3 of the Twentieth Amendment.
12. See the Twenty-sixth Amendment.
13. This Amendment was repealed by section 1 of the Twenty-first Amendment.
14. See the Twenty-fifth Amendment.

Source: U.S. Congress, House, Committee on the Judiciary, *The Constitution of the United States of America, As Amended Through July 1971*, H. Doc. 93-215, 93rd Cong., 2nd sess., 1974.